Santore, Modern European History

To my wife

Frances

and our new son

John Vincent

Selected Reading Lists and Course
Outlines from American Colleges
and Universities

Modern European History: 1789 to the Present
Vol. I: Chronological and National Courses

edited by John Santore
New York University

MARKUS WIENER PUBLISHING, INC.

016.940
S 337
v. 1

ISBN 0-910129-07-X
Library of Congress Card No. 83-061359
Printed in America

TABLE OF CONTENTS

Volume One:

Chronological and National Courses

1

Volume Two:

Topical and Thematic Courses

Military

Diplomatic

Economic and Social

Historical Methodology and Historiography

- -

   *Institutional designations refer to the university or
college at which the course was taught, and not necessarily to
the school at which the author presently teaches. In all but a
few instances, the syllabi have been reproduced exactly as submitted, with little modification or change. All college courses,
of course, are subject to annual revision and updating, and the
reader is advised to check the syllabus for format and date. [Ed.]

Introduction

Over the last two decades, the teaching of European history in American universities has undergone a remarkable transformation. Beginning almost imperceptibly in the early 1960s, colleges across the country have gradually increased their number of offerings in social history, and developed whole new areas of historical research. Indeed, since 1970 in particular, courses on such topics as the history of women, labor, and ethnic minorities, regional and local history, the history of the professions, medicine, and psychoanalysis, and the use of quantitative methods and computers have multiplied rapidly. Even the older political and diplomatic histories are no longer taught from the same perspective, and their future popularity among young historians may very well depend on their ability to adapt to new historical methods and concerns.

The courses presented in these two volumes reflect this changed emphasis among American historians. Designed by some of the country's leading teachers and scholars, they show a marked shift towards social history as a primary or secondary concern. In addition, they also illustrate the growing tendency among history departments to deepen their curriculum by adding courses on special topics, and the astonishing diversity which now characterizes the historical field. Although highly individualistic and difficult to categorize, they provide a prime example of the degree to which contemporary political and social problems affect the teaching of history as a whole.

The courses themselves have been divided into four sections, each representing a traditional area of historical interest or a specific pedagogical approach. Volume I deals with those courses which have been organized chronologically or nationally. Among the chronological courses, special

attention has been given to the survey of Western Civilization
(of which there are four examples) and a number of critical
historical periods or events (such as the French Revolution
and the Second World War). In the national section, emphasis
has been placed on the Great Powers - Britain, France,
Germany, and the USSR. This decision to emphasize the larger
nations, it should be mentioned, reflects the current distribution of history courses in the United States. As partial
compensation, the volume also includes a selection of offerings
on the lesser Powers - Italy, Poland, Spain, Portugal, Austria,
Hungary, and the Netherlands, in particular.

In contrast to volume I, volume II provides a list of
courses in which the materials have been organized topically or
thematically. Among them are several which stand at the very
cutting edge of current historical research and are thus
illustrative of many contemporary historical trends. Included
in this list are courses on the history of medicine and mental
illness, the development of the European working class and
proletarian culture, women in European society and politics,
and comparative Fascism, Communism, and political terrorism.
In addition, there are also courses on general social and
economic history, and selections on diplomatic and military
history (including the so-called "new military history") as
well.

Finally, some mention should be made about the way in
which the courses were selected. In choosing from among the
hundreds of courses submitted, I have tried to select those
which, in my estimation, would be of maximum use to students,
teachers, and scholars. As such, I have tended to favor those
which display the highest measure of clarity and organization,
as well as a mastery of existent literature in the field.
Within these parameters, I have also attempted to provide
the reader with examples of courses taught in the widest

variety of formats and at different instructional levels
(undergraduate lectures, graduate seminars, independent
reading courses, etc.) and to maintain a balance between
divergent political and pedagogical points of view. Finally,
I have never lost sight of the fact that the basic function
of a syllabus is to inform the student about the content,
readings, and other requirements needed for the course under
discussion, and that its ultimate justification lies in its
effectiveness as a pedagogical tool.

New York   John Santore
June 1983

New York University

History of Western Civilization Since 1648

Spring 1983
M. Nolan
A57.0002

Between the seventeenth century and the present the modern
Western world came into being. This course will introduce
the main economic, social, political and cultural forces
which shaped and reshaped European society and Europe's
relationship to the world in this period. Topics include the
rise of capitalism and the Industrial Revolution; such diverse
political movements as absolutism, liberalism, socialism,
and fascism; and major intellectual developments, such as
the scientific revolution, the Enlightenment, Darwinism and
Freudian psychoanalysis. The course concludes with an
exploration of post World War II Europe.

The course will meet twice a week. Some weeks there will be
two lectures, others will have one lecture and one discussion
section. Students should do the reading each week so that
they can benefit from lectures and participate in discussion
sections.

Course requirements are: two short (5 page) papers, a mid-
term exam, and a final exam.

The following books are required reading and have been
ordered at the NYU book store. They are also on reserve in
Bobst.

  McKay, J.; Hill, B.; and Buckler, J.: History of Western
      Society, vol. II. second edition.

  Tocqueville, A.: The Old Regime and the French Revolution

  Marx, K.: The Communist Manifesto

  Freud, S.: Civilization and Its Discontents

  Allen, W.S.: The Nazi Seizure of Power

  Rosenberg, W., and Young, M.: Transforming Russia and China

  Fanon, F.: The Wretched of the Earth

For some weeks you will be required to read an article or a
few primary sources which will be on reserve in Bobst. Those
assignments are marked on the syllabus with an asterisk. They
will be on reserve under my name in the personal copy file and
will have the title listed on the syllabus.

9

Week I: The Transition from Feudalism to Capitalism

Jan. 31:   The European World in the Seventeenth Century
Feb. 2:   Economy and Society

    McKay, Hill and Buckler, History of Western Society
        Chap. 19 & 20.

Week II: The State and Politics

Feb. 7:   Absolutism in Eastern and Western Europe
Feb. 9:   The English Civil War and Revolution

    McKay, Hill and Buckler, Chap. 16 & 17.
    *Vann, Richard, "Toward a New Lifestyle: Women in
        Preindustrial Capitalism", in: R. Bridenthal and
        C. Koonz (eds.), Becoming Visible: Women in
        European History,(1977)

Week III: The Rise of Rationalism

Feb. 14:   The Scientific Revolution (part lecture, part
               discussion)
Feb. 16:   The Enlightenment (part lecture, part discussion)

    McKay, Hill and Buckler, Chap. 18.
    *"The Scientific Revolution" (documents), in: Introduction
        to Contemporary Civilization in the West, (Columbia
        University Press) 1960.
    *"The Enlightenment" (documents), in: Ibid.

Week IV: Causes of the French Revolution

Feb. 21:   Holiday
Feb. 23:   Discussion of Tocqueville, The Old Regime...

    Tocqueville, A.: The Old Regime and the French Revolution,
        entire.

Week V: Age of Revolutions

Feb. 28:   The French Revolution and Napoleon
Mar. 2:   The Industrial Revolution

    McKay, Hill and Buckler, Chap. 21, 22, and 24.
    *"Condition of the Working Class." (documents), in:
        ICCW.
    *McDougall, M. "Working-class Women During the Industrial
        Revolution," in: Bridenthal and Koonz.

Week VI: Liberalism, Nationalism and Marxism

Mar. 7:   Liberalism, Nationalism and National Unification
Mar. 9:   Discussion of Marx, The Communist Manifesto

    McKay, Hill and Buckler, Chap. 23.

Marx, The Communist Manifesto, entire.

FIRST PAPER IS DUE MARCH 7.

Week VII: Europe and the World

Mar. 14:   Imperialism and the Second Industrial Revolution
Mar. 16:   MIDTERM

    McKay, Hill and Buckler, Chap. 25 & 26.
    *"Imperialism" (documents), in: ICCW.

Week VIII: Politics and Social Thought, 1890 - 1914

Mar. 21:   Socialism, Liberalism, and Conservatism
Mar. 23:   Discussion of Freud, Civilization and Darwin.

    Freud, S. Civilization and its Discontents, entire.
    *"Darwin" (documents), in ICCW.

March 28 and 30: SPRING VACATION

Week IX: Crisis of the Old Order

Apr. 4:   Women, Work, and Politics
Apr. 6:   World War I (film)

    McKay, Hill and Buckler, Chap. 27.
    *"Bourgeois Women" (documents), in: E. Riemer and John Fout (eds.),
        European Women: A Documentary History (1980).

Week X: End of the Old Order?

Apr. 11:   War, Revolution and Counterrevolution
Apr. 13:   Discussion of Rosenberg and Young, Transforming...

    Rosenberg and Young, Transforming Russia and China, Chap. 1-5

Week XI: Political and Economic Crisis

Apr. 18:   Rise of Italian Fascism
Apr. 20:   Troubled Twenties and the Depression

    McKay, Hill and Buckler, Chap. 28.
    *Bridenthal, R. "Something Old, Something New: Women Between
        the Two World Wars", in: Bridenthal and Koonz.

Week XII: Fascism

Apr. 25:   Discussion of Allen, Nazi Seizure of Power
Apr. 27:   Germany and Italy in the 1930s

    Allen, William S., The Nazi Seizure of Power, entire.

11

Week XIII: War

May 2:   Popular Front and Spanish Civil War
May 4:   World War I and Postwar Settlements

    McKay, Hill and Buckler, Chap. 29 - 31.
    Rosenberg and Young, pp. 189-220, 238-244

SECOND PAPER IS DUE MAY 4.

Week XIV: Contemporary Europe and the World

May 9:   Economics and Politics, 1950 - 1980
May 11:   Discussion of Fanon, Wretched of the Earth

    Fanon, F. The Wretched of the Earth, pp. 1- 249.

History 12

Main Currents in the Modern European World: The French Revolution to Today.

Spring 1979
Barnard College

Professor Levy
Professor Santore

Syllabus

This course will survey the main developments in modern European history from 1789 to the present. Among the topics which will be discussed are the French Revolution and its Napoleonic sequel; the nineteenth-century industrial revolutions; romanticism, liberalism, socialism, conservatism, nationalism, and imperialism; nineteenth-and-twentieth century art and science; and twentieth-century wars, revolutions, dictatorships, and aspirations.

Lectures will be given on Mondays, Wednesdays, and Fridays. On each alternate Friday, the class will be divided into smaller sections, and the ideas presented during the previous two weeks will be discussed. The reading and lecture schedule is as follows:

Readings

January 22-February 2:

R.R. Palmer and Joel Colton, A History of the Modern World (Fifth edition), xii-xxxii. (Purchase)
Georges Lefebvre, The Coming of the French Revolution. (Purchase)
Albert Soboul, The Sans-Culottes, chaps. 1,6.
Richard Cobb, "The Revolutionary Mentality in France", in Cobb, The Second Identity, pp. 122-141.

February 3-16:

Palmer and Colton, A History of the Modern World, pp. 417-38.
Jeffry Kaplow.(ed.), Western Civilization: Mainstream Readings and Radical Critiques, II, 49-120 (The Industrial Revolution).
Robert Heilbroner, The Worldly Philosophers, chaps. III (Adam Smith), IV (Malthus), and V (Ricardo).
Carl Cohen (ed.), Communism, Fascism, and Democracy: The Theoretical Foundations, pp. 488-95.
Frank Manuel and Fritzie Manuel (eds.), French Utopias, pp. 299-327.

February 17-March 2:

Palmer and Colton, A History of the Modern World, pp. 438-461.

13

Henry Kissinger, "The Congress of Vienna: A Reappraisal";
and "Metternich: A Reappraisal of his Impact on
International Relations", in Clough, Gay, Warner,
Cammett (eds.), The European Past, 2nd Edition, II,
pp. 5-17, 21-24.
Jack Lively (ed.), The Works of Joseph de Maistre, pp.
147-81.
Jacob Bronowski and Bruce Mazlish, The Western Intellectual
Tradition: From Leonardo to Hegel, pp. 415-29 (Edmund
Burke).
Edmund Burke, Reflections on the Revolution in France, in
Charles Hirschfeld (ed.), Classics of Western Thought,
III, 233-50.
Jacques Barzun, Classic, Romantic, Modern. (Purchase)

March 3-23:

Palmer and Colton, A History of the Modern World, pp.
462-501.
Francois Fejto, "Europe on the Eve of the Revolutions", in
Fejto (ed.), The Opening of an Era, 1848: A
Historical Symposium.
Robert Tucker (ed.), The Marx-Engels Reader, pp. 3-23,
52-106, 302-384, 469-511. (Purchase)

March 24-April 6:

Palmer and Colton, A History of the Modern World, pp.
502-654.
Henry Kissinger, "The White Revolutionary: Reflections on
Bismarck", in D.A. Rustov (ed.), Philosophers and
and Kings: Studies in Leadership.
Boulding and Meekerjev, "Introduction"; Hobson, "The
Economic Taproot of Imperialism; D.K. Fieldhouse,
"Imperialism: A Historical Revision", in Boulding
and Meekerjev (eds.), Economic Imperialism.
Sigmund Freud, An Outline of Psychoanalysis. (Purchase)

April 7-20:

Palmer and Colton, A History of the Modern World, pp.
654-743.
Joachim Remak, The Origins of the First World War, pp.
60-96, 132-150.
Theodore H. Von Laue, Why Lenin? Why Stalin? (Purchase)

April 21-May 2:

Palmer and Colton, A History of the Modern World, pp.
735-943.
Walter Langer, The Mind of Adolph Hitler. (Purchase)
Peter Loewenberg, "Nazi Youth Cohort", AHR, 1977.
Robert Heilbroner, An Inquiry into the Human Prospect.
(Purchase)

January 22: Introductory session: discussion of syllabus and course requirements.

January 24: The late enlightenment and the pre-revolutionary mentality: French connections. (Levy)

January 26: The revolutions of 1788-1789 in France. (Levy)

January 20-31: The radicalization of the revolution, 1790-1794. (Levy)

February 2: First discussion session.

February 5: The Thermidorian reaction and Napoleon, 1795-1810. (Levy)

February 7: The fall of Napoleon and the Congress of Vienna, 1810-1815. (Santore)

February 9-12: The Industrial Revolution (Santore)

February 14: The advent of the "isms" (I): Liberalism, Radicalism, and Republicanism. (Santore)

February 16: Second discussion session.

February 19: The advent of the "isms" (II): Utopian Socialism and Nationalism. (Santore)

February 21: Conservatism. (Levy)

February 23: Romanticism. (Levy)

February 26-28: Europe between revolution and reaction, 1815-1848. (Santore)

March 2: Third discussion session.

March 5-7: The revolutions of 1848. (Santore)

March 9: Marxism. (Levy)

March 19: The Second Empire. (Levy)

March 21: The unification of Italy, 1848-1871. (Santore)

March 23: Fourth discussion session.

March 26: The unification of Germany, 1848-1871. (Santore)

March 28: The development of late 19th century science: Darwin. (Levy)

March 30: The history of psychoanalysis: Freud. (Levy)

April 2: Imperialism. (Levy)

April 4: Europe at the beginning of the 20th century. (Levy)

April 6: Fifth discussion session.

April 9-11: The diplomatic background to the First World War, 1871-1914. (Santore)

April 13: The First World War and the Treaty of Versailles, 1914-1919. (Santore)

April 16: The Bolshevik Revolution and the Stalin Era. (Santore)

April 18: European diplomacy in the 1920s and the triumph of Fascism in Italy. (Santore)

April 20: Sixth discussion session.

April 23: The collapse of the Weimar Republic and the advent of Hitler, 1919-1933. (Santore)

April 25: Nazi Germany: leader's led and victims. (Levy)

April 27: The diplomatic background to the Second World War, 1929-1933. (Santore)

April 30: World War II and the beginnings of the Cold War, 1945-1952. (Levy)

May 2: The history of the future. (Levy)

History 181,   COMPARATIVE STUDIES IN HISTORICAL CULTURES II   Winter 1983

John Broomfield, University of Michigan

"PROGRESS OR DECAY? CONFLICTING IDEAS ON THE DEVELOPMENT OF THE MODERN WORLD"

This course differs from the usual introductory course in two important
ways. First, it stresses the value of comparison in understanding civilizations and cultures, including our own civilization. Unlike traditional American, Western or Asian civilization courses, it will not limit itself to a
single historical culture but will try to draw on the experience of many cultures, classical and modern, Western and non-Western. Secondly, the course
will be problem oriented, not survey oriented. It will not follow the "one
damned thing after another" approach, by attempting to summarize the entire
history of any of the cultures studied. Rather, it will emphasize the relevance of history as a tool for social analysis by examining the cross-cultural
ramifications of major human problems.

The focus will be the question: "Progress or Decay? Conflicting Ideas
on the Development of the Modern World." At the outset there will be con-
sideration of the widespread belief in Western Civilization throughout the
past 300 years that humans have progressed. Specific topics will then be
chosen for more careful scrutiny. As each is examined it will be shown that
there have been (and remain) schools of thought in the West that have denied
that humans have progressed in such areas of activity. Similarly it will be
shown that when there has been an intrusion into non-Western cultures, the
fundamental differences of perception have resulted in even more radical disagreements.

The course will explore the nature of "history" itself, and its fundamental importance to Western Civilization. Students will be asked to consider
some novel propositions: that there is not one history, but many histories;
that a history is the perception in the present of the past; that in the study
of history, uncontested fact is of relatively little significance compared
with conflicting interpretations and varying perceptions of the past. History
is a great debate. Students in this course will be asked to think for themselves. They will be offered challenging interpretations of the past and the
present, and they will be invited to return the challenge to the instructors,
and the books and articles they are asked to read.

"I do not think it matters much to the fortunes of man what abstract notions one may entertain concerning nature and the principles of things.... For my part I do not trouble myself with such speculative and unprofitable matters. My purpose, on the contrary, is to try whether I cannot in very fact lay more firmly the foundations, and extend more widely the limits, of the power and greatness of man."
          --Francis Bacon (1561-1626)

"It's sometimes argued that there's no real progress; that a civilization that kills multitudes in mass warfare, that pollutes the land and oceans with ever larger quantities of debris, that destroys the dignity of individuals by subjecting them to a forced mechanized existence can hardly be called an advance over the simpler hunting and gathering and agricultural existence of prehistoric times. But this argument, though romantically appealing, doesn't hold up. The primitive tribes permitted far less individual freedom than does modern society. Ancient wars were committed with far less moral justification than modern ones. A technology that produces debris can find, and is finding, ways of disposing of it without ecological upset. And the school-book pictures of primitive man sometimes omit some of the detractions of his primitive life--the pain, the disease, famine, the hard labor needed just to stay alive. From the agony of bare existence to modern life can be soberly described only as upward progress, and the sole agent for this progress is quite clearly reason itself."
          --Robert M. Pirsig: Zen and the Art of Motorcycle Maintenance (1974)

"The process of change in the modern era is of the same order of magnitude as that from prehuman to human life and from primitive to civilized societies; it is the most dynamic of the great revolutionary transformations in the conduct of human affairs. What is distinctive about the modern era is the phenomenal growth of knowledge since the scientific revolution and the unprecedented effort at adaptation to this knowledge that has come to be demanded of the whole of mankind."
          --C.E. Black: The Dynamics of Modernization (1966)

"Contemporary Western man in the overwhelming majority considers himself fundamentally different and distinct from the living world that gives him both substance and sustenance. This imagined separation between man and "nature' has provided the conceptual framework for a further doctrine, that of absolute human power and authority over the nonhuman. These ludicrous but terrifying notions have become solidified in our collective thought in a ridiculously brief period of human and Earth history.
          --John A. Livingston: One Cosmic Instant: Man's Fleeting Supremacy
          (1973)

Western civilization is dangerous "because in the interest of this growth it does not hesitate to destroy any other form of humanity whose difference from us consists in having discovered not merely other codes of existence but ways of achieving an end that still eludes us: the mastery by society of society's mastery over nature."
          --Marshall Sahlins: Culture and Practical Reason (1976)

"The reasonable man adapts himself to the world: the unreasonable one persists in trying to adapt the world to himself. Therefore all progress depends on the unreasonable man."
          --George Bernard Shaw: Man and Superman

TOPICS AND READINGS

*SELECTIONS AVAILABLE IN COURSE PACK (Albert's Copying, 535 E. Liberty Street)
+AVAILABLE IN BOOKSTORES FOR PURCHASE

1. THE IDEA OF PROGRESS

Carl Becker: "Progress," Encyclopedia of the Social Sciences, 1937 edition
+Herbert Butterfield: The Origins of Modern Science, 1300-1800 (Free Press
      paperback)
Larry Laudan: Progress and Its Problems: Towards a Theory of Scientific
      Growth (California paperback)
William Leiss: The Domination of Nature (Beacon paperback)
*John A. Livingston: One Cosmic Instant: Man's Fleeting Supremacy (Delta
      paperback)
*John T. Marcus: "Time and the Sense of History: West and East," Comparative
      Studies in Society and History, vol. III, no. 2, January 1961, pp. 123-139
*Sidney Pollard: The Idea of Progress: History and Society

2. SCIENCE

*Kenneth E. Boulding: "Science: Our Common Heritage," Science, vol. 207,
      no. 4433, February 22, 1980, pp. 831-836
+Herbert Butterfield: The Origins of Modern Science, 1300-1800 (Free Press
      paperback)
+Fritjof Capra: The Turning Point: Science, Society, and the Rising Culture
      (Simon & Schuster)
*Clifford Geertz: The Interpretation of Cultures (Basic Books paperback)
Sally Gregory Kohlstedt: "In From the Periphery: American Women in Science,
      1830-1880," Signs, vol. 4, no. 1, Autumn 1978, pp. 81-96
+Thomas S. Kuhn: The Structure of Scientific Revolutions (Chicago paperback)
*Sara Ruddick & Pamela Daniels, eds.: Working It Out: 23 Women Writers,
      Artists, Scientists and Scholars Talk About Their Lives and Work
      (Pantheon paperback)
*James P. Spradley & David W. McCurdy, eds.: Conformity and Conflict: Readings
      in Cultural Anthropology
*Benjamin Lee Whorf: Language, Thought and Reality: Selected Writings (M.I.T.
      paperback)

3. MEDICINE

Vern L. Bullough & Bonnie Bullough: The Care of the Sick: The Emergence of
      Modern Nursing (Prodist paperback)
+Herbert Butterfield: The Origins of Modern Science, 1300-1800 (Free Press
      paperback)
+Fritjof Capra: The Turning Point: Science, Society, and the Rising Culture
      (Simon & Schuster)
Ralph C. Croizier: Traditional Medicine in Modern China
*Rene Dubos: Man Adapting (Yale paperback)
*John Ehrenreich, ed.: The Cultural Crisis of Modern Medicine
*Maureen A. Flannery: "Simple Living and Hard Choices," Hastings Center Report,
      vol. 12, no. 4, August 1982, pp. 9-12
Sally Guttmacher: "Whole in Body, Mind, and Spirit: Holistic Health and the
      Limits of Medicine," Hastings Center Report, vol. 9, no. 2, April 1979,
      pp. 15-21

19

+Ross Hume Hall: <u>Food For Nought: The Decline in Nutrition</u> (Harper paperback)
+Joshua S. Horn: <u>Away With All Pests: An English Surgeon in People's China</u>
      (Monthly Review paperback)
+Ivan Illich: <u>Medical Nemesis: The Expropriation of Health</u> (Bantam paperback)
+Michael Kidron & Ronald Segal: <u>The State of the World Atlas</u> (Simon &
      Schuster paperback)
  Charles Leslie, ed.: <u>Asian Medical Systems: A Comparative Study</u> (California
      paperback)
  Thomas McKeown: <u>The Role of Medicine: Dream, Mirage, or Nemesis?</u>
*Vincente Navarro: <u>Medicine Under Capitalism</u> (Prodist paperback)
*James P. Spradley & David W. McCurdy, eds.: <u>Conformity and Conflict: Readings
   in Cultural Anthropology</u>
  Virgil J. Vogel: <u>American Indian Medicine</u>

4. FOOD

  Richard J. Barnet: <u>The Lean Years: Politics in an Age of Scarcity</u>
  Lester R., Brown: <u>By Bread Alone</u> (Praeger paperback)
+Fritjof Capra: <u>The Turning Point: Science, Society, and the Rising Culture</u>
      (Simon & Schuster)
  Erik P. Eckholm: <u>Losing Ground: Environmental Stress and World Food
      Prospects</u>
*Wade Greene: "Triage: Who Shall Be Fed? Who Shall Starve?," <u>New York Times
      Magazine</u>, January 5, 1975, pp. 9-11, 44-45, & 51
+Ross Hume Hall: <u>Food For Nought: The Decline in Nutrition</u> (Harper paperback)
*Marvin Harris: <u>Cows, Pigs, Wars, and Witches</u> (Vintage paperback)
  Jim Hightower: <u>Eat Your Heart Out: Food Profiteering in America</u> (Random
      House paperback)
*E.L. Jones & S.J. Woolf, eds.: <u>Agrarian Change and Economic Development: The
      Historical Problems</u>
+Michael Kidron & Ronald Segal: <u>The State of the World Atlas</u> (Simon &
      Schuster paperback)
  Frances Moore Lappe, Joseph Collins, & David Kinley: <u>Aid As Obstacle: Twenty
      Questions About Our Foreign Aid and the Hungry</u> (I.F.D.P. paperback)

5. POPULATION

*Richard J. Barnet: "No Room in the Lifeboats," <u>New York Times Magazine</u>,
      April 16, 1978, pp. 32-38
*Robin Clarke, ed.: <u>Notes for the Future: An Alternative History of the Past
      Decade</u>
*Wade Greene: "Triage: Who Shall Be Fed? Who Shall Starve?," <u>New York Times
      Magazine</u>, January 5, 1975, pp. 9-11, 44-45, & 51
+Michael Kidron & Ronald Segal: <u>The State of the World Atlas</u> (Simon &
      Schuster paperback)
*Mahmood Mamdani: <u>The Myth of Population Control: Family, Caste and Class in
      an Indian Village</u>
*Thomas McKeown: <u>The Modern Rise of Population</u>
+Louise A. Tilly & Joan W. Scott: <u>Women, Work and Family</u> (Holt, Rinehart &
      Winston paperback)
  E.A. Wrigley: <u>Population and History</u> (World University Library paperback)

6. TECHNOLOGY

  Richard J. Barnet: The Lean Years: Politics in an Age of Scarcity
  John Broomfield: "High Technology: The Construction of Disaster," Alternative
       Futures, vol. 3, no. 2, Spring 1980, pp. 31-44
+Fritjof Capra: The Turning Point: Science, Society, and the Rising Culture
       (Simon & Schuster)
  Robin Clarke, ed.: Notes for the Future: An Alternative History of the Past
       Decade
*Robin Clarke: "The Pressing Need for Alternative Technology," Impact of
       Science on Society, vol. 23, no. 4, 1973, pp. 257-271
+Ross Hume Hall: Food For Nought: The Decline in Nutrition (Harper paperback)
+Ivan Illich: Medical Nemesis: The Expropriation of Health (Bantam paperback)
*Hans Jonas: "Toward a Philosophy of Technology: Knowledge, Power, and the
       Biological Revolution," Hastings Center Report, vol. 9, no. 1, February
       1979, pp. 34-43
+Michael Kidron & Ronald Segal: The State of the World Atlas (Simon & Schuster
       paperback)
*David S. Landes: The Unbound Prometheus: Technological Change and Industrial
       Development in Western Europe from 1750 to the Present
*Katherine Stone: "The Origin of Job Structures in the Steel Industry,"
       Radical America, vol. 7, no. 6, November-December 1973, pp. 19-64
  E.P. Thompson: "Time, Work-Discipline, and Industrial Capitalism," Past and
       Present, no. 38, December 1967, pp. 56-97
*Peter Harper: "In Search of Allies for the Soft Technologies," Impact of
       Science on Society, vol. 23, no. 4, 1973, pp. 287-305

21

READING ASSIGNMENTS

* Available in course pack

+ Available in bookstores for purchase

IT IS RECOMMENDED THAT THE ASSIGNMENTS BE READ IN THE ORDER LISTED.

FOR WEEK
BEGINNING:

1. January 10   *Pollard, pp. 9-30 and 185-205
                      *Livingston, pp. 16-23 and 148-182
                      *Marcus

2. January 17   +Butterfield, Chap. V
                      +Capra, Chaps. II and IV
                      *Boulding
                      +Kuhn, Chaps. II-IV

3. January 24   +Kuhn, Chaps. V-IX, XI, and XIII

4. January 31   *Evelyn Keller in Ruddick & Daniels, pp. 77-91
                      *Naomi Weisstein in Ruddick & Daniels, pp. 241-250
                      +Capra, Chap. III
                      *Dorothy Lee in Spradley & McCurdy, pp. 81-95
                      *Geertz
                      *Whorf

5. February 7   +Butterfield, Chap. III
                      +Capra, Chap. V
                      *Barbara Ehrenreich & Deidre English in Ehrenreich,
                           pp. 123-143
                      *Leonard Stein in Spradley & McCurdy, pp. 185-193

6. February 14   +Illich, parts I & II
                      *Navarro

7. February 28   *Flannery
                      +Horn, pp. 53-65, 70-80, and 129-146
                      +Capra, Chap. X
                      *Dubos
                      +Kidron & Segal, maps 36, 45

8. March 7   *Jones & Woolf
                      +Hall, pp. 129-171
                      +Capra, pp. 252-260
                      *Harris
                      +Kidron & Segal, maps 18, 21, 40, 44

9. March 14   +Hall, pp. 83-128 and 7-52
                      +Kidron & Segal, maps 53, 54

10. March 21   *McKeown: Population, pp. 1-6, 18-43, and 152-163
                    +Tilly & Scott, pp. 24-30, 89-103, 167-175, 216-225

11. March 28   *Linda Gordon in Ehrenreich, pp. 144-184
                    *Mamdani
                    *Greene
                    *Barnet: "No Room in the Lifeboats"
                    +Kidron & Segal, maps 32, 38, 49, 52, 63

12. April 4   *Landes
                    *Stone
                    *Jonas
                    +Kidron & Segal, maps 19, 20

13. April 11   +Capra, Chap. XII
                    +Illich, Chap. VIII
                    *Clarke: "The Pressing Need for Alternative Technology"
                    *Harper

LECTURES

Week #

	January	5	Course introduction
		7	Idea of progress
1		10	Linear & cyclical time
		12	Idea of progress: Bacon & Descartes
		14	Idea of progress: Bentham & Marx
2		17	Idea of progress: Darwin & Wollstonecraft
		19	Science: the clockwork universe
		21	Normal science & scientific revolutions
3		24	Science as a field of power
		26	Social construction of scientific facts
		28	Linear & non-linear perception
4		31	Quantum mechanics & the participatory universe
	February	2	In reserve
		4	Traditional history of modern medicine
5		7	Presuppositions of scientific medicine
		9	History of U.S. medical profession
		11	Medical nemesis
6		14	Movie: "Are You Doing This For Me Doctor, Or Am I Doing It For You?"
		16	Movie: "Daughters of Time"
		18	In reserve
7		28	Medicine as a field of power
	March	2	Holistic health care: China & India
		4	Movie: "Eduardo the Healer"
8		7	What is disease?
		9	Technology, Food, Population
		11	Modern agricultural revolutions
9		14	Modern agricultural revolutions
		16	The shrewd peasant
		18	Real food or "fun food"?
10		21	Population & resources
		23	Population & resources
		25	Tape: "Population Control: the new fascism" – Germaine Greer
11		28	Population planning: discussion
		30	Populations & fossil fuel depletion
	April	1	Good Friday: no lecture
12		4	Humans & their technologies
		6	Movie: "Energy & Morality"
		8	High technology: the construction of disaster
13		11	Progress or decay?
		13	Progress or decay?
		15	Progress or decay?

EXTRA MOVIE (evening this week to be arranged): "Life & Times of Rosie the Riveter"

| | | 18 | In reserve |

24

Columbia University

CONTEMPORARY CIVILIZATION[*]

This course is intended as an introduction to some of the classic works which have shaped the western political and philosophical traditions. Obviously, any course which moves from the ancient Greeks to 18th century France in one semester can make no claims to comprehensiveness, and the works selected for study are only offered as a representative sampling. Still, this survey allows us to approach some of the central problems and tendencies in western thought, and the course should also provide students with a firm foundation to continue work in this area, whether in philosophy, history, or political science. Perhaps even more importantly and of even more general relevance, the course will provide students with ample opportunity to learn how to read critically. The assigned readings are, for the most part, primary sources, that is, texts written by major western thinkers, not secondary works, that is, analyses of these thinkers. The work of analysis will thus fall on your shoulders. In every case, it will be important to ask of the text: who is writing? What is the author's perspective? In what historical context is the text written? For whom? With what purpose in mind? At the center of the course are the fundamental questions of the ways in which people's perceptions and understanding of the world around them have changed over time, and in particular, the implications which this has had for political behavior, understood in the broadest sense of the word.

Course requirements will include two short papers (approx. 7 typed pages), one brief oral report, a mid-term and a final. Unexcused lateness for papers will be penalized. Class participation will provide an essential basis for the evaluation of your work in this course and will constitute 25% of your semester grade. The class will be conducted almost exclusively as a discussion seminar, not a lecture, and its success or failure will depend on your ability to contribute to our work in the course. Reading assignments should be prepared before class. As you'll see from the list of topics that follows, we will be marching forward relentlessly in the course of the semester, and it is absolutely essential that you keep up with assignments.

I will provide some historical background for class discussions, and class members will do the same in assigned oral reports. In general, students totally unfamiliar with the

_____

[*] Contemporary Civilisation in the West is part of Columbia University's "Core curriculum." Along with courses in "literature and humanities", "art humanities," "music humanities," and the sciences, it is required of all Columbia College Students. Instructors teach a basic list of "great books" and can fill in the remainder of the semester with books of their own choosing.

historical background of any given text are strongly encouraged
to consult a standard western civilization textbook, e.g.,
Chambers, Grew, Herliny, Rabb and Woloch, The Western Experience.
Another valuable textbook, useful for the study of the historical
development of political theory, is George H. Sabine and Thomas
L. Thorson, A History of Political Theory (fourth edition). If
you want additional suggestions for readings on any given topic,
please consult with me.

The mid-term will be on Monday, October 24. Due dates and
assignments for the papers will be announced early in the
semester.

Although all readings for the course will be on reserve in
the College Library, students are strongly advised to purchase
the following texts, since we will be reading substantial parts
of them:

- Plato, The Republic (Penguin, trans. Lee)
- Aristotle, The Politics (Oxford, trans. Barker)
- Susan Moller Okin, Women in Western Political Thought
  (Princeton)
- Lefkowitz and Fant, Women in Greece and Rome (Samuel
  Stevens)
- Augustine, City of God (Doubleday Image, trans. Walsh)
- Eileen Power, Medieval Women (Cambridge)
- Marc Bloch, Feudal Society, v. 2 (Chicago)
- Machiavelli, The Prince (any edition)
- Hillerbrand, ed., The Protestant Reformation (Harper
  and Row)
- Descartes, Discourse on Method and Meditations on First
  Philosophy (trans. Donald Cress, Hackett)
- Hobbes, Leviathan (ed. Michael Oakeshott, Collier)
- Locke, Two Treatises on Government (ed. Laslett,
  Mentor)
- Rousseau, The First and Second Discoursesb (ed.
  Masters, St. Martin's)
- Rousseau, The Social Contract (trans. Cranston,
  Penguin)

If at all possible, try to make use of these editions.
Discussions will obviously be facilitated if we can all refer
easily to the same texts. I have not ordered any specific
edition of the Bible, since we will be reading so little of this
book, and any edition will suffice. Some other readings will be
available only on reserve or in the form of handouts.

READING ASSIGNMENTS:

W 9/7   General Introduction

M 9/12   The Republic, Parts I-IV

W 9/14   The Republic, Parts V-VIII

M 9/19   The Republic, Part IX

W 9/21   The Politics, Book I, i-x, xii-xiii; Book II, i-
           v, vii-x

M 9/26   The Politics, Book III, entire; Book IV, 1-iii,
           vii-xii

W 9/28   The Politics, Book V, entire; Book VI, i-iii, vi-
           viii, Book VII, entire

M 10/3   Lefkowitz and Fant, Women in Greece and Rome, pp.
           18-43, 47-51, 56-84; Okin, Women in Western
           Political Thought, pp. 3-27.

W 10/5   Review, Republic, Part VI; Politics, Book II
           selections; Okin, pp. 28-96.

M 10/10   Bible-Genesis 1-22; Exodus, 1-7, 10-14, 18-24,
           32-34; 1 Samuel, 8-10, 12, 15-17; I Kings, 2-5,
           9; Matthew, 1:1-17; Luke, 1-6:1-20, 9, 10:25-42,
           12, 15, 17:20-37, 18, 22:39-71, 23:1-48, 24;
           Romans; I Corinthians 12

W 10/12   Augustine, City of God, XI, 1-3, 5, 6, 10, 21,
           22, 24, 26; XII, 1-9, XIII, 1-3, 13-15; XIV, 1-6,
           11-15, 28; XV, 1, 2, 4; XVI, 41; XVIII, 1, 2, 53-
           54; XIX, 4-5, 7, 13-15, 26; XXI, 1, 2, 22, 24

M 10/17   Bloch, Feudal Society, v. 2, 283-92, 320-31, 345-
           55, 375-93, 408-37

27

W 10/19	Power, _Medieval Women_, entire
M 10/24	Mid-Term Exam in Class
W 10/26	Machiavelli, _The Prince_, i-iii, v, vi, ix-xi, xiv-xix, xxii-xxvi
M 10/31	Joan Kelly-Gadol, "Did Women Have a Renaissance?" in Bridenthal and Koonz, _Becoming Visible_, pp. 137-64; Fracesco Barbaro, "On Wifely Duties," in Kohl and Witt, _The Earthly Republic_, pp. 189-228.
W 11/2	Hillerbrand, ed., _The Protestant Reformation_, pp. 1-28, 43-87, 172-221.
M 11/7	HOLIDAY!!!
W 11/9	Descartes, _Discourse on Method_ (entire); _Meditations_ (third meditation)
11/14-16	Hobbes, _Leviathan_, Chapters 1-6, 10-13, 14-21, 26, 28-29
11/21-23	Locke, "Second Treatise," chapters i-viii; ix-end
M 11/28	Rousseau, "Discourse on the Origin and Foundations of Inequality (Second Discourse)" (pay particular attention to Notes i, and 1)
W 11/30	Rousseau, _Social Contract_, Books I-II
M 12/5	Rousseau, _Social Contract_, Books III and IV (omit Ch. 4-7)
W 12/7	Okin, pp. 96-166; Zillah R. Eisenstein, "John Locke: Patriarchal Antipatriarchalism," in _The Radical Future of Liberal Feminism_, pp. 33-54.
M 12/7	Review

Moeller
Contemporary Civilization
Spring Semester 1983

In the spring semester, we will read all or most of the following books:

I. Kant, Foundations of the Metaphysics of Morals (Library of Liberal Arts)
E. Burke, Reflections on the Revolution in France and T. Paine, The Rights of Man
   (bound together in a Doubleday edition)
Adam Smith, Selections from the Wealth of Nations (AHM-Crofts Classics)
Mary Wollstonecraft, A Vindication of the Rights of Woman (Norton, ed. Carol
   Poston)
J.S. Mill, A Selection of His Works (Bobbs-Merrill)
J.S. Mill, The Subjection of Women (MIT)
The Marx-Engels Reader, ed. Robert Tucker (Norton, red edition)·
P. Appleman, ed., Darwin (second edition, includng essays on Darwin, Norton)
F. Nietzsche, On the Genealogy of Morals (Vintage)   ·
A. Kollontai, Selected Writings of Alexandra Kollontai (ed. A. Holt, Norton)
M. Foucault; The History of Sexuality, Vol. 1: An Introduction (Vintage)
S. Freud, Three Essays on the Theory of Sexuality (Basic Books, Harper)
S. Freud, Civilization and Its Discontents (Norton)
Lenin, State and Revolution (International Publishers)
A. Gramsci, The Modern Prince (International Publishers)
V. Woolf, Three Guineas (Penguin)

All of these books have been ordered in these editions in the University
Bookstore. They will also be on reserve in the College Library. In addition,
we will read selections from Susan Moller Okin, Women in Western Political
Thought (Princeton) which most of you purchased in the first semester.

M 1/24. Introduction

W 1/27   Kant, Foundations, Hume, selections from ICCW reader (on reserve
         in College Library; since we will begin with Kant, you might want
         to get a head start on him before the semester begins)

M 1/31   Burke, Reflections, 16-65, 71-76, 85-85, 91(bottom)- 92, 106-111,
         138-47, 153-55, 179-90, 263-66
         Documents on French Revolution (hand-out)

W 2/2   Paine, Rights, 269-332, 379-83, 387-420

M 2/7   Rousseau, Emile, Book V, selections (hand-out)
         Wollstonecraft, Vindication, 1-52, 115-21, 140-50

W 2/9   Smith, Wealth, selections

M 2/14   Smith, Wealth, selections; Bowditch, ed., Voices of the Industrial
         Revolution, (Malthus) ; Marx-Engels Reader, 203-17, 579-86

W 2/16 Mill, A Selection (On Liberty)

M 2/21 Mill, A Selection (On Utilitarianism); Bowditch, ed., Voices, (Bentham)

W 2/23 Marx-Engels Reader, 80-81, 133-35, 147-200

M 2/28 Marx-Engels Reader, 303-28, 336-61, 431-35

W 3/2   Marx-Engels Reader, 439-42, 469-500, 520-73

M 3/7   Darwin, 35-61, 74-87, 108-31

W 3/9   Darwin, 132-38, 196-208

SPRING BREAK!!!!!!

M 3/21 Mill, On the Subjection of Women

W 3/23 Okin, selections on Mill; Marx-Engels Reader, 734-59; John Stuart Mill
        and Harriet Taylor Mill, Essays on Sex Equality; Selections from
        Harriet Taylor; Kollontai, Selected Writings, 39-76, 127-39

M 3/28 Nietzsche, On the Genealogy of Morals

W 3/30

M 4/4   S. Freud, Three Essays (essays 2 and 3)

W 4/6   S. Freud, Civilization

M 4/11 M. Foucault, History of Sexuality

W 4/13 M. Foucault, History of Sexuality

M 4/18 Lenin, State and Revolution

W 4/20 Kollontai, Selections, 216-92

M 4/25 Max Weber, "Politics as a Vocation," in Gerth and Mills, eds.,
        From Max Weber, 77-128.

W 4/27 V. Woolf, Three Guineas (Complete)

M 5/2   A. Gramsci, Modern Prince (On Culture, "Modern Prince")

University of California, Berkeley

History 280B   Lynn Hunt
Old Regime and the French Revolution: Course Outline

Week 1.   Please read for the first meeting Pierre Goubert, The
Ancien Régime (Harper TB). This book and all others
starred on the list will be available at Ed Hunolt's
book store. All of the reading listed will be on
reserve at HGS and some of it will be available as
well in the History Library.

Those who have trouble reading French or who plan to
concentrate in another national history (Italy, Germany)
will be able to substitute reading for some of the reading
in French.

Week 2.   General Interpretations

*A. de Tocqueville, The Old Regime and the French Revolution.

*John McManners, "The Historiography of the French Revolution,"
in The New Cambridge Modern History, vol. VIII: The American and French Revolutions, 1763-93, pp. 618-652.

Albert Soboul, "The Classic Historiography of the French
Revolution and its Critics," Proceedings of the Western
Society for French History (1974), 443-63.

Week 3.   The Enlightenment and the Revolution

Daniel Mornet, Les Origines Intellectuelles de la Révolution
française (1933). Do not read every word. Look it over
to get a sense of his sources, structure of argument, and
conclusions.

Robert Darnton, "The Encyclopédie Wars of Pre-revolutionary
France," American Historical Review, 78 (Dec., 1973),
1331-52.

Daniel Roche, "Milieux académiques provinciaux et société des
lumières," in G. Bollème, et al., Livre et société dans la
France du XVIIIe siècle, vol. 1 (1965), pp. 93-184. (This
will be in the History Library)

      If you cannot handle Roche, you may substitute:

Robert Darnton, "Trade in the Taboo," in Paul J. Korshin, ed.,
The Widening Circle: Essays on the Circulation of Literature
in Eighteenth Century Europe (Phila., 1976), pp. 12-83.

AND

31

Carolyn Lougee, "The Enlightenment and the French Revolution: Some Recent Perspectives," Eighteenth Century Studies, 11 (Fall, 1977), 84-102.

Week 4   The Aristocratic Reaction: Rural France

*Douglas Dakin, "The Breakdown of the Old Regime in France" ch. 21 of The American and French Revolutions.

- *Georges Lefebvre, The Coming of the French Revolution, part I.

*Alfred Cobban, The Social Interpretation of the French Revolution, chs. 4 and 5.

François Furet, "Le Catéchisme révolutionnaire," Annales: E.S.C., 26 (1971), 255-289.

Pierre de Saint-Jacob, Les Paysans de la Bourgogne du Nord au dernier siècle de l'Ancien Régime (Paris, 1960). Read in the same way you read Mornet.

Week 5   The Aristocratic Reaction: Ideology and Institutions

David Bien, "La Réaction aristocratique avant 1789," Annales: E.S.C., 29 (1974), 23-48 and 505-534. This is very important and worth the effort to read in French, even though it's a translation from the English!

Colin Lucas, "Nobles, Bourgeois and the Origins of the French Revolution," Past and Present, no. 60 (1973), 84-126.

*Jules Michelet, History of the French Revolution, pages to be announced in class.

You might read ahead this week in order to leave yourself more time for writing the paper due Week 6.

Week 6   The Economic and Constitutional Crisis.

David Bien, "The Secrétaires du roi: Absolutism, Corps, and Privilege under the Ancien Régime," this article will be available only in the History Library.

*J. F. Bosher, "French administration and Public and Finance in their European Setting," ch. 20 of The American and French Revolutions.

George V. Taylor, "Revolutionary and Nonrevolutionary Content in the Cahiers of 1789: An Interim Report," French Historical Studies, 7 (1972), 479-502.

*Lefebvre, The Coming..., part II.

Ernest Labrousse, La Crise de l'économie française à la
fin de l'Ancien Régime et au début de la Révolution
(Paris, 1944).
Read for sources and main argument.

A 7-10 pp. PAPER SUMMING UP YOUR VIEWS OF THE ARISTOCRATIC REACTION
WILL BE DUE IN CLASS THIS WEEK.

Week 7.   1789

George V. Taylor, "Noncapitalist Wealth and the Origins
of the French Revolution," American Historical Review,
72 (1967), 469-496.

*Lefebvre, The Coming...., finish.

Elizabeth Eisenstein, "Who Intervened in 1788?" American
Historical Review, 71 (1965), 77-103.

Jeffrey Kaplow, et al., "Class in the French Revolution,"
American Historical Review, 72 (1967), 469-522.

Lynn Hunt, "Committees and Communes: Local Politics and
National Revolution in 1789," Comparative Studies in
Society and History, 18 (1976), 321-346.

Week 8.   The Terror

*Michelet, History, pp. numbers to be announced.

*Cobban, chs. 6, 8-11.

Albert Soboul, The Parisian Sans-Culottes and the French
Revolution, tr. Gwynne Lewis (1964). Look through for
main arguments.

*Richard Cobb, The Police and the People (1970), pp. 118-211.

Lynn Hunt, "The Rhetoric of Revolution in France", paper
available only in the History Library.

Week 9.   The Directory

*Martyn Lyons, France under the Directory (1975).

Lynn Hunt, et al., "The Failure of the Liberal Republic in
France," Journal of Modern History, 51 (Dec., 1979),
available only in History library.

33

Week 10.   Napoleon

        *Felix Markham, <u>Napoleon and the Awakening of Europe</u>.

        G. Chaussinand-Nogaret et al., "Les Notables du 'Grand
          Empire' en 1810", <u>Annales: E.S.C.</u>, 26 (1971), 1052-
          1075.

        Edward A. Whitcomb, "Napoleon's Prefects," <u>American</u>
          <u>Historical Review</u>, 79 (1974), 1089-1118.

        *Cobban, chs. 7 and 12.

FINAL 10 pp. PAPER DUE MONDAY OF FINALS WEEK. THIS PAPER SHOULD
        FOCUS ON TOCQUEVILLE AND CONTRAST HIS INTERPRETATION TO
        REST OF READING, in particular to Lefebvre-Soboul and to
        Cobban.

HISTORY 549: THE OLD REGIME AND THE REVOLUTION IN FRANCE

BACKGROUND

Bibliography: The older literature is surveyed in detail in the old "Clio" series. Edmond Préclin and Victor-L. Tapié, LE XVIIIe Siecle (Paris, 1952), 2 vol. For a survey of work since 1952 and a penetrating synthesis of it, see the "Nouvelle Clio" by Robert Mandrou. LA FRANCE AUX XVIIe ET XVIIIe SIECLES (Paris, 1967). For research and reading-in-depth, consult the systematic bibliographies: the current BIBLIOGRAPHIE ANNUELLE DE L'HISTOIRE DE FRANCE (Paris, 1953- and its predecessors; A. Martin, BIBLIOGRAPHIE DES TRAVAUX PUBLIES DE 1866 A 1879 SUR L'HISTOIRE DE FRANCE DE 1500 A 1789 (Paris, 1932-38), 2 vols.; G. Brière and P. Caron, REPERTOIRE METHODIQUE DE L'HISTOIRE MODERNE ET CONTEMPORAINE DE LA FRANCE (Paris, 1899-1924), 9 vols.; and P. Caron and H. Stein, REPERTOIRE BIBLIOGRAPHIQUE DE L'HISTOIRE DE FRANCE (Paris, 1923-38), 6 vols. A Cioranesco, BIB- LIOGRAPHIE DE LA LITTERATURE FRANÇAISE DU DIX HUITIEME SIECLE (Paris, 1969).

Journals: The two main tendencies in French historiography are represented by ANNALES: ECONOMIES, SOCIETES, CIVILISATIONS and ANNALES HISTORIQUES DE LA REVOLUTION FRANÇAISE, organs respectively of the VIe Section of the Ecole Pratique des Hautes Etudes ("Annales school") and the Société des Etudes Robespierristes (the "Sorbonne"). Two learned societies, among the many in this field, publish periodicals that should be followed, although they tend to be literary in character: DIX-HUITIEME SIECLE (published by the French Société d'étude du dix-huitième siècle) and EIGHTEENTH CENTURY STUDIES (published by the American Society for Eighteenth Century Studies). A great deal of material on the literary side also crops up in STUDIES ON VOL- TAIRE AND THE EIGHTEENTH CENTURY by Theodore Bestermann, who is a learned society unto himself. Among journals devoted to French history, see REVUE D'HISTOIRE MODERNE ET CONTEMPORAINE, REVUE HIS- TORIQUE, and FRENCH HISTORICAL STUDIES. A great many lesser-known journals have excellent material -- the ANNALES DE NORMANDIE, for instance. L'INFORMATION HISTORIQUE contains regular historiographical essays. And general journals, notably PAST AND PRESENT, have published much important work recently.

Textbooks: The best by far is Pierre Goubert, L'ANCIEN REGIME (Paris, 1969 and 1973), 2 vols. Robert Mandrou, LA FRANCE AU XVIIe ET XVIIIe SIECLES (Paris, 1967) is briefer, more bibliographical and also incisive. The most useful works in English are John Lough, AN INTRODUCTION TO EIGHTEENTH CENTURY FRANCE (London, 1960 -- beware, should you want to assign it to students; it contains long citations of sources in French); Alfred Cobban, A HISTORY OF MODERN FRANCE (London, 1957), vol. i; and Lionell Gossman, FRENCH SOCIETY AND CUL- TURE (Englewood Cliffs, 1972). For more detail and more information on the European context, see the volumes in the "Peuples et civili- sations" series, although they are largely outdated for social and economic history, and in English the "Langer" or "Rise of Modern Europe" series, which suffers from the same defect. More up-to-date are individual volumes in the "Collection U" series in French (uneven quality) and several recent French works of synthesis; Pierre Chaunu,

LA CIVILISATION DE L'EUROPE DES LUMIERES (Paris, 1971); Roland Mous-
nier and Ernest LaBrousse, LE XVIIIe SIECLE (Paris, 1967); Fernand
Braudel and Ernest Labrousse, et al, HISTOIRE ECONOMIQUE ET SOCIALE
DE LA FRANCE (Paris, 1973).

For literary history, see Claude Bellessort et al, MANUEL D'HISTOIRE
LITTERAIRE DE LA FRANCE (Paris, 1969), vol. III.

Research tools: For research it is crucial to understand the organization of French libraries and archives. Begin with Pierre Caron,
MANUEL PRATIQUE POUR L'ETUDE DE LA REVOLUTION FRANÇAISE (Paris, 1947),
in order to understand the standardized "séries". Then look through
the extensive holdings of catalogues of departmental archives and
libraries in Firestone: CATALOGUE GENERAL DES MANUSCRITS DES BIBLI-
OTHEQUES PUBLIQUES DE FRANCE (Paris 1886-), 58 vols. (so far!)
arranged by département with excellent indexes. BIBLIOTHEQUE NATION-
ALE: CATALOGUE GENERAL DES MANUSCRITS FRANÇAIS (Paris, 1898-) with
various supplements. INVENTAIRE DES ARCHIVES DU DEPARTMENT DE...
(under name of département.) And, for the revolutionary period, André
Martin and Gérard Walter, CATALOGUE DE L'HISTOIRE DE LA REVOLUTION
FRANÇAISE (Paris, 1936), 4 vols. and Gérard Walter, REPERTOIRE DE
L'HISTOIRE DE LA REVOLUTION FRANÇAISE (Paris, 1941), 2 vols." For
printed material, you will have to rely heavily on the great catalogues of the Bibliothèque Nationale and the British Museum, but
first make the acquaintance of the new NATIONAL UNION CATALOGUE, a
superb instrument of research, which identifies anonymous works and
gives their location in American libraries. You will often run into
problems of attribution and so should consult Barbier's DICTIONNAIRE
DES OUVRAGES ANONYMES (Paris, 1822) and Querard's LES SUPERCHERIES
LITTERAIRES DEVOILEES (Paris, 1845-56). France has no equivalent of
the British DICTIONARY OF NATIONAL BIOGRAPHY, although one is now
beginning to rise off the ground; but you can get information, not
always reliable, about many 18th-century figures in Michaud's
DICTIONNAIRE DE BIOGRAPHIE UNIVERSELLE as well as other "unscienti-
fic" sources, like Querard's LA FRANCE LITTERAIRE (Paris, 1826-42),
10 vol. and Bachaumont's MEMOIRES SECRETS POUR SERVIE A L'HISTOIRE
DE LA REPUBLIQUE DES LETTRES (London, 1787-89), 36 vol. (use the
index of personal names); and the superb scholarly editions of Voltaire (Theodore Bestermann, ed.), Rousseau (Ralph Leigh, Ed.), and
Diderot (Georges Roth, ed.) -- they contain information on a wide
variety of topics, not just on literature and have excellent indexes
and notes. Eighteenth-century periodicals provide an enormous and
insufficiently explored source of information. For an introduction
to them, see Claude Bellanger, Jacques Godechot, et al, HISTOIRE
GENERALE DE LA PRESSE FRANÇAISE (Paris, 1969), vol. I; but it has
not replaced Eugéne Hatin, HISTOIRE POLITIQUE ET LITTERAIRE DE LA
PRESSE EN FRANCE (1859-61), 8 vol., and especially Hatin's BIBLIOG-
RAPHIE HISTORIQUE ET CRITIQUE DE LA PRESSE PERIODIQUE FRANÇAISE
(Paris, 1866), where you can get background information on each
journal under an alphabetical listing by title.

History 549

THE OLD REGIME AND THE REVOLUTION IN FRANCE   Prof. R. Darnton

Weekly Readings:

I.   The Regime: an overview and a close-up

Alexis de Tocqueville, THE OLD REGIME AND THE FRENCH REVOLUTION.
ETAT ET DESCRIPTION DE LA VILLE DE MONTPELLIER FAIT EN 1768 in
J. Berthelé, ed., MONTPELLIER EN 1768...(Montpellier, 1909).

II. Peasant Society

Pierre Goubert, L"ANCIEN REGIME (Paris, 1969), I, chaps. 4,5,6.
Restif de la Bretonne, LA VIE DE MON PERE (Neuchâtel, 1779).

III. Nobles and Bourgeois

Goubert, chaps. 7,8,9,10,11.
Robert Foster, THE NOBILITY OF TOULOUSE (Baltimore, 1960).
François Furet and Adeline Daumard, STRUCTURES ET RELATIONS SOC-
   IALES A PARIS AU XVIIIe SIECLE (Paris, 1961), pp. 7-41.
L.-S. Mercier, TABLEAU DE PARIS (Paris, 1783). Read the following
   brief chapters (they vary according to the editions and are
   scattered in volumes I through VIII): "Coup d'oeil général,"
   "Le bourgeois," "Petites bourgeoises," "Des Grosses fortunes,"
   "Rentiers," "Bonne compagnie," "Oisifs," "Etats indéfiniss-
   ables." "Capitalistes." "Ton du monde," "Sots usages abolis,"
   "Légères observations," "Le nouveau débarqué," "Financières."

IV. Economics and Demography

Goubert, chaps 2,3.
Ernest Labrousse, LA CRISE DE L"ECONOMIE FRANÇAISE (Paris, 1944),
   introduction only.
Michel Morineau, "Was There an Agricultural Revolution in 18th-
   Century France?" in Rondo Cameron, ed., ESSAYS IN FRENCH
   ECONOMIC HISTORY (Homewood, Ill., 1970), 170-182.
George V. Taylor, "Non-capitalist Wealth and the Origins of the
   French Revolution," AMERICAN HISTORICAL REVIEW vol. 72(1967),
   469-96.
Jacques Dupâquier, "French Population in the 17th and 18th
   Centuries," in Cameron, ed., ESSAYS IN FRENCH ECONOMIC HISTORY.
Jacques Dupâquier, "Revolution française et révolution démo-
   graphique," in Ernst Hinrichs, Eberhard Schmitt, and Rudolph
   Vierhaus, eds., VOM ANCIEN REGIME ZUR FRANZOSISCHEN REVOLUTION,
   FORSCHUNGEN UND PERSPEKTIVEN (Göttingen, 1978), 233-260.
Emmanuel Le Roy Ladurie, "Les Paysans françeis au XVIIIe siècle,
   dans la perspective de la Révolution française," Ibid, 261-278.

V.   Religion

Jean Delumeau, LE CATHOLICISME ENTRE LUTHER ET VOLTAIRE, "Nouvelle
   Clio" (Paris, 1971), pp. 155-330.
John McManners, "FRENCH ECCLESIASTICAL SOCIETY UNDER T HE ANCIEN
   REGIME: ANGERS (Manchester, 1960).
Geneviève Bollème, LA BIBLIOTHEQUE BLEUE ("Collection Archives"
   Paris, 1971), pp. 211-266.

VI. Enlightenment

> Robert Shackleton, "The Enlightenment: Free Inquiry and the World
> of Ideas," in Alfred Cobban, ed., THE EIGHTEENTH CENTURY:
> EUROPE IN THE AGE OF ENLIGHTENMENT (New York and London, 1969),
> 259-278.
> Ernst Cassirer, THE PHILOSOPHY OF THE ENLIGHTENMENT (Boston, 1955),
> Chaps. 1,2,3.
> François Furet, "La 'librairie' du royaume de France au 18e siècle,"
> in Furet et al, LIVRE ET SOCIETE DANS LA FRANCE DU XVIIIe
> SIECLE (Paris and The Hague, 1965), 3-32.
> Jean Le Rond d'Alembert, "Discours préliminaire" to the Encyclo-
> pédie of Diderot and d'Alembert. (There are many editions of
> the Discourse and a good translation into English by Richard
> Schwab, Indianapolis,1976).

VII. Politics and Administration

> J. F. Bosher, "French Administration and Public Finance in Their
> European Setting," in THE NEW CAMBRIDGE MODERN HISTORY, vol.
> VIII (Cambridge, 1965), 565-591.
> Jean Egret, LOUIS XV ET L'OPPOSITION PARLEMENTAIRE (Paris, 1970).
> E.-J.-F. Barbier, JOURNAL HISTORIQUE ET ANECDOTIQUE DU REGNE DE
> LOUIS XV, 1718-1763 (Paris, 1847-1856), vol. III, p.p. 58-112
> (entries For The Year 1749).

VIII. The Revolution: from the collapse of the monarchy to the Legis-
lative Assembly

> Douglas Dakin, "The Breakdown of the Old Regime in France," THE
> NEW CAMBRIDGE MODERN HISTORY, vol. VIII, 592-617.
> Norman Hampson, A SOCIAL HISTORY OF THE FRENCH REVOLUTION (Toronto,
> 1963), chaps. 3,4, and 5.
> J. M. Roberts and R. C. Cobb, FRENCH REVOLUTION DOCUMENTS (Oxford,
> 1966), vol. I, pp. 135-185.

IX. The Revolution: radicalization

> Hampson, chaps. 6 and 7.
> M. J. Sydenham, THE GIRONDINS (London, 1961), pp. 99-212.
> Alison Patrick, "Political Divisions in the French National Con-
> vention," JOURNAL OF MODERN HISTORY vol. 41 (1969), pp. 421-474.
> J. M. Roberts and John Hardman, FRENCH REVOLUTION DOCUMENTS
> (Oxford, 1973), vol. II, pp. 46-80.

X. The Revolution: Terror and Counter-Terror

> Hampson, chaps. 8, 9, and 10.
> Albert Soboul, THE PARISIAN SANS-CULOTTES AND THE FRENCH REVO-
> LUTION (translation and abridgment by Gwynne Lewis, Oxford,
> 1964).
> Roberts and Hardman, FRENCH REVOLUTION DOCUMENTS, vol. II,
> pp. 116-132 and 161-181.

H 549

XI. The Meaning of it All

François Furet, PENSER LA REVOLUTION FRANÇAISE (PARIS, 1978), pp. 1-172.
Jacques Godechot, review of Furet in ANNALES HISTORIQUES DE LA REVOLUTION FRANÇAISE, No. 235 (Jan.-March, 1979), pp. 135-141.
Alfred Cobban, THE SOCIAL INTERPRETATION OF THE FRENCH REVOLUTION (Cambridge, 1964).
Albert Soboul, "L'Historiographie classique de la Révolution française," HISTORICAL REFLECTIONS vol. I, no. 2 (winter, 1974), pp. 141-163.
Albert Soboul, "Foreword to the English-language edition" and "Preface" in Soboul, THE FRENCH REVOLUTION 1787-1799 (New York, 1975).
Antoine Casanova, Claude Mazauric, Régine Robin, "La Révolution française, a-t-elle eu lieu?", LA NOUVELLE CRITIQUE: POLITIQUE, MARXISME, CULTURE, no. 52, nouvelle série (April, 1972), pp. 22-37.

RD:lah 1/7/80

THE UNIVERSITY OF WISCONSIN
Department of History
Semester I   1971-72

HISTORY 353   (History of Europe 1815-1871)   MR. HAMEROW

Textbook: Gordon A. Craig, Europe since 1815

LIST OF TOPICS

I.   Eighteenth Century Antecedents. Textbook: Pp. 3-10.
        R. B. Mowat. The Age of Reason, Chaps 1 and 20
        A. Aulard. The French Revolution, Vol. III, Ch. 5
        G. Bruun. ·Europe and the French Imperium, Ch. 11

II.   Vienna and the Post-War Alliance System. Textbook: Pp. 11-35.
        H. Nicolson. The Congress of Vienna, Chaps. 15-16
        C. K. Webster. The Congress of Vienna, Pt. III
        Introduction to Contemporary Civilization, Vol. II. Pp. 174-179 (3rd ed.)

III.   The Age of Reform in England. Textbook: Pp. 91-122, 221-228.
        E. L. Woodward. The Age of Reform, Book I, Ch. 2
        H. C. F. Bell. Lord Palmerston, Vol. I, Ch. 12
        J. F. Scott, A. Baltzly. Readings in European History, Pp. 94-112

IV.   Reaction and Revolution in France. Textbook: Pp. 64-90.
        E. Bourgeois, History of Modern France, Vol. I. Ch. 3
        F. B. Artz. France under the Bourbon Restoration, Ch. IV
        F. M. Anderson. Constitutions and Other Select Documents, Pp. 485-514

V.   Nationalism and Liberalism in Germany. Textbook: Pp. 44-50, 54-63.
        H. von Treitschke. History of Germany, Vol. III, Pp. 168-206
        W. O. Henderson. The Zollverein, Ch. 3
        J. G. Legge. Rhyme and Revolution, Book III, Ch. I

VI.   The Rise of Italian Nationalism. Textbook: Pp. 186-190.
        B. King. History of Italian Unification, Vol. I, Ch. 7
        K. R. Greenfield. Economics and Liberalism in the Risorgimento, Part II , Ch. 7
        Introduction to Contemporary Civilization, Vol. II, Pp. 539-544 (3rd ed.)

VII.   Austria: The Supra-National State. Textbook: Pp. 50-54.
        O. Jaszi. The Dissolution of the Habsburg Monarchy, Chs. 12-13
        R. A. Kann. The Multinational Empire, Vol. I, Chs. 1-2
        The Memoirs of Metternich, (N.Y. ed.), Vol. II, Pp. 281-337

VIII.   The Russian Autocracy. Textbook: Pp. 36-44, 230-234.
        V. O. Kluchevsky. A History of Russia, Vol. V, Ch. 19-20
        J. Mavor. An Economic History of Russia, Book II. Ch. 8
        J. F. Scott, A Baltzly. Readings in European History, Pp. 31-44

IX.   The Balkan Problem. Textbook: Pp. 153-167.
        W. Miller. The Ottoman Empire, Ch. 5
        V. J. Puryear. England, Russia, and the Straits, Ch. 2
        J. F. Scott, A Baltzly. Readings in European History, Pp. 352-362

X.   1848. Textbook: Pp. 123-142, 190-192.
        D. C. McKay. The National Workshops, Introduction and Ch. I.
        D. Valentin. 1848: Chapters of German History, Chs. 8-10
        J. C. Legge. Rhyme and Revolution, Book VII, Chs. I and II

XI.   Second Republic and Second Empire in France. Textbook: Pp.168-185.
        F. A. Simpson. Louis Napoleon and the Recovery of France, Ch. 6
        A. L. Dunham. The Anglo-French Treaty of Commerce of 1860. Ch. 5
        F. M. Anderson. Constitutions and Other Select Documents, Pp. 514-560

XII.   The Diplomatic Revolution in Central Europe. Textbook: Pp.204-220.234-238, 339-342.
        H. Friedjung. The Struggle for Supremacy in Germany, Chs. 15-17,
            Conclusion
        H. von Sybel. The Founding of the German Empire, Vol. III, Book X., Ch. 2
        O. von Bismarck. The Man and the Statesman, Vol. II, Ch. 19

XIII.   The Achievement of Italian Unification . Textbook: Pp. 192-203.
        W. R. Thayer. The Life and Times of Cavour, Vol. II, Ch. 24
        G. M. Trevelyan. Garibaldi and the Making of Italy. Chs. 14-15
        J. F. Scott, A. Baltzly. Readings in European History, Pp. 255-267

XIV.   Europe and the Industrial Revolution. Textbook: Pp. 262-271.
        B. Russell. Freedom versus Organization, Chs. 8-13
        C. Gide, C. Rist. A History of Economic Doctrines (2nd English ed.) Bk, II, Ch. 3
        J. F. Scott, A Baltzly. Readings in European History, Pp. 78-94, 113-39

XV.   From Romanticism to Realism. Textbook: Pp. 145-152.
        J. Barzun. Romanticism and the Modern Ego, Ch. 5
        J. H. Randall. The Making of the Modern Mind. Ch. 17
        Introduction to Contemporary Civilization, Vol. II, Pp. 106-113, 124-147 (3rd ed.)

HISTORY W3837y
Spring, 1980
Monday 4:10-6

ISTVAN DEAK
Internatl. Affairs Bldg. 1229
Office hours: Tu. 11-12, 2-5
Columbia University

THE REVOLUTIONS OF 1848

The revolutions of 1848 as a course topic requires some justification. After all, the only concrete achievement of that year was the abolition in Central Europe of feudal agrarian obligations. The other reforms adopted by revolutionary assemblies-- representative parliament, responsible government, equality before the law, freedom of the press, the abolition of guilds and similar restrictions on trade and industry, a republican state, and national unity-- were subsequently revoked, or at least substantially altered by the triumphant counterrevolution. Nonetheless, 1848 was a turning point in modern European history. In many ways it marked the beginning of our era. Never again could the governments, however reactionary, ignore public opinion or the force of democracy and nationalism. Within a few decades, liberal constitutions similar to those of 1848 were introduced in most European countries. The suppression of feudal obligations by the revolutionaries opened the way to a capitalist agriculture and, indirectly, to the development of a market economy and industrial mass production. Moreover, while in 1789 revolutionary France was dominated by country lawyers, shopkeepers, and peasants, 1848 brought to the fore those who would play a major role in modern European history: the urban bourgeois, industrial workers, students, and intellectuals. 1848 was the only truly international revolution in modern history and in 1848, for the first time, youth clashed with its elders. The defeat of the revolution also marked the temporary triumph of the fathers over their children.

Our task will be to examine the background of 1848 (we shall begin around the turn of the 19th century), as well as the how's and why's of the revolutions. Particular attention will be paid to the question of why, of all the major states, only highly advanced England and very backward Russia escaped a revolution.

At the risk of being branded an authoritarian, I opted for a rather strict working program. Experience shows the contrary to be very frustrating. Naturally, you will have considerable freedom in choosing topics for debate, in directing work in the classroom, and in deciding on your research paper. You will be expected to do a good deal of reading for each seminar meeting; you will have to prepare topics for discussion, and you will write a research paper of at least 20 pages during the semester. There will be no examination.

At the beginning of the semester, we shall concentrate on the background of 1848 and the role played in the revolution by such institutions and social classes as the monarchy, army, parliaments, literary clubs, industrial bourgeoisie, peasants, workers, and students. Later, we shall discuss events in a few countries.

Your research papers should focus on a relatively narrow topic. You will be expected to begin your essay early in the semester and to discuss in class your thoughts on the subject. Team-work is highly recommended. First drafts ought to be read by every member of the seminar and discussed in class.

All the required readings but one are available in paperback, and they are rather slim volumes.

COURSE OUTLINE

Jan. 21.   Introduction. Discussion of the bibliography and the course
            outline. Some general remarks on 1848.

Jan. 28/   Background to the revolutions. Changes in European society
Feb. 4.   and politics between the Great French Revolution and 1848.
            Conservatives, liberals, democrats, and socialists. Landowners,
            peasants, manufacturers, artisans, and workers.

            Reading: E.J. Hobsbawm, The Age of Revolution, 1789-1848.

Feb. 11.   The Springtime of Peoples. A survey.

            Readings: Priscilla Robertson, Revolutions of 1848. A Social
                        History. Chapter I.
                      Peter N. Stearns, 1848: The Revolutionary Tide in
                        Europe. Chapters 1-3.

Feb. 18/   The revolution in France. The second republic, the June revolt,
Mar. 3   conservative success and the triumph of Louis Napoleon.

            Readings: Robertson, Chapters II-VI.
                      Stearns, Chapter 4.
                      Karl Marx, Class Struggles in France, 1848-1850.

Mar. 11/   The revolutions in Germany. The Frankfurt parliament and the
Mar. 24   failure of German unification.

            Readings: Robertson, Chapters VII-IX.
                      Stearns, Chapter 7.
                      Lewis Namier, 1848: The Revolution of the Intellectuals.
                      Friedrich Engels, "Germany: Revolution and Counter-
                        Revolution," in Fr. Engels, The German Revolutions,
                        ed. Leonard Krieger.

Mar. 31/   Revolutions in Vienna and Prague. Liberal bourgeoisie and radical
Apr. 7   students. The emancipation of the peasants and the conservative-
            peasant alliance.

            Readings: Robertson, Chapters X-XII.
                      Stearns, Chapter 5.

Apr. 14/   Revolution in Hungary. The triumph of the liberal lesser nobility.
Apr. 21   Political and social mobilization. Habsburg-Slav-Romanian and
            Russian alliance against Hungary. The long war.

            Readings: Robertson, Chapters XIII-XIV.
                      Istvan Deak, The Lawful Revolution. Louis Kossuth and
                        the Hungarians, 1848-1849.

Apr. 28   The new absolutism.

Readings: Robertson, Chapter XXI.
            Stearns, Chapters 8-11.

Documents in Frank Eyck, ed., The Revolutions of 1848-1849.

Recommended readings:

Francois Fejtö, ed., The Opening of an Era: 1848. A Symposium.
Gustave Flaubert, Sentimental Education.
Theodore S. Hamerow, Restoration, Revolution, Reaction. Economics and
    Politics in Germany, 1815-1871.
William L. Langer, Political and Social Upheaval, 1832-1852.

Fall 1983   Columbia University
Robert Moeller
History W3205x

European Politics and Society, 1870-1919

This course is intended as an introduction to society and
politics in Europe in the period from 1870 to 1919. At the center
of the course are the questions: Who are holders of political
power? How have they come to acquire it? What are the decision-
making rules of the political system? Who can influence political
decisions? Who is excluded from political decision-making? What
channels are open for outsiders to become insiders? How does
the structure of political power change over the time period
covered by the course? What forces are pressuring for change,
and what forces are attempting to preserve the status quo? In
the first four weeks of the semester, we will survey the varieties
of political institutions, the structure of society and the
outlines of economic development in the major European powers.
Against this background, in the following five weeks we will
proceed with a more thematic approach, considering some of the
major developments which changed the nature of European society
and politics in the years from 1870 to the eve of the First World
War. This will also provide students with an introduction to some
of the most important problems treated in recent historical
scholarship, and, in addition, to the variety of methods which
historians have employed to approach the problems of social and
political change. The last four weeks of the semester will be
devoted to the study of the origins and impact of the First
World War, the outbreak of revolutionary upheaval in Europe at
the end of the war, and the restoration of order in the years
1918-19.

Complete required readings before class, since lectures
will presume a knowledge of this material. Recommended readings
are intended for the student who wishes to pursue a given
subject further. Other course requirements will include an
in-class mid-term exam, a brief book review (a list of acceptable
possibilities will be provided), and a final exams.

All readings are on reserve in the College Library.
Many are available in paperback, and where this is the case, I
have indicated it on the attached syllabus. Books marked with
an asterisk are also available in the University Bookstore.
Although you are not required to purchase any of these texts,
I recommend that you acquire at least:

*J.M. Roberts, Europe 1880-1945, New York, 1967 (paper)
(the basic background text for the course)

*Tom Kemp, Industrialization in Nineteenth-century Europe,
London and Harlow, 1969 (a country-by-country survey
which also will be a central part of the reading assignments in the first four weeks of the semester, also
available in paper).

For those who feel that their background in the basic
political events of the period is shaky, I recommend:

Norman Rich, The Age of Nationalism and Reform, 1850-1890,
New York, London, 1977 (paper)

Felix Gilbert, The End of the European Era. 1890 to the
Present, New York, London, 1979 (paper)

Carlton J.H. Hayes, A Generation of Materialism, 1871-1900,
New York, Evanston, London, 1963 (paper)

Oron J. Hale, The Great Illusion: 1900-1914, New York, 1971
(paper)

James Joll, Europe since 1870: An International History,
London, 1973 (paper)

I. Introduction: Society and Politics in Late Nineteenth
Century Europe

Required: *J.M. Roberts, Europe 1880-1945, 17-88
          *Tom Kemp, Industrialization in Nineteenth Century
          Europe, Chapters 1 and 2
          ✝E.J. Hobsbawm, The Age of Capital, 1848-1875,
          New York, 1975 (paper), Chapters 12, 13 and 16
          *Geoffrey Barraclough, An Introduction to
          Contemporary History, New York, 1964 (paper),
          Chapters 2, 3 and 5

II. The Democratic Systems: France and England

Required: Roberts, 123-157
           Kemp, Chapters 3 and 7
           Henry Pelling, Modern Britain 1885-1955,
           New York, 1960 (paper), 1-62
           R.D. Anderson, France 1870-1914. Politics and
           Society, London, Henley and Boston, 1977,
           Introduction, Chapters 1, 4, 5, and 9

III. The New Nations: Italy and Germany

      Required: Roberts, 202–214, 165–175
                  Kemp, Chapters 4 and 6
                  Arthur Rosenberg, Imperial Germany. The Birth
                  of the German Republic 1871–1918, Boston,
                  1964 (paper), chapters 1 and 2
                  Denis Mack Smith, Italy. A Modern History,
                  Ann Arbor, 1959, 101–48, 162–242, 254–262

IV. Eastern European Autocracies: Russia and Austria–Hungary

      Required: Roberts, 176–202
                  Kemp, Chapter 6
                  Nicholas V. Riasanovsky, A History of Russia,
                  New York, 1969 (second edition), 408–61
                  C.A. Macartney, The House of Austria. The
                  Later Phase 1790–1918, Edinburgh, 1978, Chapters 13–16

V. Peasants and Lords in Industrial Societies: The Transformation
   of European Agriculture

      Required: Jerome Blum, The End of the Old Order in Rural
                  Europe, Princeton, 1978, Chapter 19
                  Gavin Lewis, "The Peasantry, Rural Change and
                  Conservative Agrarianism: Lower Austria at the
                  Turn of the Century," Past & Present, Nr. 81,
                  1978, 119–143
                  Tony Judt, "The Origins of Rural Socialism in
                  Europe: Economic Change and the Provencal
                  Peasantry, 1870–1914," Social History, 1,
                  1, 1976
                  Ian Farr, "Populism in the Countryside: The
                  Peasant Leagues in Bavaria in the 1890s," in
                  R.J. Evans, ed., Society and Politics in Wilhelmine
                  Germany, New York, London, 1978, 136–159
                  F. M. L. Thompson, "Britain," in David Spring,
                  ed., European Landed Elites in the Nineteenth
                  Century, Baltimore and London, 1977

VI. Reshaping the Right: Anti-Democratic Forces in Democratic
Societies
                   Roberts, 225-29
     Required: Carl E. Schorske, "Politics in a New Key:
Schönerer," in Leonard Krieger and Fritz Stern,
eds., The Responsibility of Power, Garden City,
New York, 1969, 251-270
Geoff Eley, Reshaping the German Right. Radical
Nationalism and Political Change after Bismarck,
New Haven & London, 1980, 19-40, 349-355
Shulamit Volkov, "The Social and Political Function
of Late 19th Century Anti-Semitism," in Hans-
Ulrich Wehler, Sozialgeschichte Heute, Göttingen, 1974
R.D. Anderson, France 1870-1914, Chapter 8
G.R. Searle, "Critics of Edwardian Society:
The Case of the Radical Right," in Alan O'Day, ed.,
The Edwardian Age: Conflict and Stability 1900-
1914, Hamden, CT, 1979, 79-96

VII. The Working Class, Trade Unions and Political Socialism

     Required: Roberts, 230-236
Harvey Mitchell, "Labor and the Origins of
Social Democracy in Britain, France and
Germany, 1890-1914," in Stearns and Mitchell,
The European Labor Movement, pp. 12-117
Dick Geary, European Labour Protest 1848-1939,
pp. 13-133
Victoria Bonnell, "Trade Unions, Parties, and
the State in Tsarist Russia: A Study of Labor
Politics in St. Petersburg and Moscow," Politics
and Society, 9, 3, 1980, 299-322

VIII. Feminism and the Women's Movement

     Required: Richard J. Evans, The Feminists: Women's Emanci-
pation Movements in Europe, America, Australasia,
1840-1920, London, 1977, 1-43, 63-69, 91-203,
209-212, 212-224, 223-245
Marilyn J. Boxer and Jean H. Quataert, Socialist
Women. European Socialist Feminism in the
Nineteenth and Early Twentieth Centuries, New
York, Oxford, Shannon, 1978, 1-18

IX. Imperialism

     Required: Roberts, 100-123
Heinz Gollwitzer, Europe in the Age of Imperialism,
1880-1914, New York, 1969, Chapters 5-10, 14
William L. Langer, The Diplomacy of Imperialism
1890-1902, New York, 1951, 67-96
Geoff Eley, "Social Imperialism in Germany. Reformist
Synthesis or Reactionary Sleight of Hand?" in
J. Radkau and I. Geiss, eds., Imperialismus im 20.
Jahrhundert, Munich, 1976, 71-86.

X.   Origins of the First World War

    Required: Roberts, 239-262
                 Barraclough, chapter IV
                 Michael R. Gordon, "Domestic Conflict and the
                 Origins of the First World War: The British
                 and the German Cases," Journal of Modern History,
                 46, 2, June 1974, 191-226
                 Wolfgang J. Mommsen, "The Debate on German
                 War Aims," Journal of Contemporary History,
                 1, 3, 1966, 47-72
                 Paul W. Schroeder, "World War I as Galloping
                 Gertie: A Reply to Joachim Remak," Journal
                 of Modern History, 44, 3, September 1972, 319-46

XI.   The First World War

    Required: Roberts, 263-303
                 *Gerd Hardach, The First World War 1914-1918,
                 London, 1977 (paperback edition from University
                 of California Press)

XII. Revolutionary Europe

    Required: Sheila Fitzpatrick, The Russian Revolution,
                 pp. 1-84
                 *James Cronin and Carmen Sirianni, eds., Work,
                 Community, and Power. The Experience of Labor
                 in Europe and America, 1900-1925, articles
                 by Cronin, "Labor Insurgency and Class Formation";
                 Nolan, "Workers and Revolution in Germany";
                 and Sirianni "Workers' Control in Europe"

XIII. Peace and Restoration

    Required: Roberts, 304-324
                 Arno J. Mayer, Political Origins of the New
                 Diplomacy, 1917-1918, New Haven, 1959, 1-58.
                 Arno J. Mayer, Politics and Diplomacy of
                 Peacemaking. Containment and Counterrevolution
                 at Versailles, 1918-1919, New York, 1967, 3-30
                 Charles Maier, "Political Crisis and Partial
                 Modernization: The Outcomes in Germany, Austria,
                 Hungary, and Italy after World War I," in
                 Bertrand, ed., Revolutionary Situations, 119-132

Robert Moeller
History W3205x

European Politics and Society, 1870-1919

Recommended Readings

I. Introduction: Society and Politics in Late Nineteenth
Century Europe

David Landes, The Unbound Prometheus. Technological Change
and Industrial Development in Western Europe from 1750
to the present, Cambridge, 1969 (paper), Chapters 3-5

Carlo M. Cipolla, ed. The Fontanta Economic History of
Europe, v. 4, parts 1 and 2 (country-by-country
accounts of industrial development, available in paper)

Peter Stearns, European Society in Upheaval. Social History
since 1750, New York and London, 1975 (paper), chapter 5

Patricia Branca, Women in Europe since 1750, London, 1978,
chapters 1-4

A. Milward and S.B. Saul, The Development of the Economies
of Continental Europe, 1977

Edward R. Tannenbaum, 1900. The Generation Before the
Great War, Garden City, New York, 1976

II. France and England

Donald Read, England, 1868-1914: The Age of Urban Democracy,
New York, 1979

Henry Pelling, Popular Politics and Society in Late Victorian
Britain, London, 1968

Donald Read, Edwardian England 1901-1915. Society and
Politics, London, 1972

Aaron Lawrence Levine, Industrial Retardation in Britain
1880-1914, New York, 1967

Samuel Hynes, The Edwardian Turn of Mind, Princeton, 1968

David Thompson, Democracy in France since 1870, Oxford,
1969 (paper)

D. W. Brogan, France Under the Republic. The Development
of Modern France (1870-1939), New York and London, 1940

Georges Dupeux, French Society 1789-1970, 1976

Theodore Zeldin, France. 1848-1945, volume one, Oxford, 1973

Tom Kemp, Economic Forces in French History, London, 1971

Gordon Wright, France in Modern Times. 1760 to the present,
Chicago and London, 1966, part III

II. France and England (cont'd)

Stewart Edwards, The Paris Commune of 1871, London, 1971

Karl Marx, The Civil War in France, New York, 1968 (paper)

III. Germany and Italy

Richard J. Evans, ed.,Society and Politics in Wilhelmine Germany, London and New York, 1978

Gordon Craig, Germany, 1866-1945, Oxford, 1978 (paper)

Eckart Kehr, Economic Interest, Militarism, and Foreign Policy, Berkeley, Los Angeles, London, 1977

James J. Sheehan, ed., Imperial Germany, New York, 1976 (paper) (especially articles by Born, Rosenberg, Sheehan)

A. William Salomne, Italy in the Giollittian Era: Italian Democracy in the Making, Philadelphia, 1960

Christopher Seton-Watson, Italy from Liberalism to Fascism, 1870-1925, London, 1967

Edward R. Tannenbaum and Emiliana P. Noether, eds., Modern Italy. A Topical History Since 1861, New York, 1974, especially chapters 2, 6, and 14

Benedetto Croce, A History of Italy, 1871-1915, Oxford, 1929

Shepard B. Clough and Salvatore Saladino, eds., A History of Modern Italy. Documents, Readings, and Commentary, New York and London, 1968

IV. Russia and Austria-Hungary

C.A. Macartney, The Habsburg Empire 1790-1918, 1968

Arthur J. May, The Hapsburg Monarchy 1867-1914, New York, 1951 (paper)

A.J.P. Taylor, The Habsburg Monarchy, 1809-1918, London, 1948

R.A. Kann, A History of the Habsburg Empire 1526-1918, Berkeley and Los Angeles, 1974

Cyril Black, ed., Aspects of Social Change since 1861: The Transformation of Russian Society, Cambridge, MA, 1960

Hugh Seton-Watson, The Russian Empire, 1801-1917, Oxford, 1967

Hugh Seton-Watson, The Decline of Imperial Russia 1855-1918, London, 1955

J. Walkin, The Rise of Democracy in Pre-Revolutionary Russia: Political and Social Institutions under the Last Three Tsars, New York,1962

Theodore H. von Laue, Sergei Witte and the Industrialization of Russia, New York, 1963

Sidney Harcave, The Russian Revolution of 1905, London, 1964 (paper)

V. Peasants and Lords

Eugen Weber, _Peasants into Frenchmen: The Modernization of Rural France, 1870-1914_, Stanford, 1976

Jerome Blum, _Lord and Peasant in Russia from the Ninth to the Nineteenth Century_, Princeton, 1961

Geroid Tanquary Robinson, _Rural Russia Under the Old Regime. A History of the Landlord-Peasant World and a Prologue to the Peasant Revolution of 1917_, New York, 1949

Teodor Shanin, _The Awkward Class. Political Sociology of Peasantry in a Developing Society: Russia 1910-1925_, Oxford, 1972

Robert Edelman, _Gentry Politics on the Eve of the Russian Revolution. The Nationalist Party 1907-1917_, New Brunswick, New Jersey, 1980

Wayne S. Vucinich, ed., _The Peasant in Nineteenth-Century Russia_, Stanford, 1968 (paper)

F.M.L. Thompson, _English Landed Society in the Nineteenth Century_, London, 1963

J.P.D. Dunbabin, _Rural Discontent in 19th-Century Britain_, 1974

J. Harvey Smith, "Agricultural Workers and the French Wine-Growers' Revolt of 1907," _Past & Present_, 79, 1978, 101-25

Rudolph M. Bell, _Fate and Honor, Family and Village. Demographic and Cultural Change in Rural Italy since 1800_, Chicago, 1979

Leopold H. Haimson, ed., _The Politics of Rural Russia, 1905-1914_, Bloomington, 1979

S. Tirrell, _German Agrarian Politics after Bismarck's Fall_, New York, 1951

Alexander Gerschenkron, _Bread and Democracy in Germany_, Berkeley and Los Angeles, 1943

James C. Hunt, "The 'Egalitarianism' of the Right: The Agrarian League in Southwest Germany, 1893-1914," _J of Contemp Hist_, 10, 1975, 513-30

Frank B. Tipton, Jr., "Farm Labor and Power Politics in Germany, 1850-1914," _J of Ec History_, 34, 4, 1974, 951-74

Michael Tracy, _Agriculture in Western Europe. Crisis and Adaptation since 1880_, London, 1964

Suzanne Berger, _Peasants against Politics. Rural Organization in Brittany 1911-1967_, Cambridge, MA, 1972

VI. Reshaping the Right

Hans Rogger and Eugen Weber, eds., The European Right. A
Historical Profile, Berkeley and Los Angeles, 1965 (paper)

David Shapiro, ed., The Right in France. Three Studies,
London, 1962

Fritz Stern, The Politics of Cultural Despair, Berkeley, 1961

René Rémond, The Right Wing in France. From 1815 to
de Gaulle, Philadelphia, 1969 (esp. chapters 5-7)

Eugen Weber, The Nationalist Revival in France, 1905-1914,
Berkeley and LA, 1959

Zeev Sternhall, "Paul Déroulède and the Origins of Modern
French Nationalism," J of Contemp History, 6, 4, 1971, 46-71

Alexander Sedgwick, The Ralliement in French Politics
1890-1898, Cambridge, MA, 1965

Arno J. Mayer, "The Lower Middle Class as Historical Problem,"
J of Modern Hist, 47, 3, 1975

Geoffrey Crossick, ed., The Lower Middle Class in Britain,
1870-1914, London, 1977

Abraham J. Peck, Radicals and Reactionaries: The Crisis
of Conservatism in Wilhelmine Germany, Washington, DC,
1978

Shulamit Volkov, The Rise of Popular Antimodernism in Germany:
The Urban Masters, 1873-1896, Princeton, 1978

Peter G.J. Pulzer, The Rise of Political Anti-Semitism in
Germany and Austria, New York, 1964

Robert F. Byrnes, Antisemitism in Modern France. The Prologue to the Dreyfus Affair, New York, 1969

Peter M. Rutkoff, "The Ligue des Patriotes: The Nature of
the Radical Right and the Dreyfus Affair," French
Historical Studies, VIII, 1974, 584-603

Reinhard Rürup, "Emancipation and Crisis: The 'Jewish
Question' in Germany, 1850-1890," Leo Baeck Institute
Yearbook, v. 20, 1975

Salo W. Baron, The Russian Jew under Tsar and Soviets,
New York, London, 1964

Colin Holmes, Anti-Semitism in British Society, 1876-1939,
New York, 1979

Alexander J. DeGrand, The Italian Nationalist Association
and the Rise of Fascism in Italy, Lincoln, 1978

VII. The Working Class

Wolfgang Abendroth, <u>A Short History of the European Working Class</u>, New York and London, 1972 (paper)

Val Lorwin, "Working-Class Politics and Economic Development in Western Europe," <u>Am Hist Rev</u>, 63, 1958, 338-51

Peter N. Stearns and Daniel J. Walkowitz, ed., <u>Workers in the Industrial Revolution: Recent Studies of Labor in the United States and Europe</u>, New Brunswick, NJ, 1974 (articles by Crew, Schofer, Hobsbawm, Stearns)

James Joll, <u>The Second International 1889-1914</u>, London and Boston, 1955

E.J. Hobsbawm, <u>Labouring Men. Studies in the History of Labour</u>, London, 1964

Standish Meacham, <u>A Life Apart: The English Working Class, 1890-1914</u>, London, 1977

Henry Pelling, <u>Short History of the Labour Party</u>

David Kynaston, <u>King Labour. The British Working Class 1850-1914</u>, London, 1976

Gerald W. Crompton, "Issues in British Trade Union Organization 1890-1914," <u>Archiv für Sozialgeschichte</u>, 20, 1980 219-63

Tony Judt, <u>Socialism in Provence. A Study of the Origins of the Modern French Left</u>, Cambridge, 1979

Val Lorwin, <u>The French Labor Movement</u>

James E. Miller, "Reformism and Party Organization. The Italian Socialist Party, 1900-1914," <u>Politico</u>, 40, March 1975, 102-26

D. L. Horowitz, <u>The Italian Labor Movement</u>, Cambridge, MA, 1963

Carl. E. Schorske, <u>German Social Democracy, 1905-1917. The Development of the Great Schism</u>, New York, 1972 (paper)

Barrington Moore, Jr., <u>Injustice: The Social Bases of Obedience and Revolt</u>, White Plains, New York, 1978

Dick Geary, "The German Labour Movement, 1848-1918," <u>European Studies Review</u>,VI, 1976, 297-330

Guenther Roth, <u>The Social Democratis in Imperial Germany: A Study of Working Class Isolation and Negative Integration</u>, Totowa, 1963

Leopold Haimson, "The Problem of Social Stability in Urban Russia, 1905-1917," <u>Slavic Review</u>, 23, 4, 1964, 620-42, and 24, 1, 1965, 1-22

Leopold Haimson, <u>The Russian Marxists and the Origins of Bolshevism</u>, Boston, 1966

Charles Tilly and Edward Shorter, Strikes in France, 1830-1968, Cambridge, 1974

James E. Cronin, Industrial Conflict in Modern Britain, Totowa, 1979

Gerhard A. Ritter, "Workers' Culture in Imperial Germany: Problems and Points of Departure for Research," J of Contemporary Hist, 13, 1978

Gareth Stedman Jones, "Working-Class Culture and Working Class Politics in London, 1870-1900: Notes on the Remaking of a Working Class," J of Soc History, 7, 1974, 460-507

Peter N. Stearns, "The Effort at Continuity in Working-Class Culture," J of Modern History, 52, Dec. 1980, 626-55

Donald H. Bell, "Worker Culture and Worker Politics: The Experience of an Italian Town, 1880-1915," Social History, 3, 1, 1978, 1-21

VIII. Feminism and the Women's Movement

Eleanor S. Riemer and John C. Fout, eds., European Women. A Documentary History, 1789-1945, New York, 1980 (extensive bibliography)

Joan W. Scott and Louise A. Tilly, Women, Work, and Family, New York, Chicago, San Francisco, etc., 1978

Theresa McBride, The Domestic Revolution: The Modernization of Household Service in England and France 1820-1920, London, 1976

Marilyn J. Boxer and Jean H. Quataert, eds., Socialist Women: Feminism in the 19th and early 20th centuries, NY, 1978 (articles on feminist socialists in various European countries)

Renate Bridenthal and Claudia Koonz, eds., Becoming Visible. Women in European History, Boston, 1977 (articles by McDougall, McBride, Pope, Hurwitz, Engel, Rosenthal)

Andrew Rosen, Rise up, Women: The Militant Campaign of the Women's Social and Political Union, 1903-1914, London, Boston, 1974

Brian Harrison, Separate Spheres: The Opposition to Women's Suffrage in Britain, London, 1978

Patricia Branca, Silent Sisterhood. Middle Class Women in the Victorian Home, London, 1975

Martha Vicinus, ed., Suffer and Be Still. Women in the Victorian Age, Bloomington and London, 1972

Martha Vicinus, ed., A Widening Sphere. Changing Roles of Victorian Women, Bloomington and London, 1977

Patricia Hollis, ed., Women in Public 1850-1900. Documents of the Victorian Women's Movement, London, 1979

Marilyn J. Boxer, "French Socialism, Feminism, and the Family," Third Republic, 3/4, 1977, 128-67

Karen Honeycutt, "Socialism and Feminism in Imperial Germany," Signs, 5, Autumn 1979, 30-41

Richard J. Evans, "German Social Democracy and Women's Suffrage 1891-1918," J of Contemp Hist, 15, 3, 1980, 533-59

Richard J. Evans, The Feminist Movement in Germany, 1894-1933, London, 1976

Amy Hackett, "The German Women's Movement and Suffrage, 1890-1914: A Study of National Feminism," in Robert J. Bezucha, ed., Modern European Social History, Lexington, MA, 1972

Rose L. Glickman, "The Russian Factory Woman, 1880-1914," D. Atkinson, ed., Women in Russia, Stanford, 1977, 63-84

Richard Stites, The Women's Liberation Movement in Russia: Feminism, Nihilism, and Bolshevism, 1860-1930, Princeton,

IX. Imperialism

D.K. Fieldhouse, The Colonial Empires. A Comparative Survey from the Eighteenth Century, London, 1966

Bernard Semmel, Imperialism and Social Reform. English Social-Imperial Thought 1895-1914, Cambridge, MA 1960

George Lichtheim, Imperialism, New York, Washington, 1971

Richard Price, An Imperial War and the British Working Class: Working-Class Attitudes and Reactions to the Boer War 1899-1902, Londton and Toronto, 1972

Harrison M. Wright, ed., The "New Imperialism." Analysis of Late-Nineteenth-Century Expansion, Lexington, MA, 1976 (in particular, selections from Hobson, Lenin, Langer, Robinson and Gallagher)

Tom Kemp, Theories of Imperialism, London, 1967

Joseph A. Schumpeter, Imperialism and Social Classes, New York, 1951

Leonard Woolf, Economic Imperialism, New York, 1970

Hartmut Pogge von Strandmann, "Domestic Origins of Germany's Colonial Expansion under Bismarck," Past & Present, No. 42, 1969, 140-59

W.L. Langer, The Diplomacy of Imperialism, 1890-1902, Cambridge, MA, 1960

Hans-Ulrich Wehler, "Bismarck's Imperialism, 1862-1890," in Sheehan, ed., Imperial Germany, New York, London, 1976

M.E. Townsend, The Rise and Fall of Germany's Colonial Empire, 1884-1918, New York, 1930

(IX. cont'd)

    H. Brunschwig, <u>Myths and Realities of French
      Colonialism, 1871-1914</u>, London, 1966

    D.K. Fieldhouse, <u>Economics and Empire, 1830-1914</u>

X. Origins of the First World War

    L.C.F. Turner, <u>Origins of the First World War</u>, New York,
      1970 (paper)

    Joachim Remak, "1914 -- The Third Balkan War: Origins
      Reconsidered," <u>J of Mod History</u>, 43, Sept. 1971, 353-66

    Samuel R. Williamson, Jr., <u>The Politics of Grand Strategy:
      Britain and France Prepare for War, 1900-1914</u>, Cambridge,
      MA, 1969

    A.J.P. Taylor, <u>The Struggle for Mastery in Europe, 1848-1914</u>,
      London, 1954

    Immanuel Geiss, ed., <u>July 1914: The Outbreak of the
      First World War: Selected Documents</u>, New York, 1967 (paper)

    James Joll, <u>1914: The Unspoken Assumptions</u>, London, 1968

    Laurence Lafore, <u>The Long Fuse. An Interpretation of the
      Origins of World War I</u>, Philadelphia, NY, Toronto, 1971 (paper)

    Fritz Fischer, <u>Germany's Aims in the First World War</u>, New
      York, 1967 (paper)

    Fritz Fischer, <u>War of Illusions</u>

    Wolfgang T. Mommsen, "Domestic Factors in German Foreign
      Policy before 1914," <u>Central European History</u>, 6, 1,
      March 1973, 3-43

XI. The War

    John Williams, <u>The Home Fronts: Britain, France and Germany,
      1914-1918</u>, London, 1972

    Georges Haupt, <u>Socialism and the Great War. The Collapse
      of the Second International</u>, Oxford, 1972

    Gerald D. Feldman, <u>Army, Industry and Labor in Germany
      1914-1918</u>, Princeton, 1966

    Marc Ferro, <u>The Great War 1914-1918</u>, London, 1973

    Arthur Marwick, <u>Women at War 1914-1918</u>, London, 1977

    Arthur Marwick, <u>The Deluge. British Society and the
      First World War</u>, New York, 1970 (paper)

(XI. cont'd)

    Jürgen Kocka, "The First World War and the 'Mittelstand,'"
       J of Contemp History, 8, 1973, 101-23

    Gerald D. Feldman, ed., German Imperialism 1914-1918: The
       Development of a Historical Debate, New York, 1972 (paper)

XII. Revolutionary Upheaval in Europe, 1917-1919

    William Henry Chamberlain, The Russian Revolution 1917-1921,
       Vol. 1, 1917-1918, New York, 1965 (paper)

    Alexander Rabinowitch, The Bolsheviks Come to Power.
       The Revolution of 1917 in Petrograd, New York, 1976 (paper)

    Oskar Anweiler, The Soviets: The Russian Workers', Peasants'
       and Soldiers' Councils, 1905-1921, New York, 1974

    John L.H. Keep, The Russian Revolution. A Study of Mass
       Mobilization, New York, 1976

    Marc Ferro, The Russian Revolution of February 1917,
       Englewood Cliffs, NJ, 1972

    Gwyn A. Williams, Proletarian Order. Antonio Gramsci, Factory
       Councils and the Origins of Italian Communism 1911-1921,
       London, 1975

    Martin Clark, Antonio Gramsci and the Revolution that Failed,
       New Haven and London, 1977

    Roberto Vivarelli, "Revolution and Reaction in Italy
       1918-1922," J of Italian History, 1, 2, 1978, 235-63

    J. Hinton, The First Shop Stewards' Movement, London, 1973

    Reinhard Rürup, "Problems of the German Revolution, 1918-1919,"
       J of Contemp Hist, 13, 1968, 165-89

    Dick Geary, "Radicalism and the Workers: Metalworkers
       and Revolution, 1914-23," in Richard Evans, ed.,
       Society and Politics in Wilhelmine Germany, 267-86

    Gerald D. Feldman, "Economic and Social Problems of the German
       Demobilization 1918-1919," J of Modern Hist, 47, 1975,
       1-45

    Jürgen Tampke, The Ruhr and Revolution. The Revolutionary
       Movement in the Rhenish-Westphalian Industrial Region
       1912-1919, Canberra, 1978

    Allan Mitchell, Revolution in Bavaria 1918-1919. The
       Eisner Regime and the Soviet Republic, Princeton, 1965

    Frances Ludwig Carsten, Revolution in Central Europe,
       1918-1919, London, 1972

XIII. Peace and Restoration

Arno J. Mayer, <u>Political Origins of the New Diplomacy, 1917-1918</u>, New Haven, 1959

Charles S. Maier, <u>Recasting Bourgeois Europe. Stabilization in France, Germany and Italy in the Decade after World War I</u>, Princeton, 1975

Marc Trachtenberg, "Reparation at the Paris Peace Conference," <u>J of Mod Hist</u>, 51, March 1979, 24-55

Harold Nicolson, <u>Peacemaking 1919</u>, New York, 1965

Harvard University
Graduate Course

Donald H. Bell
Robinson L-24
Fall, 1980

HISTORY 1334:

WESTERN EUROPE, 1890-1970: THE CRISIS OF INDUSTRIAL SOCIETY

This course deals primarily with West European social,
economic,and political life from the "Great Depression" of the
late-nineteenth century to the equally climactic changes which
have occurred in recent decades. Lecture topics as well as
required and recommended readings are listed below. It would be
especially useful to read the required material before it is
discussed in class (and, at any rate, you should complete the
required assignments before the section meeting). Recommended
readings will help broaden your understanding and will aid in
paper writing.

There will be two lectures a week on Tuesday and Thursday
and a section meeting to discuss the reading at a time to be
arranged. There will be a mid-term exam (on Thursday, October 23),
and a final examination. There will be, in addition, a ten-page
paper, the topic of which you will choose from a list of available
topics. The paper will be due on the last day of class, December 18.

All required readings are on reserve in Lamont and Hilles,
as are most recommended ones. All books marked (P) are for student
purchase at the Coop. Xeroxed material (on reserve) is marked (X)
on the list below.

My office is in Robinson L-24; my office hours will
(tentatively) be Wednesday, 2:00-4:00. My office telephone is 495-5146.

If you need to consult a general text for background
information, see, either R.R. Palmer, A History of the Modern World
(4th ed.), or H. Hearder, Europe in the Nineteenth Century. Both
are on reserve.

Sometime during the term (preferably at the beginning, but
at least before writing your paper) please read: George Orwell,
"Politics and the English Language" in A Collection of Essays by
George Orwell (on reserve, and also available in Xerox reserve).

TOPIC I: THE EUROPEAN WORLD IN 1890: INDUSTRY AND EMPIRE

1. Industrialization and its Impact.

2. The "Great Depression" and the Response of Industrial
Capitalism

Required:

Geoffrey Barraclough, An Introduction to Contemporary History (P),
Chapters 1-3,5.

D.S. Landes, The Unbound Prometheus (P), Chapter 5.

E.J. Hobsbawm, Industry and Empire (P), Chapters 6,8,9.

TOPIC II: IMPERIALISM AND THE CRISIS OF LIBERAL SOCIETY

    1. The "New" Imperialism

    2. The Changing Character of European Liberalism

Required:

    Heinz Gollwitzer, Europe in the Age of Imperialism,
       Chapters 1,3,5,6,10.
    E.J. Hobsbawm, Industry and Empire (P), Chapter 7
    Carlton J.H. Hayes, A Generation of Materialism, Chapter 9.
Recommended:

    William Langer, The Diplomacy of Imperialism
    J.A. Hobson, A Study of Imperialism
    V.I. Lenin, Imperialism
    George Lichtheim, Imperialism
    B. Semmel, Imperialism and Social Reform
    J. Schumpeter, Imperialism and Social Classes
    Arthur Rosenberg, Imperial Germany (esp. Ch. 1-2).

TOPIC III: WORLD WAR I: SOURCES AND IMPACT

    1. Diplomatic and Domestic Sources of War

    2. "Us and Them": The War at the Front and at Home

Required:

    Geoffrey Barraclough, An Introduction to Contemporary History,
       Chapter 4.

    Arno Mayer,"Domestic Causes of World War I,", in Kreiger
       and Stern, The Responsibility of Power ,(also X).

    Robert O. Paxton, Europe in the Twentieth Century (P),
       Chapters 1-4.

    Robert Graves, Goodbye to All That, Chapters 20-21

    Ernest Hemingway, "Now I Lay Me","Soldier's Home", in
       The Short Stories of Ernest Hemingway

Recommended:

    Paul Fussell, The Great War in Modern Memory (esp. recommended)
    Arthur Marwick, The Deluge
    Fritz Fischer, Germany's Aims in the First World War
    S.B. Fay, The Origins of the World War
    L. Lafore, The Long Fuse
    Walter Laqueur, 1914: The Coming of the Great War
    J. Thayer, Italy and the Great War
    Barbara Tuchman, The Guns of August

TOPIC IV: THE WORLD AT THE END OF WORLD WAR I

    1. Politics and Society

    2. "Biennio Rosso": A Revolution that Failed?

Required:
>Robert Paxton, Europe in the Twentieth Century, Chapters 5-6.
>Shepard Clough, Thomas and Carol Moodie, (eds)., Economic
>   History of Europe: The Twentieth Century . Pt. I, Chapters
>   1,2,4, Part II, Chapters 1,2,4,
>Robert Graves and Alan Hodge, The Long Weekend, Chapters 1-3,5.

Recommended:

>Renè Albrecht-Carrie, The Meaning of the First World War,
>   esp. Chapters 3-4.
>Paolo Spriano, The Occupation of the Factories: Italy, 1920
>Gwyn Williams, Proletarian Order
>A.J. Ryder, The German Revolution of 1918
>R. Hunt, "Friedrich Ebert and the German Revolution of 1918",
>   in Stern and Kreiger, The Responsibility of Power
>R. Comfort, Revolutionary Hamburg

TOPIC V: THE 1920s: " A RETURN TO NORMALCY"

    1. Normalcy and Reality

    2. Economic Change

Required:

>Paxton, Chapters 8-9
>Charles Maier, Recasting Bourgeois Europe, Preface, Introduction,
>   Chapter 1, (Chapters 2-3, optional)
>D.S. Landes, The Unbound Prometheus, Chapter 6, pp. 359-401,
>   418-485.
>E.J. Hobsbawm, Industry and Empire, Chapters 11-12
>Jack Russell, "The Coming of the Line: The Ford Highland Park
>   Plant, 1910-1914", Radical America, XII, 3,May-June, 1978,
>   (or X).
>Clough and Moodie, Part III, Chapters 15,16,17, Part IV,
>   Chapters 18,20 (21 and 22 optional)

Recommended:
>R.J. Sontag , A Broken World
>Maurice Dobb, Studies in the Development of Capitalism
>The Fontana Economic History of Europe:
>   Claude Fohlen, "France, 1920-1970" (X)
>   Sergio Ricossa, Italy, 1920-1970"
>   Angus Maddison "Economic Policy and Performance" (X)

TOPIC VI: THE RISE OF FASCISM

    1. The Nature of Fascism

    2. Italian Fascism: A Case Study?

Required:
    Paxton, Chapters 7,12.
    Renzo De Felice, Interpretations of Fascism, Chapters 1,2,
    . Conclusions.
    William Sheridan Allen, The Nazi Seizure of Power (P),
      Chapters 1-11, Conclusions.
    S.J. Woolf, "Italy ", in S.J. Woolf, ed., European Fascism
    Clough and Moodie, Part VII, Chapters 34,37.
Recommended:

    Angelo Tasca, The Rise of Italian Fascism (esp. Chapters I-III,
      V,pp. 52-56, Chapters VI-VIII, Epilogue
    Christopher Seton-Watson, Italy from Liberalism to Fascism,
      esp. pp. 585-629.
    H.J. Trevor-Roper,"The Phenomenon of Fascism", in S.J. Woolf(ed.),
      European Fascism , pp. 18-38.
    Dennis Mack Smith, Italy, A Modern History
    Roland Sarti, Fascism and Industrial Leadership in Italy
             , The Axe Within ,esp. Chapters 6-9.
    Herman Finer, Mussolini's Italy
    Adrian Littleton, The Seizure of Power
    G. Salvemini, Origins of Italian Fascism
    I. Kirkpatrick, Mussolini: A Study in Power
    Walter Laqueur, Fascism: A Reader's Guide
    Karl Dietrich Bracher, The German Dictatorship
    Ernst Nolte, Three Faces of Fascism

TOPIC VII: THE GREAT DEPRESSION

    1. Sources

    2. Responses

Required:
    Paxton, Chapter 11.
    Landes, pp. 401-419.
    Maurizio Vaudagna, "The New Deal and Corporativism in Italy",
      in Radical History Review,IV, 2-3, Sp.-Summer,1977,pp.3-35.
      (also, Xerox).
    Clough and Moodie, Part VI, pp. 213-214, 224-263.
    H.N. Brailsford, "An English View of the Crash", in Aaron and
      Bediner,The Strenuous Decade, pp. 23-27.

Recommended:

>George Orwell, The Road to Wigan Pier (P)
>J.K.Galbraith, The Great Crash
>Charles Kindleberger, The World in Depression
>Maurice Dobb, Studies in the Development of Capitalism
>James Agee, Let Us Now Praise Famous Men
>Stanley Hoffmann, ed. In Search of France, esp. pp. 21-41.

TOPIC VIII: SOCIAL CHANGE IN THE 1930s

>1. Nazi Germany

>2.Class Conflict in the 1930s

Required:

>Paxton, Chapters 10, 13 (pp. 373-389, 398-400)
>George Orwell, "England, Your England", in A Collection
>   of Essays by George Orwell (Also X).
>Graves and Hodge, The Long Weekend, Chapters 15,18-20,24.
>Molly Nolan, "Class Struggles in the 3rd Reich," in Radical
>   History Review IV,2-3,1977,pp. 138-159.
>A.J. Nicholls,Nazi Germany, in S.J. Woolf, (ed.),European
>   Fascism

Recommended:

>Maurice Dobb, Studies in the Development of Capitalism

>Karl Dietrich Bracher, The German Dictatorship
>David Schoenbaum,Hitler's Social Revolution
>Tim Mason, "Women in Nazi Germany", History Workshop Journal,
>   Issues 1 and 2, 1976.
>Sohn-Rethel, Economy and Class Structure of German Fascism

TOPIC IX: THE SPANISH CIVIL WAR

>1. Origins: "The Spanish Labyrinth"

>2. International Reprecussions

Required:

>Gerald Brenan, The Spanish Labyrinth , Book I (pp. 1-110),
>   Epilogue
>Hugh Thomas, The Spanish Civil War, Parts I and II.
>George Orwell, "Looking Back on the Spanish War", in A Collection
>   of Essays by George Orwell, pp. 193-215.
>D. Aaron and R. Bediner, The Strenous Decade: "Writers and the
>   War in Spain" (also X)

Recommended:
>Gabriel Jackson, The Spanish Republic and the Civil War
>George Orwell, Homage to Catalonia

TOPIC X: TOTAL WAR AND RESISTANCE

      1. The Origins and Course of War

      2. War Mobilization and Resistance

Required:

      Paxton, Chapters 14-15.
      Gordon Wright, The Ordeal of Total War (P), Chapters 1-5,7,9.
      A.J.P. Taylor, The Origins of the Second World War, Preface,
          Chapters 1-4,7-8,10-11.
      Clough and Moodie, Part VIII.

Recommended:

      Charles Delzell, Mussolini's Enemies
      Albert Speer, Inside the Third Reich
      David Schoenbrun, Soldiers of the Night:The Story of the
          French Resistance
      Marc Bloch, Strange Defeat
      A.J.P. Taylor, English History,1914-1945, Chapters 8-9.
      A.L. Rowse, Appeasement and All Souls
      Lucy Dawidowicz, The War Against the Jews, 1933-1945
      R. Hilberg, The Destruction of the European Jews
      Hannah Arendt, Eichmann in Jerusalem

TOPIC XI: THE POST-WAR WORLD

      1. Cold War and Divided Europe

      2. Recovery, Boom, and Social Change (Britain, France,
         Germany , Italy)

Required:

      Paxton, Chapters 16-18.
      Landes, Chapters 7-8.
      E.J. Hobsbawm, Industry and Empire, Chapters 13-14
      Clough and Moodie, Part IX.

Recommended:

      Stanley Hoffmann, ed., In Search of France,(esp. selections
         by Hoffmann, Kindleberger, Wylie).
      Gordon Wright, France in Modern Times, Chapters 33-35.

TOPIC XII: THE CHANGING NATURE OF WORK AND LEISURE

      1. Work

      2. Leisure

65

Required:

Edward Shorter, ed.,Work and Community in the West, articles
     by Shorter, Alaine Touraine,Serge Mallet (article by
     Elinor Langer--optional). (also X)

Richard Sennett and J. Cobb, The Hidden Injuries of Class (P),
     pp. 1-51, 91-118, 245-262.

Michael Marrus, ed.,The Emergence of Leisure, Introduction,
     articles by deGrazia, Touraine, Dumazedier and Latouche
     (pp. 1-10, 69-143); (also X).

Robert F. Wheeler, "Organized Sport and Organized Labour: The
     Workers' Sports Movement" (X).

Recommended:

Harry Braverman, Labor and Monopoly Capital
Hunnius, Garson, Case, Workers' Control,(esp. Part III).
Studs Terkel, Working
Stuart Ewen, Captains of Consciousness,(esp. Preface, Chapters 1-2,
     Conclusion).
David A. Steinberg, " The Workers' Sports International,1920-28"(X).
Charles P. Korr, "West Ham United Football Club and the Beginnings
     of Professional Football in East London, 1895-1914" (X).
Frederic L. Paxon, "The Rise of Sport" (X).

TOPIC XIII: THE RECENT PAST AND THE FUTURE

1. Contemporary Europe: The End of the Long Boom

2. Future Scenarios:"Stuck Society" and the Alternatives:
     A Third Industrial Revolution?

Required:

Paxton, Chapters 19-20
Barraclough, Chapter 6.
Charles Lindblom, Politics and Markets (P), Preface, Chapters
     1,7,8,10,13,19,22,24,25.
Dedalus, Winter, 1979 : articles by Stanley Hoffmann, Suzanne
     Berger, and Albert Bressand.

Recommended:

Neil McInnes, The Communist Parties of Western Europe
Jane Kramer, Unsettling Europe
Dedalus,Winter 1979, Spring, 1980--entire.

Harvard University

Spring Term, 1982-83
Mon.-Wed.-Fri.

Professor Charles Maier
Center for European Studies
5 Bryant St.; 495-4303/4304
or: Robinson 101; 495-2157

History 1330b

Europe since 1930

This course covers Western European politics, economics, and society since the economic crisis and the ideological polarization of the 1930s. Lectures will treat the impact of the Depression, the rise of Nazism in Germany and of dictatorships elsewhere; the pre-war Popular Fronts and the transformation of European socialism; the Second World War and the resistance; the welfare state and Cold-War politics; the effects of decolonization, economic growth, renewed ideological clashes since the late 1960's, and the economic difficulties since the early 1970's. The emphasis of the lectures and readings is upon developments in France, Germany, Italy, Spain, and Britain with occasional reference to Eastern and Northern Europe. Although diplomatic history is not stressed, the origins of World War II, and the Cold War, and European integration will be outlined; likewise some cultural history will be sketched.

Monday and Wednesday class hours will be devoted primarily to lectures; Friday sessions will involve discussions. The reading list (required and recommended) is designed to allow exploration of specific topics. No general text is assigned, but if you feel the need for one I suggest Robert Paxton, Europe in the Twentieth Century. Requirements include an hour exam, a term essay (some suggested topics will be provided later), and a final examination.

The lecture schedule is subject to modification.

Dates	Topics
Wed., February 2:	Introduction: Europe after World War One.
Fri., February 4:	The International Economy of the 1920's and the Causes of the Great Depression.
Mon., February 7:	The Politics of Unemployment; Policies to Meet the Depression: Deflation vs. Expansionary.
Wed., February 9:	The Collapse of the Weimar Republic and the Advent of Nazism.
Fri., February 11:	Discussion: Could Weimar have been saved?
Mon., February 14:	The Nazi Regime.
Wed., February 16:	The Nazi Regime.
Fri., February 18:	The Nazi Regime: Discussion.

Dates	Topics
Mon., February 21:	Washington's Birthday Holiday
Wed., February 23:	The Austrian Republic Between Socialism and Clerical-Fascism, 1918-1938.
Fri., February 25:	The French Popular Front.
Mon., February 28:	The Spanish Republic and the Background of the Civil War.
Wed., March 2:	The Spanish Civil War.
Fri., March 4:	Discussion: The Spanish Civil War (Fraser: Blood of Spain).
Mon., March 7:	The Approach of World War II and Hitler's successes, 1935-40.
Wed., March 9:	Vichy France and the Salò Republic in Italy, 1940-45.
Fri., March 11:	Discussion: Collaboration; the Holocaust.
Mon., March 14:	The Resistance: Ideas and Music (tape).
Wed., March 16:	The Resistance and the Big Powers, 1943-45.
Fri., March 18:	Hour Examination in Class.
Mon., March 21:	Origins of the Cold War.
Wed., March 23:	The Politics of the Cold War: France, Italy, and the Marshall Plan.
Fri., March 25:	Discussion: Intellectuals and Communism (Merleau-Ponty, Humanism and Terror).
Week of March 27-April 3:	Spring Vacation
Mon., April 4:	Slide Lecture: The Triumph of Modern Art and Architecture.
Wed., April 6:	Britain under Labour and the Modern Welfare State
Fri., April 8:	Discussion: The Welfare State and its limits.
Mon., April 11:	The Rebirth of Germany.
Wed., April 13:	Sources and Trends of Economic Growth, 1948-71; Common Market.
Fri., April 15:	Mendès-France, the Algerian War, and de Gaulle's Republic; (Discussion: A Savage War of Peace).
Mon., April 18:	Reform and its Limits, 1954-63 (Russia after Stalin; Geneva, 1954 & 1955; John XXIII; socialism in Italy and Germany).
Wed., April 20:	Movement on the Left, 1965-72: Currents in Marxism, university protests, labor militance.
Fri., April 22:	Discussion: The European Left, 1968-1982.

Dates   Topics

Mon., April 25:   A Decade of 'Stagflation': Economic
                         Difficulties Since the '70s
Wed., April 27:   Democratization in Spain, Portugal, and
                         Greece: 1974-82.
Fri., April 29:   European Problems in the 1980s: The End
                         of Postwar Consensus?

Course Papers due: Friday, May 6; Final Examination: Thursday,
                    May 19.

Required and Suggested Readings

1. The Depression:
    Charles P. Kindleberger, The World in Depression, 1929-1939
    (U.Cal. PB), at least chapters 3-8, 14, are required. For
    an alternative approach to the whole period, 1920-50, you may
    substitute I. Svennilson, Growth and Stagnation in the European
    Economy (U.N. Economic Commission for Europe, 1954).

    For policies toward the Depression, you can read: Robert Ski-
    delsky, Politicians and the Slump: The Labour Government of
    1929-1931 (Penguin PB), esp. chaps. 1-3, 8, 10, 12-14; Ross
    McKibbin, "The Economic Policy of the Second Labour Government,
    1929-1931," Past & Present, 68 (August 1975): 95-123; Robert
    Gates, "German Socialism and the Crisis of 1929-33," Central
    European History, VII, 4 (1974): 332-359; Donald Winch, Eco-
    nomics and Policy (Fontana PB)--on the advent of Keynesianism.

    For the impact of the Depression, read Paul Lazarsfeld, Maria
    Yahoda, and H. Zeisel, Marienthal: The Sociography of an Un-
    employed Community (Chicago, 1971)--about an industrial suburb
    of Vienna; or E. Wight Bakke, Citizens without work (Yale UP,
    1940); the Pilgrim Trust, Men without Work (Cambridge, England,
    1938); George Orwell, The Road to Wigan Pier (orig. Left Book
    Club); or Walter Greenwood's novel of Manchester life, Love
    on the Dole (Penguin PB); or Hans Fellada, Little Man, What Now?
    (a German novel).

2. Nazi Germany:
    Martin Broszat, The Hitler State (Longman PB), at least chaps.
    1-3, 5-6, 8-11, are required. For an alternative approach you
    may substitute Alan Bullock, Hitler: A Study in Tyranny (Harper
    Torchbook), at least chapters 1-8.

2. Nazi Germany, Continued:

        Broszat's is frankly a fairly dry institutional study,
    but an important analysis of the regime that stresses how it
    worked as a "system." For a brilliant earlier analysis from
    a quasi-Marxian perspective, Franz Neumann, Behemoth: The
    Structure and Practice of National Socialism, 1933-1944 (New
    York, 1944; later Harper Torchbook ed.) is still valuable.
    An encyclopaedic survey is provided by Karl Dietrich Bracher,
    The German Dictatorship (Praeger PB). David Schoenbaum, Hitler's
    Social Revolution (Anchor PB) examines the effect of the regime
    on different social sectors. For accounts of how Nazism came
    to power see William Sheridan Allen, The Nazi Seizure of Power:
    The Experience of a Single German Town 1930-1935 (Quadrangle PB)
    and Jeremy Noakes, The Nazi Party in Lower Saxony (Oxford UP).
    Alfred Speer's Inside the Third Reich (PB) is a revealing memoir
    of rivalries around Hitler; see also Joachim Fest's, The Face
    of the Third Reich for Nazi portraits.

3. The Spanish Civil War.

    Ronald Fraser, Blood of Spain (Pantheon PB), pp. 1-185, 201-
    272, 321-394, 499-585, is required--a history of the Civil
    War built upon oral interviews.

    In addition, Gabriel Jackson, The Spanish Republic and the Civil
    War, 1931-1939 (Princeton PB) provides a good narrative of the
    whole period; Stanley Payne, The Spanish Revolution (Norton PB)
    is helpful from the viewpoint of the moderate center; Gerald
    Brenan, The Spanish Labyrinth (Cambridge PB) has splendid studies
    of agrarian problems and social currents; Bernard Bolloten, The
    Spanish Revolution (UNC Press; original ed.: The Grand Camouflage)
    is a painstaking expose of Communist maneuvering; Edward Malefakis,
    Agrarian Reform and Peasant Revolution in Spain (Yale UP) covers
    an important issue. Jerome Mintz, The Peasants of Casas Viejas
    (Chicago, 1982) is a fine revisionist reconstruction of anarchism
    and the early Civil War. For personal testimony, George Orwell,
    Homage to Catalonia and Franz Borkenau, The Spanish Cockpit (both
    PBs) are revealing; or read Peter Stansky and William Abrahams,
    Journey to the Frontier (PB) about two young English poets in
    Spain. The survey by Hugh Thomas, The Spanish Civil War is detailed
    but less preferable than the studies above.

4. Occupation and Resistance:

    Required: Robert O. Paxton, Vichy France: Old Guard and New
    Order (Norton PB), pp. 3-148, 168-243, 280-383; AND
        H. R. Kedward, Resistance in Vichy France (OUP, 1978),
    chaps. I, II, V, VII, X, XI.

4. Occupation and Resistance Continued:

    The required reading focuses on France. For the Popular Front
    background read Joel Colton, Léon Blum: Humanist in Politics
    (MIT: PB). A general survey of Resistance movements is in
    Henri Michel, The Shadow War and M.R.D. Fott's Resistance
    (Paladin PB); and for Italy and Mussolini during the period
    of the Salò Republic (1943-45) see F. W. Deakin, The Brutal
    Friendship (Harper & Row, Anchor PB). An interesting study
    is Jan Tomasz Gross, Polish Society under German Occupation:
    The Generalgouvernement, 1939-1945 (Princeton UP); and for the
    harshest aspect, Lucy Dawidowicz, The War against the Jews,
    1933-1945 (Harper Torchook) and on economic aspects: Alan
    Milward, War, Economy, and Society, 1939-1945 (U. Cal. PB).

5. The Background of the Welfare State:
    Required: Paul Addison, The Road to 1945 (Quartet PB).

    For further reading on the background of the welfare state and
    Britain during the war, see Alan Bullock, The Life and Times
    of Ernest Bevin, vol. II, and Michael Foot, Aneurin Bevan, 2
    vols. R. M. Titmuss's advocacy of the welfare state emerges from
    his Essays on the Welfare State (Beacon PB) and he wrote a solid
    official history of welfare and family policy during the war:
    Problems of Social Policy.

6. The Cold War and Ideological Conflict:

    Required: Maurice Merleau-Ponty, Humanism and Terror (Beacon
    PB). I suggest you read in conjunction with this book Arthur
    Koestler's drama, Darkness at Noon (which provoked Merleau-
    Ponty) and Koestler's autobiographical essay in Richard Cross-
    man, ed., The God that Failed (PB). For fictional depiction of
    conflicting postwar currents see Simone de Beauvoir, The Mandarins
    (Meridian PB), and for a scholarly study, Marc Poster, Existential
    Humanism in Postwar France (Princeton UP), with discussions of
    Sartre and Merleau-Ponty.

    On the Cold War in Europe, see Charles S. Maier, ed., The Origins
    of the Cold War and Contemporary Europe (Franklin Watts PB),
    which collects essays and has extensive critical bibliography.

7. Postwar reconstruction; postwar dilemmas:
    Required: Alistair Horne, A Savage War of Peace: Algeria
    1954-1962 (Penguin PB).

    For a closer look at the collapse of the Fourth Republic under
    the impact of the Algerian War, see Charles S. Maier and Dan

7. Postwar reconstruction; postwar dilemmas continued:

    S. White, eds., The Thirteenth of May: The Advent of de
    Gaulle's Republic. By and large narrative histories for
    the two postwar decades are not outstanding. The journalistic
    compendium of Alexander Werth, France, 1940-1955 has an engaging
    narrative; Jean Lacouture has written a biography of de Gaulle.
    Richard Mayne, The Rebirth of Europe (Anchor PB) covers the moves
    toward "integration" that gave rise to the Common Market and
    European Community, while John Ardagh, The New French Revolution
    (Harper PB) stresses the socioeconomic transformations of the
    years up through the 1960's. Alfred Grosser, Germany in Our
    Time (Praeger PB) gives a general survey of the Federal Republic
    into the 1960's. Some of the political development of the
    smaller countries--Scandinavia, Low countries, Austria--is
    available in Robert Dahl, ed., Political Oppositions in Western
    Democracies (PB).

8. The "other" Europeans:
    Required: Jane Kramer, Unsettling Europe (Vintage PB).

    The Kramer is a collection of New Yorker essays about migrant
    worker families or those whom the new affluence has stranded.
    See also Ann Cornelisen, Strangers and Pilgrims (McGraw Hill,
    ed.), about Italians working in Germany; also Stephen Castles
    and Godula Kosack, Immigrant Workers and Class Structure in
    Western Europe (Oxford UP); or the essay by John Berger, The
    Seventh Man.

9. The Mirror of Fiction:
        Choose at least one of the novels suggested here:
            Andre Malraux, Man's Hope (on the Spanish Civil War);
            Albert Moravia, The Conformist (a depiction of a fascist
                        of the 1930's-40's
            Simone Beauvoir, The Mandarins (Sartre vs. Camus; cited
                        above);
            Gunther Grass, The Tin Drum (an allegory of Nazism and
                        postwar Germany).

Barnard College
SYLLABUS

HISTORY 20: THE SECOND WORLD WAR AND THE RECOVERY OF EUROPE

I. The Diplomatic Background to the Second World War.

   Required Reading:

Alan Bullock, Hitler, A Study in Tyranny (Harper Colophon),
          chaps. 6-9.
Adolph Hitler, "Race and People", "The German Postwar Policy of
          Alliances", "Germany's Policy in Eastern Europe",
          and "The Right of Self-Defense", in Mein Kampf.
William E. Scott, "Neville Chamberlain and Munich: Two Aspects
          of Power", in Leonard Krieger and Fritz Stern
          (eds.), The Responsibility of Power, pp. 353-369.
A.J.P. Taylor, The Origins of the Second World War (Penguin).
William Roger Louis (ed.), The Origins of the Second World War:
          A.J.P. Taylor and His Critics, essays by Trevor-
          Roper, Hinsley, and Bullock.
T.W. Mason, "Some Origins of the Second World War", Past and Pre-
          sent, no. 29 (December 1964), pp. 68-87.

   Recommended (Optional) Reading:

Kieth Eubank, The Origins of World War II (1969).
Laurence Lafore, The End of Glory: An Interpretation of the
          Origins of World War II (1970).
Pierre Renouvin, World War II and its Origins: International
          Relations, 1929-1945 (1969).
Norman Rich, Hitler's War Aims (1973).
Christopher Thorne, The Approach of War, 1938-1939 (1967).
Gerhard L. Weinberg, The Foreign Policy of Hitler's Germany,
          1933-1936 (1970).

II. The Second World War, 1939-1945.

   Required Reading:

Alan Bullock, Hitler, chaps. 10-14.
Gordon Wright, The Ordeal of Total War, 1939-1945 (Harper Torch
          Books).
Don W. Alexander, "Repercussions of the Breda Variant", French
          Historical Studies, v. 8, no. 3 (spring 1974).
Winston Churchill, Their Finest Hour, pp. 27-118, 138-160,
          177-223.

J.P. Nettl, <u>The Soviet Achievement</u> (Harcourt, Brace, and World)
pp. 150-180.

Recommended Reading:

Charles de Gaulle, <u>Complete War Memoirs</u>, v. 1, pp. 3-53.
Marc Bloch, <u>Strange Defeat</u> (Norton).
Basil H. Liddell-Hart, <u>The History of the Second World War</u> (1971).
Arthur Marwick, "The Second World War", in Marwick, <u>Britain in
the Century of Total War</u>.
Albert Speer, <u>Inside the Third Reich</u>, Part I, chaps. 11-13;Part II,
chap. 16; Part III, chaps. 25-26.
Robert O. Paxton, <u>Vichy France: Old Guard and New Order, 1940-
1944</u> (1970).
Henri Michel, <u>The Shadow of War: The European Resistance, 1939-
1945</u>.
Alexander Dallin, <u>German Rule in Russia, 1941-1945</u> (1957).
John A. Armstrong, "Collaborationism in World War II: The Integral
Nationalist Variant in Eastern Europe", <u>Journal of
Modern History</u>, v. 40, no. 3 (September 1968).
Herbert Feis, <u>Churchill, Roosevelt, Stalin: The War They Fought
and the Peace They Sought</u> (1957).
_ _ _ _ _, <u>The Potsdam Conference</u> (1960).
Diane Shavers Clemens, <u>Yalta</u> (1970).

III. Postwar Europe.

Required Reading:

Walter Laqueur, <u>The Rebirth of Europe: A History of the Years
Since the Fall of Hitler</u>, pp. 3-193.
Charles Robertson, <u>International Politics Since World War II: A
Short History</u> (Wiley), chaps. 1-4.
Hugh Seton-Watson, <u>The East European Revolution</u>, Part III, chaps.
8-11.
Z.K. Brzezinski, <u>The Soviet Bloc: Unity and Conflict</u>, The Second
Phase, chaps. 4-7; The Third Phase, chap. 8.
George Lichtheim, <u>The New Europe</u>, chaps. 3-5.
Stephen Graubard (ed.), <u>A New Europe?</u>
Raymond Aron, "Old Nations, New Europe".
Oliver Franks, "Britain and Europe."
Klaus Epstein, "The Adenauer Era in German History."
Altessandro Pizzorno, "The Individualistic Mobil-
ization of Europe."
Rolf Dahrendroff, "Recent Changes in the Class
Structure of European Societies."
Seymour Martin Lipset, "The Changing Class Structure
and Contemporary European Politics."
Geoffrey Barraclough, <u>An Introduction to Contemporary History</u>
(Penguin), chaps. 3-4, 6-7.

Recommended Reading:

H. Holborn, The Political Collapse of Europe (1951), pp. 162-193.
Herbert Feis, The Atomic Bomb and the End of World War II (1966).
Gabriel Kolko, The Politics of War (1968).
Charles S. Maier, "Revisionism and Cold War Origins", Perspectives
    in American History, v. 4 (1970).
John L. Gaddis, The United States and the Origins of the Cold
    War, 1941-1947 (1972).
Philip Williams, Crisis and Compromise (1966).
H. Stuart Hughes, The United States and Italy (1965, last chap.
F. Roy Willis, France, Germany, and the New Europe, 1945-1967
    (1966).
Alistair Buchan, War in Modern Society (Harper).

History 20

The Second World War and the Recovery of Europe

Lecture Schedule

January 23: Introductory session.

January 25-30: The international situation at the end of the
first postwar decade.

February 1: The world economic crisis and the return to power
politics (I): The Japanese invasion of Manchuria,
1931-1933.

February 6: The world economic crisis and the return to power
politics (II): The Nazi rise to power and the elements
of Nazi foreign policy, 1929-1933.

February 8-13: The dismantling of Versailles, 1933-1936.

February 15-20: The triumph of appeasement, 1937-1938.

February 22: The Polish Crisis and the outbreak of the Second
World War, 1939.

February 27: The question of responsibility: the historical
controversy over the origins of the Second World
War.

March 1: The war in the West, 1939-1941.

March 6: The war in the East, 1941-1943.

March 8: Midterm.

March 20: Hitler's Europe: collaboration.

March 22: Hitler's Europe: resistance.

March 27: The American entry into the war and the Allied
campaign in the West, 1941-1945.

March 29: The Soviet victory in the East, 1943-1945.

April 3: Allied diplomacy: Teheran, Yalta, Potsdam, and the
end of the war, 1943-1945.

April 5-10: The origins of the Cold War, 1945-1947.

April 12-17: Ruin and reconstruction: Western Europe, 1945-1953.

April 19: The "People's Democracies" of Eastern Europe, 1945-1953.

April 24-26: Europe in the Cold War: international relations, 1947-1962.

May 1: Decolonization, 1945-1961.

HISTORY OF MODERN BRITAIN

Rutgers University

History 510:342   Spring 1983   Professor John R. Gillis
306 Van Dyck, CAC
932-7905

This course will explore the rise of the world's first urban industrial society, its period of world dominance, and the effects of its subsequent loss of world power status. While attention will be given to the political development from aristocratic patronage to mass democracy, the lectures will focus more particularly on the social consequences of industrialization, the origins and nature of Victorianism, the domestic consequences of imperialism, and the effects of a century of total war on women and men of all classes. A variety of documents, novels, oral histories, art, music, and eyewitness accounts will illustrate how ordinary British people have experienced the epochal transformations of the past two centuries.

The lectures will be limited to fifty minutes to allow time for discussion during each class period. Discourse will be encouraged, so it is important to keep up with the readings, which have been carefully selected to complement the lectures. There will be a mid-term exam on March 16. Members of the course may select to write a final paper (8-10 pages) or take a final examination. The decision to write a paper must be indicated by April 18 and approval of topic granted.

The following books are available at the Douglass bookstore. All other readings are on reserve. One copy of purchase books can also be found on reserve.

> A. Briggs, Age of Improvement
> W. Hogarth, Engravings
> E.P. Thompson, Making of the English Working Class
> G. Orwell, Burmese Days
> P. Thompson, The Edwardians
> F. Bedarida, A Social History of England
> G. Orwell, Road of Wigan Pier
> J. Fowles, French Lieutenant's Woman

Reserve readings are marked (R)
The document package should be brought to each class and returned
  to me at the end of the course.

Week I   Introduction to the Course

Jan. 24   The Paradoxes of British History
Jan. 26   Film: Hoskins' "The Making of the English Landscape"

Read the selections from Defoe's Tour through the Whole Island of Great Britain in preparation for class.

Week II   Britain in the Eighteenth Century

Jan. 31   The World and the Moral Economy
Feb. 2   Paternalist Society and its Politics

Neither the social relations nor the politics of the eighteenth century fit into categories we are familiar with. The world that Hogarth opens to us is so strange as to seem bizarre. How was Britain governed in the eighteenth century? What was the nature of social relations, of work and leisure? Read Thompson

and Briggs and then turn to Hogarth. Examine the plates
and read the text to understand the artist's intentions.
Note that art is not to be confused with reality, but
does express the major issues of eighteenth century society.

Read: E.P. Thompson, "Patrician Society, Plebeian Culture" (R)
A. Briggs, Age of Improvement, Chapter I
Hogarth, Engravings, nrs. 18-23, 27, 51-56, 60-76, 86-89,
92-98

Week III   Britain in an Age of Revolution, 1770-1815

Feb. 7   The Atlantic Revolutions
Feb. 9   British Reaction

As an integral part of the Atlantic world, Britain could not
but be affected by a series of political upheavals that began
in North America and engulfed the European continent in
the late eighteenth century. How did Britain manage to
avoid its own political revolution and what were the consequences
of the long political reaction that set in during the 1790s?

Read: Briggs, Age of Improvement, Chapter III
E.P. Thompson, Making of the English Working Class,
pp. 102-19, 350-74, 521-52

Week IV   The First Industrial Nation

Feb. 14   Revolution on the Land
Feb. 16   From Manufacture to the Factory System

As the first society to industrialize in a modern way, Britain
was bound to experience this process differently from other
countries that drew on her experience. Remember that industrialization
is not just a neutral technological process, but a social, cultural
and political event, inextricably linked to the conditions
of the late eighteenth and early nineteenth century. Think
about Wedgwood's early experiment as a social and political
event. Consider the costs of the factory system and why
industrialization was so controversial.

Read: N.McKendrick, "The Making of the Wedgwood Factory" (handout)
E.P. Thompson, Making, pp. 213-233, 269-313, 350-375

Week V   Two Nations

Feb. 21   The Urban Revolution of the Nineteenth Century
Feb. 23   From Order to Class

Not only did the future shape of economic and social relations
but the nature of the modern city become evident in the
crucial decades of the early nineteenth century. The
function and structure of cities changed drastically. The
very meaning of community was transformed as the old
paternalist notions gave way to new concepts of a market
oriented capitalist society. Thompson describes the actual
experience of class formation during this great transformation.

Read: Briggs, Age of Improvement, Chapter IX
Thompson, Making, pp. 314-49, 401-49

Week VI   Victorianism

Feb. 28   Sex and Class in the Victorian Age
Feb. 30   The Victorian Artifact   (class participation)

This was an age not only of economic but of gender transformation.
The definition of the masculine and the feminine was
radically altered in an urban class society. We will look
at the way that the redefinition of gender reinforced
the class structure and vice versa. On Feb. 30 each of you
will bring to class something "Victorian" and be prepared
to discuss its special function and meaning to that time.

Read: John Fowles, French Lieutenant's Woman
       L. Davidoff, "Class and Gender in Victorian Britain" (R)

Week VII   Reform and Radicalism: 1830s and 1840s

March 7   Reform: Appearance and Reality
March 9   Working Class Radicalism: Chartism

In the 1830s British political institutions were reformed
to meet the realities of a capitalist industrial age. Just
how far reform represented the total triumph of the
middle classes is debatable, but it is undeniable that the
period represented a turning point in both middle and
working class politics.

Read: Briggs, Age of Improvement, Chapters V,VI
       Thompson, Making, pp. 711-45

Week VIII   The Path Not Taken

March 14   Owenism
March 16   Mid-Term

Robert Owen, one of the most successful capitalists of his
day, also became the leading figure in Britain's first
socialist movement. Early socialism differed from later
socialism in many respects, but the response to Owenism
suggests the nature of a working class consciousness
that would become an enduring feature of British history.

Read: Thompson, Making, pp. 779-806
       R. Owen, New Moral World, in document package

March 21-27   SPRING BREAK

Week IX   Apogee of Liberalism

March 28   The Great Exhibition 1851
March 30   The Voluntary Society

At the time it seemed that the liberal concensus achieved
by the 1860s had resolved the problems of the industrial
and political revolutions. British society seemed remarkably
stable and content until the mid-1870s. What accounts for
this?

Read: Briggs, Age of Improvement, Chapter X
       F. Bedarida, A Social History of England, Part I

Week X   Imperial Britain in the 1870s and 1880s

April 4   The Second Industrial Revolution
April 6   The Peculiarities of British Imperialism

As we have already seen, the history of Britain is inextricably linked to world events. What appeared at the time to be an unparalleled success in world trade and politics was in the long run to have dubious consequences for British society. Think about the relationship between the new imperialism and change within Britain itself.

Read: Bedarida, A Social History, Part II
G. Orwell, Burmese Days

Week XI   End of the Liberal Era

April 11   State and Society in the Edwardian Era
April 13   The Condition of Britain: 1914

Edwardian Britain was a society of astounding contrasts, many of which were just beginning to be recognized and acted on when the Great War intervened. From the remarkable oral histories collected by Paul Thompson you can reconstruct the Edwardian world. Note the huge gap in the experiences of different classes, as well as the differences between the world of men and women, of adults and children.

Read: P. Thompson, The Edwardians, Parts I; Part II (Chapters
7,9,11); Part III to page 276

Week XII   Origins of the Long Crisis

April 18   The Great War
April 20   War's Toll

No event in the twentieth century has done so much to shape popular consciousness as the Great War. Examine the consequences of this first total war for Britain's internal and external situation.

Read: P. Thompson, The Edwardians, pp. 276-341
J. Keegan, Face of Battle, Chapter IV (R)

Week XIII   From Depression to War

April 25   The Troubles Within
April 27   A Second Great War

The 1980s are currently being compared to the 1930s. In Britain's case many of the parallels are apt, for the problems, internal and external, evident then still plague the country today. As today, the effects of the Depression were uneven. Britain muddled through until shocked into action by the Second World War.

Read: Bedarida, A Social History of England, pp. 200-45
G. Orwell, Road to Wigan Pier, Part I

Week XIV   Britain in a Post-Imperial Age

         May 2   The Second Age of Reform
         May 4   Welfare State, Consumer Capitalism, and the Present Crisis

Bedarida explores the general societal transformation that
brought Britain through austerity to prosperity in the
1960s. His book stops short of the current economic crisis,
but suggests some of its origins. Richard Hoggart is
concerned with the question of whether the welfare state
and the new affluence have created a classless society.
Specifically, he tries to answer the question of whether
mass culture has taken over from the class cultures that
originated at the very beginning of the industrial era.

Read: Bedarida, <u>A Social History of England</u>, pp. 247-98
       R. Hoggart, <u>The Uses of Literacy</u>, pp. 15-37, 238-282 (R)

Modern Britain:
The 19th and 20th Centuries

J.A. Thompson
University of Kentucky

GENERAL AIDS TO READING FOR GRADUATES IN MODERN BRITAIN

For the 19th century there is an excellent general bibliography, Josef L. Altholz, Victorian England, 1837-1901, a part of a series sponsored by the Conference on British Studies. This can be supplemented by the bibliographies published annually in the Journal Victorial Studies.

For the period since 1901 the best place to begin is A.F. Havighurst, Modern England, 1901-70, also a handbook in the Conference on British Studies series. The final volume in the Oxford History of England series, A.J.P. Taylor's English History 1914-1945, contains a wealth of material, intelligently interpreted; it provides, in its notes and bibliographical section, an excellent guide to further work in the period. The American Historical Association has issued a brief bibliographical pamphlet on Twentieth Century Britain, compiled by Henry R. Winkler.

There is a brief, general bibliography (available in paperback) which covers Modern Britain: G.R. Elton's Modern Historians on British History, 1485-1945. This volume reviews the historical literature written in the 25 years after World War II.

Beyond these general aids there are a variety of useful bibliographical sources, including:

1) Writings on British History. This is an annual publication but considerably behind schedule. Publications of 1901-45 covered in 15 vols. Publications of 1946-64 are in 7 vols. The most recent vols. are for 1962-64 and 1965-66.

2) The relevant volumes of the English Historical Documents Series (each of these volumes includes a general bibliography, plus specialized additional lists for the various subjects covered-- politics, religion, etc.):

Vol. XI: 1783-1832 (A. Aspinall and E.A. Smith, eds.)
Vol. XII: (1): 1833-1874 (G.M. Young & W.D. Handcock, eds.)
Vol. XIII: (2): 1874-1914 (W.D. Handcock, ed.)

Some of these volumes exclude foreign or imperial matters, on the theory that these have been covered adequately by such other collections as: A. Berriedale Keith, Selected Speeches & Documents on Colonial Policy; H. Temperly & L.M. Penson, Foundations of British Foreign Policy from Pitt to Salisbury; or George P. Gooch and Harold W.V. Temperley, eds., British Documents on the Origins of the War, 1898-1914.

3) The relevant volumes of the Oxford History of England. (Each contains a critical bibliography organized by subject).

J. Steven Watson, The Reign of George III, 1760-1815 (sic)
E.L. Woodward, The Age of Reform, 1815-1870
R.C.K. Ensor, England, 1870-1914
A.J.P. Taylor, England, 1914-1945

4) The Cambridge History of the British Empire (This is a collaborative, multi-volume work). For the recent Empire and Commonwealth see Robin Winks, ed., Historiography of the British Empire-Commonwealth, as well as the bibliographical notes in such reliable general studies as Bernard Porter, The Lion's Share: A Short History of British Imperialism, 1850-1970 and W. David McIntyre, The Commonwealth Of Nations: Origins and Impact, 1869-1971.

5) The Cambridge History of British Foreign Policy (Also a collaborative milti-volume work). For foreign affairs since World War I there is a series of documents comparable to Gooch & Temperley (above) but not yet quite complete: Woodward & Butler, Documents on British Foreign Policy 1919-1939. For events since 1939 see the annual Survey of International Affairs published under the auspices of the Royal Institute of International Affairs, Chatham House (the series began in 1924 and ended in 1963).

Items 2-5 above are useful substantive works, too, of course. Students of modern British history should also be familiar with the classic multi-volume general histories of the period: Spencer Walpole, History of England from the Conclusion of Great War in 1815 (5 vols. 1878-90). Elie Halevy, History of the English People in the 19th Century (an incomplete work. After a masterly opening survey, England in 1815, Halevy went on to write narrative volumes taking the story almost to mid-century, after which he shifted to the end of his period and wrote an Epilogue, (2 vols. in 3 covering 1895-1914; then he died, without ever closing the gap).

Finally, to keep up with recent articles on all phases of modern history you can use the periodical, Historical Abstracts. Main publishers of scholarly articles in British history include: English Historical Review (not many articles on the 20th century); History (somewhat more sympathetic to modernists); the Historical Journal (formerly the Cambridge Historical Journal); the Bulletin of the Institute of Historical Research; the Journal of Imperial and Commonwealth History; Past and Present; the Economic Historical Review; and (in the USA), the Journal of British Studies; Albion; the Journal of Modern History and occasionally the American Historical Review. The British also published a popular yet-serious historical journal called History Today. It sells for one pound ($2.95) and is hence obviously intended for something other than coffee-table display.

EARLY VICTORIAN ENGLAND

General

Despite its age and size, Halevy's first volume (England in 1815) remains one of the best introductions to the Victorian period. Asa Briggs, The Age of Improvement (1783-1867) is difficult but does well in meshing social with political and economic developments. The leading historian of this age is Norman Gash, whose recent study, Aristocracy and People, 1815-1865, is excellent for the general student.

Special Topics

Repudiation of the 18th-Century Constitution: On parliamentary reform, J.R.M. Butler, The Passing of the Great Reform Bill (1914, new impression, 1964), is probably still the best. The most recent introduction to 1832 is The Great Reform Act (1973) by Michael Brock. For the constitutional and political adjustments after the bill see especially Norman Gash, Reaction and Reconstruction in English Politics. Good on politics is G. Kitson Clark's Peel and the Conservative Party and Gash's Politics in the Age of Peel: A Study in the Technique of Parliamentary Representation, 1830-1850.

Reform and Dissent

On church reform and the position of the dissenters see O. Chadwick, The Victorian Church (a monumental treatment in two-volumes) and R. G. Cowherd, The Politics of English Dissent. The reaction of the Established Church to the "Condition of England" question is described in G. Kitson Clark's Churchmen and the Condition of England, 1832-1885. M. Hovell, The Chartist Movement, still has the best single study of the Chartists, but it should be supplemented by A. Briggs, ed. Chartist Studies, a collection of essays.

Standard of Living Controversy

An essential primary text is Frederick Engel's The Condition of the Working Class in England (1844) but the introductions to the two modern editions, by W. H. Choloner and W. O. Henderson (1958) and E. J. Hobsbawm (1969), should both be read for their contrary views as to its usefulness. Hobsbawm and R. H. Hartwell debate the issue in "The Standard of Living during the Industrial Revolution: a discussion," Economic History Review, 2nd series, vol. xvi, no. 1 (August 1963). A useful discussion of the problems involved is also found in A. J. Taylor, "Progress and Poverty in Britain 1780-1850," Essays in Economic History, vol. 3 (London, 1962).

Mid-Victorian England

General:

Gash, <u>Aristocracy and People</u>, brings us up to 1965. He places his emphasis on the elements of continuity rather than change, as does W. L. Burn, <u>The Age of Equipose</u>. A valuable interpretative work suggesting the social forces pressing for change is G. Kitson Clark's, <u>The Making of Victorian England</u>. Finally there is a splendid essay by Geoffrey Best, <u>Mid-Victorian Britain, 1851-75</u>, appearing in the History of British Society series edited by Hobsbawm.

Special Topics:

The "Victorian Compromise": In addition to the general work cited above see Walter Haughton, <u>The Victorian Frame of Mind, 1830-1870</u>; Walter Bagehot, <u>The English Constitution</u> and Robert Robson, ed., <u>Ideas and Institutions of Victorian Britain</u>

Invaluable original works are John Stuart Mill's Autobiography (1873), Samuel Smiles, <u>Self-Help</u> (1859) and the novels of Trollope.

Britain and the World: Several chapters in J.P.T. Bury, ed., <u>The Zenith of European Power, 1830-1870</u>, vol. X of the New Cambridge Modern History are important. See especially the essay by Gordon Craig. A readable study of the Crimean War is Cecil Woodham-Smith, <u>The Reason Why</u>. On the domestic impact, especially politics, see Oliver Anderson, <u>A Liberal State at War</u>. C.K. Webster, <u>The Foreign Policy of Palmerston</u>, 2 vols., is basic for Lord Palmerston but see also Donald Southgate, <u>The Most English Prime Minister</u>.

Second Reform Epoch: Begin with James B. Conacher, ed., <u>The Emergence of British Parliamentary Democracy in the Nineteenth Century</u>, a collection of commentary and documents comparing the reform acts of 1832, 1867 and 1884. F.B. Smith, <u>The Making of the Second Reform Bill</u> is a fine recent account. F.E. Gillespie, <u>Labor and Politics, 1850-1867</u>, approaches reform from the side of the working class. Robert Blake now has the best biography of Disraeli and Philip Magnus of Gladstone. But see also a recent biographical essay of Peter Stansky, <u>Gladstone: A Progress in Politics</u>.

LATE VICTORIAN ENGLAND: THE GREAT DEPRESSION

General

The fullest account is still Robert Ensor's England 1870-1914
but it is somewhat out-of-date on pre-World-War-I diplomacy.
Donald Read, England 1868-1914, which appeared in 1979, is an
adequate substitute. A concise introduction to the topic of the
week is given, with some supporting documents, in the Anvil
paperback by Herman Ausubel, The Late Victorians.

Special Topics

1) The Economic Impact:

See the standard economic histories, such as William Ashworth, An
Economic History of England, 1870-1939. A most valuable volume
of essays and documents is W.H.B. Court, British Economic History,
1870-1914: Commentary and Documents.

For a summary and bibliography of professional opinion on "the
Great Depression" see S.B. Saul, The Myth of the Great Depression,
1873-1896. Articles of special value are C.H. Wilson "Economy
and Society in Late Victorian Britain," Economic History Review,
1965, and T.W. Fletcher, "The Great Depression of English
Agriculture," Economic History Review, 1961.

2) Moves Towards the Interventionist State:

A fine book, often neglected, is Helen M. Lynd, England in the
Eighteen-Eighties. For the history and origins of the Labour party
the best accounts are Henry Pelling, The Origins of the Labour
Party 1880-1900, and Philip Poirier, The Advent of the British
Labour Party. See also A.V. Dicey, Lectures on the Relation between
Law and Public Opinion in England during the Nineteenth Century,
Lecture VIII (the rise of collectivism), and Samuel H. Beer, British
Politics in the Collectivist Age, chapter IX.

3) Revival of Imperialism:

For a discussion of some of the literature on imperialism, see
William A. Green, "The Crest of Empire," in Victorian Studies,
March 1975. On the expansion into Africa there is R.E. Robinson
and John Gallagher, Africa and the Victorians. For the reaction
in Britain to the "imperial idea" see A.P. Thornton, The Imperial
Idea and its Enemies. And sample some of the great publicists'
works of the period, such as Charles Dilke's Greater Britain,
or Seeley's Expansion of England.

"The Strange Death of Liberal England"

General

Donald Read provides good general coverage. For a good survey
covering the entire century, see Alfred H. Havighurst, <u>Twentieth
Century Britain</u>. The title of this week's session is taken from
the well-written, lively and provocative book of the same name
by George Dangerfield.

Special Topics

1) "The British New Deal":

A straightforward account is Peter Rowland, <u>The Last Liberal
Governments</u>. Bentley B. Gilbert's <u>The Evolution of National
Insurance: The</u> Origins of the Welfare <u>State</u>, is a more thorough
examination of the social legislation passed before the war. Two
older accounts should not be neglected: W.J. Braithwaite, <u>Lloyd
George's Ambulance Wagon</u>, and Lucy Masterman, <u>C.F.G. Masterman</u>
(a biography).

2) Politics of Violence--Women, Workers and Irish:

Dangerfield will start you off but essays by Henry Pelling in
<u>Popular Politics and Society in Late Victorian Britain</u> are a
healthy corrective. For the women see Andrew Rosen, <u>Rise Up Women!</u>
and on labor and industry, E. H. Phelps Brown, <u>The Growth of British
Industrial Relations</u>. Roy Jenkins has a useful and lively account,
<u>Mr. Balfour's Poodle: An Account of the Struggle between the House
of Lords and the Government of Mr. Asquith</u>.

3) Britain and the War:

On the coming of the war see Zara S. Steiner, <u>Britain and the
Origins of the First World War</u>, an excellent and brief account,
and A.J.P. Taylor, <u>The Struggle for the Mastery in Europe 1848-1918</u>.
For the war itself the fullest account is E. Llewellyn Woodward's
<u>Great Britain and the War of 1914-1918</u>. Briefer and good is M.F.
Cruttwell, <u>A History of the Great War</u>. The politicians and the
generals are examined in Paul Guinn's <u>British Strategy and Politics,
1914-1918</u>. On the domestic front there is Arthur Marwick, <u>The
Deluge</u>, and for a participant's point of view on the war see Robert
Graves, <u>Goodbye to All That</u>.

Special Topic: The Women's Movement

As yet no fully satisfactory account of the women's movement has
appeared. There is a brief and lively discussion from a socialist
standpoint in Sheila Rowbotham's Hidden From History: 300 Years of
Women's Oppression and the Fight Against It (1973). Constance Rover's
Love, Morals and the Feminists (1970) outlines the outlook and strategy
of the feminists but it is not comprehensive. J.A. and Olive Banks seek to
explain the connection between the decline of the birth rate and the rise
of the feminist movement in Feminism and Family Planning in Victorian
England (1964). More recently there is the full biography of Marie Stopes by
Ruth Hall (1979). H. G. Wells gives a portrait of a feminist in Ann
Veronica (1909), which is well worth reading.

Scholarly suffrage studies are appearing. We have looked at Andrew
Rosen, Rise Up Women! It might be useful to look at the other side,
which is given in Brian Howard Harrison, Separate spheres: the opposition
to women's suffrage in Britain (1978). It is his thesis that the full
dimension of the suffrage movement in the late Victorian and Edwardian
eras cannot be understood without reference to the antisuffrage movement.

THE INTERWAR YEARS: 1918-1940

General

For this period we have a solid general study, with copious bibliographical apparatus, Charles L. Mowat's Britain Between the Wars. Those already tolerably familiar with the period can read this to good advantage. Those less familar had better begin with R.K. Webb or Alfred Havinghurst.

Special Topics

1) Economic Dilemmas:

Begin with Mowat, passim, and especially Chapter V, "The World's Workshop on Short Time." Sidney Pollard, The Development of the British Economy, 1914-1950, is a reliable survey. A fine study, frnm which few politicians emerge with credit, is Robert Skidelsky, Politicians and the Slump. In a recent (1978) study John Stevenson and Chris Cook, The Slump: Society and Politics During the Depression. challenge many traditional views.

2) Foreign Policy in the 1920s and 1930s

The standard--and brief--survey is G. M. Gathorne-Hardy's, A Short History of International Affairs. A fuller history is F. S. Northedge, The Troubled Giant: Britain among the great powers, 1916-1939. Harold Nicolson provides color and drama in his Peacemaking 1919, and in the first volume (covering 1930-1939) of his Diaries and Letters. John W. Wheeler-Bennett's Munich: Prologue to Tradegy is still the best traditional account of appeasement. See the second edition for an up-to-date bibliographical essay on the subject. Recent additions to the literature are R. K. Middlemas, Diplomacy of Illusion, and M. Gilbert, The Roots of Appeasement.

3) Social

Several well-written and sprightly accounts, of which we should mention Robert Graves and Alan Hodge, The Long Weekend, John Montgomery, The Twenties: An Informal Social History and Ronald Blythe, The Age of Illusion. But they should be contrasted with a new social history, Noreen Branson and Margot Heineman, Britain in the 1930's.

Britain After World War II

General: In this period there is less terra firma beneath our feet but
Alfred Havighurst brings us into the 1970s; and C.J. Bartlett, A History
of Postwar Britain 1945-1974, and David Childs, Britain since 1945: A
Political History (1980), are good readable surveys.

Special Topics:

1) Trial by Planning:

E. Barry O'Brien, Nationalisation in British Politics, gives the
historical background. Ben W. Lewis, British Planning and Nationalization
(1952) is a good American study. On the British side W.A. Robson,
Nationalised Industry and Public Ownership (1960) is favorable and R. Kolf-Cohen,
Nationalization in Britain: The End of Dogma (1958) rather unfavorable.
John Jewkes, Ordeal by Planning (1948) is a plemic against planning, Labor
Government style.

2) The Welfare State:

For perspective see Arthur Marwick, "The Labour Party and the Welfare
State in Britain, 1900-1948" and Kathleen Woodroofe, "The Making of the
Welfare State in England," reprinted in Henry R. Winkler, ed., Twentieth
Century Britain (1976), pp. 149-195. A favorable assessment is given by
Richard M. Titmuss, Commitment to Welfare (1969) and a distinctly unfavorable
essay in R. Emmett Tyrrell, Jr., ed., The Future That Doesn't Work (1977).
Recent assessments are given by William Robson, Welfare State and Welfare
Society (1976) and David C. Marsh, The Welfare State (1970).

3) Relinquishing the Empire:

See earlier studies, such as A.P. Thornton, The Imperial Idea and
Its Enemies. They can be supplemented by Margery Perham's, The Colonial
Rechoning (1963) and John Strachey, The End of Empire (1962). M. Edwardes,
The Last Years of British India (1963) provides the background for independence
and partition.

On the Commonwealth see Frank H. Underhill, The British Commonwealth,
especially chapter 3, "The Second Commonwealth," and , MacIntyre,
The Commonwealth of Nations.

4) The State of the Economy:

For economic activity in the 1950s, Andrew Shonfield, a staff member
of the Observer, has British Economic Policy since the War; see also Norman
Macrae, Sunshades in October. More recent analysis is given in the
successive editions of Anthony Sampson, Anatomy of Britain (1962, 1965, 1972).
Useful books urging reforms are Michael Shanks, The Stagnant Society,
Samuel Brittan, The Treasury under the Tories, and Arthur Koestler,
Suicide of a Nation.

ERINDALE COLLEGE
University of Toronto

Department of History

HISTORY 338Y

From Empire to Welfare State, 1906 - Present

(Handout No. 1)

Contents: A Thought

Course Description

Lecturer

Office

Office Hours

Lectures

Tutorials

Texts and Readings

Assignments

Tests

The Grade System

Handouts

Attached: Guide to Lecture Subjects

Tutorial Schedule

Required Books

Recommended Books

General Reading List

Course Description:

This course constitutes a topical analysis of political, economic and social issues in modern British history: a case study in the decline and fall of an imperial power. The primary aim, therefore, is to further the student's understanding of problems affecting Britain today. The method used will be to analyze those themes which have been instrumental in shaping the nature of British society since 1906. Among the subjects to be discussed are the decline of the Liberal Party as the instrument of progressive change, the decisive effects of the two world wars in impoverishing Britain, the shaping and effectiveness of the welfare state, the impact of the decline of Empire, the records of the alternating post-war Labour and Conservative Governments, and the election surprises of the 1970's.

Lecturer: Sidney Aster.

Office: Room 206, North Building.

Office Hours: To be announced.

Lectures: Lecture and/or tutorial hours are from 1 - 2 p.m., Tuesday and Thursday. A 'Guide to First Term Lecture Subjects' is attached. This list is intended as a general indication of the main subjects and themes. It can vary according to student interests, personal inclination and, possibly, the weather. Definitive lists of lectures with details of major subjects will be distributed periodically during the session. Students should find this useful for revision purposes.

Tutorials: Tutorials are an integral part of the course. Attendance is mandatory and participation is obligatory. Tutorial discussions will be based on readings from a variety of sources and material. This will include extracts from texts, required additional readings and analyses of original documents. During the course of the session each student will be asked to contribute a short oral presentation to the tutorial group. A written version, 300-400 words, must be handed in for assessment within a week of presentation.

93

Texts and Readings: Attached is a list of required and recommended books for this course. Please buy personal copies of the former as they constitute the major readings for the session. The books have been chosen to provide both a general reference framework and in-depth study of some key topics. Further required readings will be mentioned periodically during lectures and tutorials. Arthur Marwick, The Explosion of British Society, 1914-1970 (available in the Library on reserve) should be read as soon as possible.

Assignments: The written work for the course will consist of a 2,000 word essay each term on a topic to be chosen from lists distributed early in the term. The essays will be due on Thursday, 20 November and Thursday, 12 March respectively.* Furthermore, papers which after the first few pages indicate that attention has not been paid to the correct use of language and punctuation will be returned un-marked for revision. The assignments should be type-written, and documented with quotations, footnotes and references to sources given in the proper form. The Library distributes a handout on the proper presentation of research papers. All students should use this for the sake of uniformity and clarity. Finally, the attention of all students is drawn to the fact that essays which are found to have been plagiarized will be returned with a zero grade. This offense is described in the Erindale College Calendar, 1980-81, pages 49-50.

Tests: There is no final examination in this course. Instead there will be two end of term tests. The nature of the tests - type, duration, etc. - will be decided in the course of each term.

Grade System: A student's grade will be determined by a combination of results intended to be fair, accurate and comprehensive. The constituents of the final grade are as follows:

```
Term Papers (2 x 20) ----------------- 40%
Term Tests (2 x 20) ------------------ 40%
Tutorial Participation and Attendance- 15%
Tutorial Presentation---------------- 5%
```

*No papers will be accepted after these deadlines and there will be no exceptions.

94

Required Books:*

Donald Read, Edwardian England, 1901-1915, Society and Politics (G.Harrap)

T.O. Lloyd, Empire to Welfare State, English History, 1906-1976 (O.U.P.)

H.R. Winkler, Twentieth Century Britain (New Viewpoints)

George Orwell, The Road to Wigan Pier (Penguin)

V. Bogdanor, R. Skidelsky, The Age of Affluence, 1951-1964 (Papermac)

Recommended Books:

Arthur Marwick, The Explosion of British Society,
    1914-1970 (Papermac)

Henry Pelling, Winston Churchill (Pan)

A. H. Halsey, Change in British Society, Based on the Reith Lectures, 1978.

*This list is subject to possible change in particular with
regards to new relevant publications.

General Reading List

The following is intended merely as a guide to some suggested further reading:

1. ### Bibliography and Reference

   David Butler and Jennie Freeman, British Political Facts, 1900-1967.
   An indispensable collection of information, facts, statistics,
   etc. on all subjects.
   Ian R. Christie, British History Since 1760, A Select Bibliography.
   Contains numerous entries, divided by subject, on the twentieth Century.
   Chris Cook and John Stevenson, Longman Atlas of Modern British History,
   A Visual Guide to British Society and Politics 1700-1970. Enormously
   useful in clarifying complex topics.
   G.R. Elton, Modern Historians on British History 1485-1945, A Critical
   Bibliography 1945-1969. Contains a substantial section on the twentieth
   century.
   Martin Gilbert, British History Atlas. A useful visual guide with very in-
   formative maps.
   A.F. Havighurst, Modern England 1901-1970. The most comprehensive bibliography
   for the modern period.
   C.L. Mowat, British History Since 1926: A Select Bibliography (revised edition).
   The best short bibliography. Well annotated.

2. ### General Surveys

   C.J. Bartlett, A History of Post-War Britain 1945-74.
   Peter Calvocoressi, The British Experience, 1945-75.
   Bentley Gilbert, Britain Since 1918.
   A.F. Havighurst, Twentieth Century Britain.
   Robert Rhodes James, The British Revolution, British Politics 1880-1939,
   2 vols.
   Trevor Lloyd, Empire to Welfare State, English History 1906-76.
   Arthur Marwick, Britain in the Century of Total War 1900-67.
   W.N. Medlicott, Contemporary England 1914-64.
   L.A. Monk, Britain 1945-70.
   C.L. Mowat, Britain Between the Wars 1918-39.
   Henry Pelling, Modern Britain 1885-1955.
   E.E. Reynolds and N.E. Brasher, Britain in the Twentieth Century 1900-1964.
   L.C.B. Seaman, Post-Victorian Britain 1902-51.
   Richard Shannon, The Crisis of Imperialism 1865-1915.
   Alan Sked and Chris Cook, Post-War Britain, A Political History.
   A.J.P. Taylor, English History 1914-45.
   David Thomson, England in the Twentieth Century.
   Anthony Wood, Great Britain 1900-1965.

3. ### Political, Constitutional and Social

   Paul Addison, The Road to 1945.
   Paul Adelman, The Rise of the Labour Party 1880-1945.
   Samuel Beer, Modern British Politics.
   Noreen Branson, Britain in the Twenties.
   Noreen Branson and Margot Heineman, Britain in the Thirties.
   Maurice Bruce, The Coming of the Welfare State.
   Lord Butler, ed., The Conservatives, A History from their Origins to 1965.

Angus Calder, The People's War 1939-45.
Chris Cook, The Age of Alignment, Electoral Politics in Britain 1922-29.
Chris Cook and John Ramsden, Trends in British Politics Since 1945.
George Dangerfield, The Strange Death of Liberal England.
Christian Davies, Permissive Britain.
Paul Foot, The Politics of Harold Wilson.
Derek Fraser, The Evolution of the British Welfare State.
Bentley Gilbert, British Social Policy 1914-39.
Sean Glynn and John Oxborrow, Inter-War Britain: A Social and Economic History.
Pauline Gregg, The Welfare State..
J.R. Hay, The Development of the British Welfare State.
T. Lindsay, The Conservative Party 1918-70.
Robert McKenzie, British Political Parties.
David McKie and Chris Cook, The Decade of Disillusion, British Politics in
      the Sixties.
Arthur Marwick, The Deluge, British Society and the First World War.
--------------, The Home Front, The British and the Second World War.
David Morgan, Suffragettes and Liberals, The Politics of Woman Suffrage
      in England.
A.J.A. Morris, ed., Edwardian Radicalism 1900-14.
Margaret Morris, The General Strike.
G. Peele and Chris Cook, eds., The Politics of Reappraisal 1918-39.
Henry Pelling, A Short History of the Labour Party.
-------------, Britain and the Second World War.
G.A. Phillips, The General Strike, The Politics of Industrial Conflict.
M. Proudfoot, British Politics and Government, 1951-70.
John Ramsden, The Age of Balfour and Baldwin 1902-40.
Peter Rowland, The Last Liberal Governments, vol. 1, 1905-10.
Judith Ryder and Harold Silver, Modern English Society.
M. Sissons and P. French, eds., The Age of Austerity 1945-51.
Robert Skidelsky, Politicians and the Slump.
John Stevenson, Social Conditions in Britain Between the Wars.
R. Emmett Tyrell, ed., The Future That Doesn't Work: Social Democracy's
      Failures in Britain.
Trevor Wilson, The Downfall of the Liberal Party 1914-35.

4. Economic

Derek Aldcroft and H. Richardson, The British Economy 1870-1939.
Derek Aldcroft, The Inter-War Economy, Britain 1919-39.
B.W.E. Alford, Depression and Recovery, British Economic Growth 1918-39.
W. Beckerman, ed., The Labour Government's Economic Record 1964-70.
Samuel Britain, The Treasury Under the Tories 1951-64.
Norman Chesler, The Nationalization of British Industry, 1945-51.
J.C.R. Dow, The Management of the British Economy 1945-60.
E.J. Hobsbawm, Industry and Empire.
Samuel Hurwitz, State Intervention in Great Britain 1914-19.
W. Arthur Lewis, Economic Survey 1919-1939.
A.S. Milward, The Economic Effects of the Two World Wars on Britain.
G.A. Philips and R.T. Maddock, The Growth of the British Economy 1918-68.
Sidney Pollard, The Development of the British Economy 1914-67.
H.W. Richardson, Economic Recovery in Britain 1932-39.
A. Shonfield, British Economic Policy Since the War.
L.J. Williams, Britain and the World Economy 1919-70.
G. Worswick and P. Edy, eds., The British Economy 1951-59.
A.J. Youngson, British Economic Growth 1920-66.

5. **Foreign Policy and Empire**

Sidney Aster, 1939, The Making of the Second World War.
Max Beloff, Britain's Liberal Empire, vol. 1, Imperial Sunset.
Colin Cross, The Fall of the British Empire.
George Dangerfield, The Damnable Question: A Study in Anglo-Irish Relations.
Roy Douglas, In the Year of Munich.
Michael Edwards, The Last Years of British India.
Martin Gilbert, The Roots of Appeasement.
Paul Hayes, The Twentieth Century 1880-1939.
F.S.L. Lyons, Ireland Since the Famine, 1850 to the Present.
N. Mansergh, The Commonwealth Experience.
James Morris, Pax Britannica, The Climax of an Empire.
W.N. Medlicott, British Foreign Policy Since Versailles 1919-63.
F.S. Northedge, The Troubled Giant, Britain Among the Powers 1916-39.
Liam de Paor, Divided Ulster.
Bernard Porter, The Lion's Share, A Short History of British Imperialism 1850-1970.
P.A. Reynolds, British Foreign Policy in the Inter-War Years.
Hugh.Thomas, The Suez Affair
A.P. Thornton, The Imperial Idea and Its Enemies.
George Woodcock, Who Killed the British Empire?
C.M. Woodhouse, British Foreign Policy Since the Second World War.
E.L. Woodward, British Foreign Policy in the Second World War.

5. **Biography and Memoirs**

Sidney Aster, Anthony Eden.
C.R. Attlee, As it Happened.
Lord Avon (Anthony Eden), Memoirs, 3 vols.
Robert Blake, The Unknown Prime Minister, Bonar Law.
Lord Butler, The Art of the Possible.
George Brown, In My Way.
A. Bullock, Ernest Bevin.
R.H.S. Crossman, Diaries of a Cabinet Minister, 3 vols.
Michael Foot, Aneurin Bevan.
Keith Feiling, Neville Chamberlain.
John Grigg, The Young Lloyd George.
-------, Lloyd George, The People's Champion 1902-1911.
George Hutchinson, Edward Heath.
Roy Jenkins, Asquith.
Stephen Koss, Asquith.
John P. Mackintosh, ed., British Prime Ministers in the Twentieth Century, 2 vols.
David Marquand, Ramsay MacDonald.
Harold Macmillan, Memoirs, 6 vols.
Keith Middlemas and John Barnes, Baldwin.
D.E. Moggridge, Keynes.
Frank Owen, Tempestuous Journey, The Life of Lloyd George.
Andrew Roth, Sir Harold Wilson, Yorkshire Walter Mitty.
Anthony Sampson, Macmillan.
Philip Snowden, Autobiography.
Lord Templewood, Nine Troubled Years.
Harold Wilson, The Labour Government 1964-70.
Lord Woolton, Memoirs.

The following is a proposed list of preliminary lectures, tutorials and readings:

Number 1 — Introductory.

Number 2 — The Victorian Legacy.

Number 3 — The Victorian Legacy, concluded.
              Some Themes of British History.
              — Donald Read, Edwardian England, 1901–1915, Society and Politics,
              pp. 13–86.

Number 4 — Tutorial One: Introductory
              · Read, pp. 87–150

Number 5 — Liberal Social Legislation, 1906–1914: Patronage, Piety
              or Self-Preservation?
              Trevor Lloyd, Empire to Welfare State, English History
              1906–1976, pp. 1–10, 12–54
              Read, pp. 151–193

Number 6 — Tutorial Two: The Liberal Welfare Reforms, 1906–1914:
              Patronage, Piety or Self-Preservation?
              As indicated on tutorial schedule.

Number 7 — The Death of Liberal England, 1910–1914?
              Read, pp. 194–243

Number 8 — Tutorial Three: The Death of Liberal England, 1910–1914
              As indicated on tutorial schedule

Number 9 — Labour and the Emergence of the Labour Party to 1918.
              Henry Pelling, A Short History of the Labour Party, pp. 1–45.

Number 10 — Labour and the Emergence of the Labour Party to 1918,
              concluded.

Number 11 — Tutorial Four: Labour and the Emergence of the Labour
              Party to 1918.
              As indicated on tutorial schedule.

                                        To be continued.

99

HISTORY 338Y

The following is a continuation schedule of proposed lectures, readings and tutorials:

Number 12: War and Society, 1914-1918: The Experience of Collectivism.
            Lloyd, pp. 54-90

Number 13: Tutorial Five. War and Society, 1914-1918: The Experience
            of Collectivism.
            As indicated on tutorial schedule.

Number 14: Politics Between the Wars, 1919-1939
            Lloyd, pp. 98-104, 119-152, 156-161
            Arthur Marwick, The Explosion of British Society, 1914-1970,
            pp. 23-96 (S)
            Henry Pelling, A Short History of the Labour Party, pp. 52-
            86 (S)
            Adelman, pp. 51-77
            Winkler, pp. 100-110

Number 15: The Inter-War Economy, I, 1919-1929
            Lloyd, pp. 104-110, 152-156
            E.J. Hobsbawm, Industry and Empire, pp. 207-224
            Alan S. Milward, The Economic Effects of the Two World Wars,
            pp. 7-24

Number 16: Tutorial Six. The Inter-War Economy, I, 1919-1929
            As indicated on tutorial schedule.

Number 17: The Inter-War Economy, II, 1929-1939
            Lloyd, pp. 161-176, 177-186

Number 18: Tutorial Seven. The Inter-War Economy, II, 1929-1939
            As indicated on tutorial schedule.

Number 19: Society Between the Wars, 1919-1939
            Lloyd, pp. 193-204
            C.L. Mowat, Britain Between the Wars, 1918-1940
            pp. 201-258, 480-531 (S)

Number 20: Tutorial Eight. The Road to Wigan Pier
            As indicated on tutorial schedule.

TO BE CONTINUED

HISTORY 336Y   (Handout No. 14)

The following is a continuation list of proposed lectures, readings and
tutorials:

Number 21:   The Erosion of Consensus, Empire Developments to 1939
                  Lloyd, pp. 110-118
                  George Woodcock, Who Killed the British Empire?
                  pp. 192-213, 225-238, 257-281 (R)

Number 22:   Appeasement and the Origins of World War Two
                  Lloyd, pp. 91-98, 187-193, 204-213
                  Anthony Adamthwaite, The Making of the Second World War,
                  pp. 19-75 (R)

Number 23::   Tutorial Nine. The Origins of World War Two
                  As indicated on tutorial schedule

Number 24:   War and Society: The Experience of Collectivism, 1939-1945
                  Lloyd, p. 244-269
                  Arthur Marwick, The Home Front, The British and the Second
                  World War, pp. 9-12, 123-149, 180-184 (R)

Number 25:   Tutorial Ten. The Domestic Impact of the Second World War
                  As indicated on tutorial schedule

Numb.r 26:   The Second World War, Foreign and Military Aspects, 1939-1945
                  Lloyd, pp. 214-243
                  Winkler, pp. 47-61

Number 27:   Tutorial Eleven. The Role of Winston Churchill: World War Two
                  As indicated on tutorial scedule

Number 28:   The Achievement of Labour: Nationalization and the Welfare
                  State, 1945-1951
                  Lloyd, pp. 284-313
                  Henry Pelling, A Short History of the Labour Party, pp. 88-104

Number 29:   Tutorial Twelve. The General Election of 1945
                  As indicated on tutorial schedule

Number 30:   Tutorial Thirteen. The Making of the Welfare State, 1945-1951
                  As indicated on tutorial schedule.

                                        TO BE CONTINUED

The following is a final list of proposed lectures, readings
and tutorials:

Lecture: The End of Empire: Labour, India and the "Wind
            of Change", 1945-1964
                Lloyd, pp. 278-82, 313-21, 363-68, 404-406
                George Woodcock, Who Killed the British Empire?
                    pp. 282-98, 327-34
                A.P.Thornton, The Imperial Idea and Its
                    Enemies, pp. 316-56

Lecture: The Age of Affluence: Tory Economics, 1951-1964
                Lloyd, pp. 321-337, 343-363, 368-393
                Arthur Marwick, The Explosion of British Society,
                    1914-1970, pp. 131-144, 159-64

Tutorial: Fourteen. "Bread and Circuses": The Conservatives
            in Office, 1951-1964
                as indicated on tutorial schedule

Lecture: From Potsdam to Suez: Foreign Policy in the Post-
            War World, 1945-1956
                Lloyd, pp. 270-78, 282-84, 313-21, 337-42

Tutorial: Fifteen. "The Lessons of Suez"
                as indicated on tutorial schedule

Lecture: Society in the 1950s and 1960s
                Lloyd, pp. 301-305, 358-65, 401-409
                Marwick, Explosion of British Society, pp. 165-86

Tutorial: Sixteen. The Meaning of Anger
                as indicated on tutorial schedule

Lecture: Wilson's Britain, 1964-1970
                Lloyd, pp. 393-429

Tutorial: Seventeen. The Balance of Payments, 1964-1970
                as indicated on tutorial schedule

Lecture: The Long Road to Europe
                Lloyd, relevant extracts
                Winkler, pp. 216-41
                V.Bogdanor and Robert Skidelsky, eds., The Age
                    of Affluence, 1951-1964, pp. 192-220

Tutorial Schedule:

Tutorial Number:

One   Introductory: discussion of tutorial work, participation,
           readings, etc.

Two   The Liberal Welfare Reforms, 1906-1914: Patronage, Piety
           or Preservation? What motives prompted the outburst of the
           Liberal welfare reforms from 1906-1914: was it patronage,
           piety or preservation?

           Henry R. Winkler, ed., Twentieth Century Britain,
                pp. 1-5, 150-167
           J.R. Hay, The Origins of the Liberal Welfare Reforms,
                1906-1914, pp. 9-63 (R)
           E.H. Phelps-Brown, "The Labour and Welfare Policies of the
                Liberal Government, 1906-1914"   (R)

Three   The Death of Liberal England? 1911-1914
           Did the Liberal Party die prior to the First World War?
           Did liberal England die? Neither or both?

           Trevor Wilson, The Downfall of the Liberal Party,
                pp. 15-19, 23-31 (R)
           Peter Rowland, The Last Liberal Governments, 1905-1910,
                IX-XI, XV-XVIII, 30, 342-344 (R)
           George Dangerfield, The Strange Death of Liberal England,
                pp. 3-73, 139-150, 214-234, 389-442 (R)

Four   Labour and the Emergence of the Labour Party to 1918.
           How and why did the labour movement turn from economics
           to politics? What explains the conversion of the Labour Party
           to socialism in 1918?

           Winkler,pp. 171-180.
           Paul Adelman, The Rise of the Labour Party, 1880-1945,
                pp. 3-51, 93-115 (R)

Five   War and Society, 1914-1918: The Experience of Collectivism.
           How did the First World War contribute towards the experience
           and shaping of collectivism? On the basis of the readings,
           assess how the views of Arthur Marwick have evolved on the
           question of war and change.

           Arthur Marwick, The Explosion of British Society, 1914-1970,
                pp. 1-22
           Winkler, pp. 24-44.
           Arthur Marwick, War and Social Change in the Twentieth Century,
                pp. 1-14 (R)

                    TO BE CONTINUED

103

HISTORY 338Y   (Handout No. 6)

Tutorial Schedule, contd.

Tutorial Number:

Six   The Inter-War Economy, I, 1919-1929
        What differences of opinion prevail about the long term
        economic consequences of the First World War? What
        were some of these consequences? Is the General Strike
        among them?

        E.J. Hobsbawm, Industry and Empire, pp. 207-224
        Alan S. Milward, The Economic Effects of the Two
            World Wars, pp. 7-24
        L.J. Williams, Britain and the World Economy, 1919-
            1970, pp. 18-60

Seven   The Inter-War Economy, II, 1929-1939
        In what particular ways did the depression affect
        Britain? What were the instruments of recovery?
        How real was this recovery?

        Williams, pp. 61-114

Eight   Society Between the Wars, 1919-1939: The Road to Wigan
        Pier. In what ways were the economics and politics of
        the inter-war period reflected in social conditions?
        Or did social and cultural change influence political
        and economic realities? What dimension of reality does
        The Road to Wigan Pier reflect?

        George Orwell, The Road to Wigan Pier

                            TO BE CONTINUED.

104

HISTORY 338Y   (Handout No. 15)

The following is a continuation list of proposed tutorials:

Tutorial Number:

Nine
The Origins of World War Two
Was the failure of the Versailles peace settlement inevitable?
What is the meaning of appeasement? In what senses was the
Munich conference an example of appeasement? Why did Britain go
to war in 1939 and not 1938 - or earlier?
   A. P. Adamthwaite, The Making of the Second World War,
   pp. 19-75 (R)
   J. W. Wheeler-Bennett, "A Judgement on Munich"; Neville
   Chamberlain, "Speech in the House of Commons, 3 Oct. 1938"
   (xerox)
   Winkler, pp. 62-77

Ten
The Domestic Impact of the Second World War, 1939-45
What did the Second World War contribute towards the experience
and direction of collectivism? How have historians divided on
the consequences of the war for Britain? What in particular were
the economic effects?
   Arthur Marwick, The Home Front, The British and the Second
   World War, pp. 9-12, 123-149, 180-184
   "The Views of Angus Calder, Henry Pelling and Arthur Marwick"
   (xerox)
   Milward, Economic Effects of the Two World Wars, pp. 24-52

Eleven
The Role of Winston Churchill: World War Two
How do Lloyd George and Churchill compare as war ministers?
Where does the balance lie in terms of Churchill's contribution
to domestic, military and foreign affairs? "What was Winston
Churchill?"
   Winkler, pp. 47-61
   A. J. P. Taylor, "Daddy, What was Winston Churchill?" (xerox)
   Paul Addison, The Road to 1945, pp. 75-102, 229-278
      (suggested additional reading)

Twelve
The General Election of 1945
How and why did the wartime coalition come to an end? What
are the points of similarity and difference in the party
political programmes? What interpretations can be placed on
the election results?
   Addison, pp. 252-269
   "The General Election of 1945" (xerox)

continued...

(Handout No. 15), continued

Tutorial Number:

Thirteen   <u>The Making of the Welfare State, 1945-1951</u>
In what ways were the activities of the Labour Government,
1945-51, facilitated by domestic developments since 1906?
How would you measure the success or failure of the Labour
Government in the areas of nationalization and welfare
legislation?
  Henry Pelling, <u>A Short History of the Labour Party</u>, pp. 88-104
  Winkler, pp. 101-110, 180-191, 197-214
  Derek Fraser, <u>The Evolution of the British Welfare State</u>,
    pp. 206-232.

ERINDALE COLLEGE
University of Toronto
Department of History
     HISTORY 338Y   (Handout No. 20)

The following is a final list of proposed tutorials:
Tutorial Number:

Fourteen   "Bread and Circuses": The Conservatives in Office,
              1951-1964
              What does the phrase "bread and circuses" mean as
              a description of Conservative economic policy?
              Did the Conservatives play politics with economics?
              Did affluence disguise underlying economic weakness?
                  Williams, pp. 114-45
                  Bogdanor and Skidelsky, pp. 17-77, 117-36, 154-60

Fifteen   The "Lessons of Suez"
              What were the lessons of Suez - if any?
                  Bogdanor and Skidelsky, pp. 168-220
                  Selwyn Lloyd, Suez 1956 (extract on reserve)

Sixteen   The Meaning of Anger
              In what ways did the C.N.D., Look Back in Anger,
              and the teddy boys reflect society in the fifties
              and sixties? Could you relate this to the changing
              political and economic background?
                  Bogdanor and Skidelsky, pp. 221-338

Seventeen   The Balance of Payments, 1964-1970
              In what ways did the balance of payments problem
              reflect long term British economic difficulties?
              How successful was the Labour Government in dealing
              with this economic problem?
                  Williams, pp. 145-84
                  Winkler, pp. 115-47
                  D.McKie and C.Cook, Decade of Disillusion, British
                      Politics in the 1960s, pp. 1-68

107

ERINDALE COLLEGE
University of Toronto
Department of History
History 431Y
Topics in Twentieth Century British Diplomacy

(Handout No. 1)

Contents: Course Description
              Lecturer
              Office and Hours
              Texts
              Assignments
              Test
              Final Grade
              Handouts

Attached: Required Books
              Reading List
              First Term Seminars

A Thought: "We are an island race, part of Europe, but with
the Atlantic breaking against our coast. An
accident of history brought the industrial
revolution to Britain before any other European
country. This, coupled with British sea power,
gave us the wherewithall to trade and invest in
almost every corner of the globe. Today, we are
members of the European Community and our future
lies with Europe. But the scale of our international interests is not such that we could
withdraw from them even if we wished to do so.
It is not a British instinct to seek to restrict
our horizons and to think and act as if in a
continental cocoon. The maritime influence is
strong within us.

David Owen, Human Rights (1978)

108

ERINDALE COLLEGE

University of Toronto

Department of History

<u>History 431Y</u>

<u>Topics in Twentieth Century British Diplomacy</u>

This course is concerned with a topical analysis of twentieth century
British diplomacy. The primary aim of the seminar is to further the student's
understanding of Britain's international position in the present day world. An
attempt will be made to trace and analyse the decline of British power in foreign
affairs. The method used will be to examine those themes and crises which have
been instrumental in leading to that decline. Among the subjects discussed
therefore are war origins, war aims and the peace settlements of the First World
War. Particular and prolonged attention will be paid to the theory and practice
of appeasement in the inter-war period. The crisis diplomacy of the 1930's
will be analysed in detail. After an examination of the record of British
foreign policy during the Second World War, the success of Labour's foreign
policy during the early Cold War period will be assessed. This will be dealt
with by questioning whether there are socialist alternatives in foreign policy.
The traumatic affair of the Suez crisis, the negotiations to enter the European
Economic Community and the Rhodesian situation will be used, among other examples,
to assess Britain's current international standing.

It must be emphasized that this seminar is primarily based on research. All
students will be expected to present a major research paper each term and act
once in each term as a critic of a colleague's paper. Independent work habits
and a wide critical interest in the topic are therefore highly desirable.

HISTORY 431Y

Lecturer: Sidney Aster

Office and Hours: Room 206; hours to be posted.

Texts: Attached is a list of required books for this seminar. They are available at the Erindale Bookstore. Each student must purchase a personal copy. The books have been chosen to provide both a general reference framework and in-depth study of several key topics.

Assignments: The written work for the course will consist of a 2500 word essay each term. The subjects will be chosen from the list of seminar topics which is attached. On the relevant date each student will present a precis of the subject for approximately 40 minutes. The precis is intended to indicate the preliminary research done and introduce the main themes and interpretations of the topic. A written summary of the precis, approximately one typewritten page, is expected for distribution to the seminar prior to its meeting. By the end of the second term therefore each student will have a personal and substantial dossier of material covering all aspects of the seminar's work. Following the precis, a pre-appointed student will act as critic to lead off the discussion. The task of the critic is to be familiar with some of the relevant material on the topic and to indicate both the strengths and weaknesses of the precis.

The final version of each term's paper will be due on the date decided in class. No papers will be accepted after the deadline. The papers should be typewritten, with adequate margins, and documented with quotations, footnotes and references to sources given in the proper form. The Library distributes a handout on the correct presentation of research papers. All students should use this for the sake of clarity and uniformity. Finally, the attention of all students is drawn to the fact that essays which are found to have been plagiarized will be returned with a zero grade. This offence is described in the

REQUIRED BOOKS

Texts:
Paul Hayes, <u>Modern British Foreign Policy</u>,
<u>The Twentieth Century, 1880-1939</u>
(A & C Black)

F.S. Northedge, <u>Descent From Power, British</u>
<u>Foreign Policy, 1945-1973</u> (Allen & Unwin)

William R. Rock, <u>British Appeasement in the 1930's</u>
(Arnold)

Additional
Reading
Martin Gilbert, <u>The Roots of Appeasement</u> (Plume)

Michael Howard, <u>The Continental Commitment, The</u>
<u>Dilemma of British Defence Policy in the</u>
<u>Era of the Two World Wars</u> (Penguin)

HISTORY 431Y
Reading List: The following are some suggestions for further
reading and research aids:

1. Bibliographies and Reference Books
   David Butler and Jennie Freeman, British Political Facts,
   1900-1967. An indispensable collection of information,
   facts, statistics, etc. on all subjects.
   Ian R. Christie, British History Since 1760, A Select
   Bibliography. Contains numerous entries on diplomacy.
   Chris Cook and John Stevenson, Longman Atlas of Modern
   British History, A Visual Guide to British Society and
   Politics 1700-1970. Useful in clarifying some complex topics.
   Martin Gilbert, British History Atlas. A visual guide with
   very informative maps on some topics in foreign affairs.
   A.F.Havighurst, Modern England 1901-1970. The best
   bibliography for the modern period. An enormous
   section on foreign affairs.
   C.L.Mowat, British History Since 1926: A Select Bibliography
   (revised edition) Well annotated entries on foreign affairs.
   Keith Sainsbury, International History 1939-1970. Annotated
   by topic. Must be consulted for the later period.

2. General Surveys, Twentieth Century Britain
   C.J.Bartlett, A History of Post-War Britain 1945-74
   Bentley Gilbert, Britain Since 1918
   A.F.Havighurst, Twentieth Century Britain
   Robert Rhodes James, The British Revolution, British Politics
   1880-1939, 2 vols.
   Trevor Lloyd, Empire to Welfare State, English History 1906-76
   Arthur Marwick, Britain in the Century of Total War, 1900-67
   W.N.Medlicott, Contemporary England 1914-64
   L.A.Monk, Britain 1945-70
   C.L.Mowat, Britain Between the Wars 1918-39
   Henry Pelling, Modern Britain 1885-1955
   L.C.B.Seaman, Post-Victorian Britain 1902-51
   Richard Shannon, The Crisis of Imperialism 1865-1915
   A.J.P.Taylor, English History 1914-45
   David Thomson, England in the Twentieth Century
   Anthony Wood, Great Britain 1900-1965

3. Surveys, Foreign Affairs
   M.R.D.Foot, British Foreign Policy Since 1898
   Joseph Frankel, British Foreign Policy 1945-73
   James Joll, Britain and Europe, 1793-1940. (Documents)
   Roy E.Jones, The Changing Structure of British Foreign Policy
   W.N.Medlicott, British Foreign Policy Since Versailles 1919-63
   F.S.Northedge, The Troubled Giant, Britain Among the Powers
   1916-1939
   Royal Institute of International Affairs, Survey of Inter-
   national Affairs - annual volumes
   Lord Strang, Britain in World Affairs, Henry Vlll to
   Elizabeth ll
   David Vital, The Making of British Foreign Policy
   William Wallace, The Foreign Policy Process in Britain
   A.J.P.Taylor, The Trouble Makers, Dissent Over Foreign Policy
   1792-1939

3. Surveys, Foreign Affairs, contd.
D.C.Watt, Personality and Policies, Studies in the Formulation
of British Foreign Policy in the Twentieth Century
John W.Wheeler-Bennett, et al., eds., Documents on International
Affairs, 1929-73
E.L.Woodward and W.N.Medlicott, et al., eds., Documents on
British Foreign Policy 1919-1939. Three Series.
Joel H. Weiner, ed., Great Britain: Foreign Policy and the
Span of Empire 1689-1971, A Documentary History, 4 vols.
C.M.Woodhouse, British Foreign Policy Since the Second World War
Kenneth Younger, Changing Perspectives in British Foreign Policy

4. Pre-1939
A.P.Adamthwaite, France and the Coming of the Second World War
A.P.Adamthwaite, The Making of the Second World War
Sidney Aster, 1939, The Making of the Second World War
Sidney Aster, ed., The "X" Documents, The Secret History of
Foreign Office Contacts with the German Resistance 1937-39
David Carlton, MacDonald Versus Henderson, The Foreign Policy
of the Second Labour Government
E.H.Carr, The Twenty Years' Crisis 1919-39
Kenneth J. Calder, Britain and the Origins of the New Europe,
1914-1918
Ian Colvin, Vansittart in Office
Ian Colvin, The Chamberlain Cabinet
Maurice Cowling, The Impact of Hitler: British Politics
and British Policy, 1933-40
Peter Dennis, Decision by Default, Peace Time Conscription
and British Defence 1919-39
J.Emmerson, The Rhineland Crisis
Stephen Endicott, Diplomacy and Enterprise, British China
Policy, 1933-37
Michael Fry, Lloyd George and Foreign Policy, vol.1
N.H.Gibbs, Grand Strategy, vol. 1, Rearmament Policy
Martin Gilbert, The Roots of Appeasement
Martin Gilbert, Britain and Germany Between the Wars
F.H.Hinsley, British Foreign Policy Under Sir Edward Grey
Michael Howard, The Continental Commitment
W.M.Jordan, Great Britain, France and the German Problem 1918-39
Frank Hardie, The Abyssinian Crisis
J.M.Keynes, The Economic Consequences of the Peace
Jon Jacobson, Locarno Diplomacy
Ivo Lederer, ed., The Versailles Settlement, Was it Foredoomed
to Failure?
Bradford A.Lee, Britain and the Sino-Japanese War 1937-39
William R. Louis, British Strategy in the Far East 1919-39
David Lloyd George, The Truth About the Peace Treaties
W.N.Medlicott, The Coming of War in 1939
W.N.Medlicott, Britain and Germany, The Search for Agreement
1930-1937
Keith Middlemas, Diplomacy of Illusion, The British Government
and Germany 1937-39
Arno J. Mayer, Politics and Diplomacy of Peacemaking
Harold I.Nelson, Land and Power, British and Allied Policy
on Germany's Frontiers 1916-19
Harold Nicolson, Peacemaking, 1919
Ritchie Ovendale, Appeasement and the English Speaking World
1937-39

113

4. Pre-1939, contd.
    Peter Padfield, The Great Naval Race, The Anglo-German Naval
        Rivalry 1900-14
    Roger Parkinson, Peace for Our Time: Munich to Dunkirk
    Lawrence Pratt, East of Malta, West of Suez, Britain's Medit-
        erranean crisis 1936-39
    P.A.Reynolds, British Foreign Policy in the Inter-War Years
    William R. Rock, British Appeasement in the 1930's
    Victor H. Rothwell, British War Aims and Peace Diplomacy 1914-18
    Ludwig Schaefer, ed., The Ethiopian Crisis
    Robert Shay, British Rearmament in the Thirties: Politics and
        and Profits
    Zara S. Steiner, Britain and the Origins of the First World War
    A.J.P.Taylor, The Origins of the Second World War
    Christopher Thorne, The Approach of War 1938-39
    Christopher Thorne, The Limits of Foreign Policy, The West,
        the League and the Far Eastern Crisis1931-33
    Ann Trotter, Britain and East Asia 1933-37
    L.F.C.Turner, The Origins of the First World War
    Telford Taylor, Munich
    D.C.Watt, Too Serious a Business, European Armed Forces and the
        Approach to the Second World War
    Frank Walters, A History of the League of Nations
    Arnold Wolfers, Britain and France Between Two Wars

5. Post-1939
    Elizabeth Barker, Britain in a Divided Europe 1945-72
    --------, Churchill and Eden at War
    Christopher J. Bartlett, The Long Retreat, A Short History
        of British Defence Policy 1945-70
    Nora Beloff, The General Says No
    C.Bell, The Debatable Alliance
    Miriam Camps, Britain and the European Community 1955-63
    Arthur Cyr, British Foreign Policy and the Atlantic Area
    Leon D.Epstein, British Politics in the Suez Crisis
    Geoffrey Goodwin, Britain and the United Nations
    Michael R. Gordon, Conflict and Consensus in Labour's Foreign
        Policy 1914-65
    M.Gowing and L.Arnold, Independence and Deterrence, Britain and
        Atomic Energy 1945-52
    H.Feis, Churchill, Roosevelt, Stalin
    M.A.Fitzsimons, The Foreign Policy of the British Labour
        Government 1945-51
    Emanuel J. de Kadt, British Defence Policy and Nuclear War
    Uwe Kitzinger, Diplomacy and Persuasion, How Britain Joined
        the Common Market
    Geoffrey McDermott, The Eden Legacy and the Decline of British
        Diplomacy
    William H.McNeill, America, Britain and Russia, Their Cooper-
        ation and Conflict 1941-46
    Ronald B. Manderson-Jones, The Special Relationship, Anglo-
        American Relations and Western Unity 1947-56
    Eugene J.Meehan, The British Left Wing and Foreign Policy, A
        Study of the Influence of Ideology
    Elizabeth Monroe, Britain's Moment in the Middle East 1914-56

5. Post-1939, contd
    Herbert George Nicholas, Britain and the U.S.A.
    Francis L. Loewenheim, ed., Roosevelt and Churchill, Their
        Secret Wartime Correspondence
    Roger Parkinson, Blood, Toil, Tears and Sweat
    Roger Parkinson, A Day's March Nearer Home
    Peter Teed, The March to Europe 1880-1972
    Hugh Thomas, The Suez Affair
    D.C.Watt, Britain Looks to Germany, British Opinion and Policy
        Towards Germany Since 1945
    Elaine Windrich, British Labour's Foreign Policy
    -------, Britain and the Politics of Rhodesian Independence
    E.L.Woodward, British Foreign Policy in the Second World War

6. Biography (Foreign Secretaries)
    Kenneth Young, A.J.Balfour
    Leonard Moseley, Curzon, The End of an Epoch
    M.A.Hamilton, Arthur Henderson
    Keith Robbins, Sir Edward Grey
    Charles Petrie, The Life and Letters of the Rt. Hon. Sir Austen
        Chamberlain
    Marquess of Reading, Rufus Isaacs
    David Marquand, Ramsay MacDonald
    Sir John Simon, Retrospect
    Sir Samuel Hoare (Lord Templewood), Nine Troubled Years
    Lord Avon (Anthony Eden), Memoirs, 3 vols.
    Sidney Aster, Anthony Eden
    Lord Halifax, Fulness of Days
    Lord Birkenhead, Halifax
    A.Bullock, Ernest Bevin
    Herbert Morrison, Autobiography
    Bernard Donoughue and G.W.Jones, Herbert Morrison. Portrait of
        a Politician
    Harold Macmillan, Memoirs, 6 vols.
    Selwyn Lloyd, Suez 1956
    Lord Butler, The Art of the Possible
    John Dickie, The Reluctant Commoner (Sir Alec Douglas-Home)
    George Brown, In My Way
    Avi Shlaim, ed., British Foreign Secretaries Since 1945

7. Biography (Others)
    Clem Attlee, As It Happened
    Robert Blake, The Unknown Prime Minister, Bonar Law
    R.H.S.Crossman, Diaries of a Cabinet Minister, 3 vols.
    David Dilks, ed., The Diaries of Sir Alexander Cadogan, 1938-45
    Keith Feiling, Nevile Chamberlain
    Nevile Henderson, Failure of a Mission, Berlin 1937-39
    Lord Kilmuir, Political Adventure
    George Hutchinson, Edward Heath
    Stephen Koss, Asquith
    John P.Mackintosh, ed., British Prime Ministers in the Twentieth
        Century, 2 vols.
    Keith Middlemas and John Barnes, Baldwin
    Anthony Nutting, No End of a Lesson
    Henry Pelling, Winston Churchill
    Peter Rowland, Lloyd George
    Harold Wilson, The Labour Government 1964-70

8. Articles
    See A.F.Havighurst, Modern England 1901-70, pp. 40-44

HISTORY 431Y

First Term Seminars
Topics and Readings*

12 September.   Introductory: Course requirements, etc.

19 September.   The British Foreign Office: History, Functions,
                     Diplomatic Constants and Themes.
                         James Joll, ed., Britain and Europe, 1793-1940,
                             1-30, 204-206, 214-231 (R)
                         Harold Nicolson, Diplomacy (R)

26 September.   The Background Surveyed: 1603-1902
                     Paul Hayes, Modern British Foreign Policy,
                     The Twentieth Century 1880-1939, pp. 1-105
                     Lord Strang, Britain in World Affairs,
                     pp. 41-245 (R)

Seminar One: Britain and the Origins of the First World War.
                     What precipitated the return from isolation?
                     How did overseas developments (e.g., the
                     Moroccan crises) and events in south-east
                     Europe (e.g., the Bosnian crises) redirect
                     British foreign policy? Why did Britain go to
                     war in August 1914?
                     Hayes, pp. 109-171
                     Strang, 249-284
                     Joel H. Wiener, ed., Great Britain: Foreign Policy
                     and the Span of Empire, 1689-1971, A Documentary
                     History, pp. 596-625.

                     Michael Howard, The Continental Commitment, pp.7-52.
                         L.C.F. Turner, Origins of the First World
                         War, pp. 1-115 (R)
                         Zara Steiner, Britain and the Origins of the
                         First World War (R)

Seminar Two: War Aims and Peace Preliminaries 1914-1918.
                     How did debate evolve during the war regarding war
                     aims? What was the position on the eve of the
                     'Coupon Election' December 1918? What influence did
                     the election have on the formulation of British aims
                     and objectives prior to the opening of the peace
                     conference?

                     Hayes, pp. 177-205
                     Martin Gilbert, The Roots of Appeasement, 1-42
                     Weiner, Documents, (Xeroxed extracts)

---

*Readings listed first are the obligatory minimum for the seminar. Readings
which follow - indented - are informative supplementary material. In addition,
for all seminars dealing with the inter-war period students must read the relevant section in the authoritative study: N. H. Gibbs, Grand Strategy, volume I;
as well as the weekly selection of distributed documents.

116

A.J.P. Taylor and R. Pares, eds., Essays in
Honour of Lewis Namier, "The War Aims of the
Allies in the First World War", 475-505 (R)
   Harold Nelson, Land and Power, 3-87,
   126-41, 321-82 (R)
   Joll, 232-238
   F.S. Northedge, The Troubled Giant, 1-44 (R)

Seminar Three:

Lloyd George and the Versailles Treaties, 1918-19.
What were the main areas of British concern at the
peace conference? Does Lloyd George's performance
at the conference bear out his reputation as a
moderate? What is the significance and impact of
the Fontainebleau Memorandum? How did British
objectives finally accord with the results of the
conference?
Hayes, 205-212
Gilbert, 43-55
Joll, 239-269
Frank Owen, Tempestuous Journey, The Life and Times
of Lloyd George, 522-555 (R)
   W.N. Medlicott, British Foreign Policy Since
   Versailles, 1919-1963, 1-17, 32-43 (R)
   Northedge, 91-124

Seminar Four:

The Roots of Appeasement, 1919-1929
What was the combined significance of a) The
Fontainebleau Memorandum, b) J.M. Keynes, The
Economic Consequences of the Peace? How was
British diplomacy influenced in the 1920's by
guilt over the Versailles settlement? What is
the significance of the Locarno settlement and
how was it followed up?
Hayes, 212-259.
Gilbert, 56-125.
William R. Rock, British Appeasement in the 1930's,
31-36.
   Joll, 270-296
   Medlicott, 18-31, 44-93
   Northedge, 160-196, 223-272

117

Seminar Five: Disarmament and the Continental Commitment, 1919-1932.
What provisions did the Versailles treaty make for
both German and general disarmament? What was the
strategic significance of the Washington Naval
Conference of 1921? What further progress was made
on this question at the League of Nations? What was
the basic conflict between disarmament and the
"continental commitment"? What was the dilemma of
British defence policy? Why did the Disarmament
Conference fail?
Michael Howard, The Continental Commitment, 53-96
Medlicott, 94-105
   Northedge, 327-347, 368-395
   Strang, 285-318

Seminar Six: The Far East 1929-1933: The Manchurian Crisis.
Was the Manchurian crisis the first case of
appeasement by the western powers? What reasons
compelled Britain to avoid force or the application
of League sanctions? Did Britain frustrate U.S.
attempts to take effective action against Japan?
Medlicott, 105-122
Northedge, 340-367
   Christopher Thorne, The Limits of Foreign
   Policy, 3-14, 78-127, 328-403 (R)
   P.A. Reynolds, British Foreign Policy in
   the Inter-War Years, 81-98 (R)

Seminar Seven: Britain and Germany: the Search for Agreement
1933-1935.
Why did the rise of Hitler add impetus to appeasement
in Britain? What efforts were made in this direction?
How did Germany react? What was the impact of the
British White Paper of March 1935? In what sense was
the Anglo-German Naval Agreement of June 1935 a
logical stage in appeasement?
Hayes, 262-273
Gilbert, 126-150
Rock, 36-40, 41-53
   Medlicott, 123-140
   Northedge, 396-407
   Anthony Eden, Facing the Dictators,
   24-83, 121-143 (R)

Seminar Eight:

The Rhineland Crisis, March 1936
What was the treaty position in regards to the
Rhineland? Why could Britain and France reach
no agreed policy? How did the re-occupation alter
the strategic situation in western Europe? Was
this crisis the last opportunity to have called a
halt to Nazi expansionism?
Hayes, 278-280
Joll, 305-319
Maurice Beaumont, "The Rhineland Crisis" (R)
   Northedge, 426-434
   Eden, 330-367
   E.M. Robertson, Hitler's Pre-War Policy and
   Military Plans, 66-81 (R)

   J. T. Emmerson, The Rhineland Crisis, 7 March 1936,
    A Study in Multilateral Diplomacy

Seminar Nine:

Crises in the Mediterranean, 1935-8: Abyssinia
and the Spanish Civil War
In strategic terms what was the significance of the
Mediterranean in British defence policy? What impact
did the Chiefs of Staff warning against a war on
three world fronts have on British policy? How
successful was the "dual policy" during the
Abyssinian crisis? Why were sanctions never applied
against Italy? How did Britain arrive at the policy
of non-intervention during the Spanish Civil War?
What strategic interests did it serve?
Hayes, 273-278, 280-284
Medlicott, 141-155
R.A.C. Parker, "Britain and Ethiopia, 1935-36" (R)
   Eden, 191-329, 395-441
   Northedge, 407-425, 436-446

Seminar Ten:

Chamberlain, Appeasement and Munich 1937-1938
What views on foreign policy did Chamberlain hold
on becoming Prime Minister in May 1937? What attitude
to appeasement did he hold? What strategic considera-
tions governed British policy towards Czechoslovakia?
How did Britain come to accept a mediating role? Were
the decisions reached at Munich a tragic necessity?
a tragic mistake? or the best of a bad situation?
Hayes, 284-297
Gilbert, 151-188
Rock, 1-30, 54-84
   Joll, 320-366
   Medlicott, 169-196
   Keith Feiling, Neville Chamberlain 295-342 (R)

Seminar Eleven: The Coming of War, From Munich to Danzig
1938 - September 1939
What explains British policy towards the occupation
of Prague? In what sense was the Polish guarantee
a return to the Continental Commitment? Did British
diplomacy from April to September indicate a search
for alliances or just the establishment of a deterrent
front? Why did Britain go to war on 3 September 1939?
Hayes, 297-326
Rock, 85-101.
Howard, 97-149
   Sidney Aster, 1939, The Making of the Second World
   War, 19-114, 152-242, 281-319, 339-390.
   Northedge, 549-630
   Medlicott, 197-233.

ERINDALE COLLEGE
University of Toronto
Department of History

HISTORY 431Y

(Handout No. 8)

Second Term Seminars: Some General Observations

At the outset of the first term I mentioned that we will be altering
the format of the seminars. Attached therefore is the new schedule for these
seminars.

Please note the following:

1. The basic structure and framework remains unaltered.

2. There is still a paper precis of research in progress and critics
   appraising this work each session.

3. However two refinements have been added:

   a) Whereas previously a paper precis was designed to examine all
      the evidence on a topic and produce a balanced judgement, the
      attempt now is to present a powerful one-sided case. My intention
      here is positively to encourage you to take a risk and get
      intimately involved in an issue.

   b) The role of the critics likewise is made more active and committed.
      Rather than acting as passive commentators, the critics will
      participate as advocates for a diametrically opposed view.

The work load for both paper precis and critic roles is in no way
increased.

Second Term Seminars

Seminar Dates: January 23 (first term papers due); 30, February 6, 13
27, March 6, 13, 20, 27; April 3, 10 (test).

Seminar One: The Socialist Alternative in Foreign Policy, 1945-1951

    Paper Precis: "To describe the foreign policy of the Labour Government
from 1945-51 as socialist is utter and complete rubbish."

    Critique: "Ernest Bevin and Herbert Morrison pursued socialist goals
in foreign policy - even if broadly interpreted."

        F. S. Northedge, Descent From Power, pp. 11-67
        Avi Shlaim, ed., British Foreign Secretaries Since 1945,
            pp. 13-26 (R)
        Joseph Frankel, British Foreign Policy, 1945-1973, pp. 1-19
        M. A. Fitzsimons, "British Labour in Search of a Socialist
            Foreign Policy", xerox article on reserve.

        Medlicott, pp. 268-294
        M. A. Fitzsimons, The Foreign Policy of the Labour Government,
            1945-51, pp. 1-54 (R)

Seminar Two: Britain and Divided Germany, From Potsdam to NATO, 1945-1949.

    Paper Precis: "Four-Power disunity on the issue of Germany in the post-1945
period was purely economic in origin."

    Critique: "Politics, as always, not economics lay at the heart of the
'German problem': security was the issue, not recovery."

    Northedge, pp. 68-97
    Fitzsimons, pp. 87-111

        D. C. Watt, Britain Looks to Germany, pp. 13-98
        Avi Shlaim, British Foreign Secretaries Since 1945,
            pp. 27-80 (R).

Seminar Three: British Defence Policy in the Nuclear Age, 1945-73.

    Paper Precis: "Considering post-1945 changes in the global balance of power,
Britain's nuclear deterrent has maintained her influence
and contributed to western defence needs."

    Critique: "Britain's experience with an independent nuclear force has
been an economic and military disaster."

        Northedge, pp. 273-301.
        C. M. Woodhouse, British Foreign Policy Since the Second
            World War, pp. 13-34 (R).
        Joseph Frankel, British Foreign Policy, 1945-1973,
            pp. 283-309 (R)
        C. J. Bartlett, The Long Retreat: A Short History of
            British Defence Policy, 1945-1970.

Seminar Three: (concl'd.)

W. P. Snyder, The Politics of British Defence Policy, 1945-1962, pp. 3-40, 205-260 (R).

Seminar Four: The 'Special Relationship' Anglo-American Relations Since 1945.

Paper Precis: "Despite recurrent problems and friction the Anglo- American connection has substance and content: it is special."

Critique: "The Anglo- American 'Special Relationship' is neither special nor is there a relationship. It is a convenient British myth to disguise Britain's post-1945 demise in international affairs.'

Northedge, pp. 173-204
Max Beloff, "The Special Relationship: an Anglo-American Myth", (xerox article on reserve.)
Frankel, pp. 203-13.
Coral Bell, The Debatable Alliance, An Essay in Anglo-American Relations, pp. 1-30, 57-73, 126-30 (R).
H. G. Nicholas, Britain and the USA, pp. 11-180 (R).
Coral Bell, "The Special Relationship", in Michael Leifer, Constraints and Adjustments in British Foreign Policy, pp. 103-119.

Seminar Five: The Suez Crisis, 1956

Paper Precis: "Eden if anyone, not Nasser, was the Hitler of 1956 with the same cloud of words and the same unscrupulousness of action."

Critique: "Selwyn [Lloyd], why did you stop? Why didn't you go through with it and get Nasser down?" (Dulles)

Frankel, pp. 213-220
Sidney Aster, Anthony Eden, pp. 141-165
Northedge, pp. 98-141
"Suez", The Times Literary Supplement, 30 November 1979, pp. 64, 67-70, etc. xerox articles.
Anthony Eden, Full Circle, pp. 419-584
Hugh Thomas, The Suez Affair, relevant extracts.

Seminar Six: The 'Wind of Change': Foreign and Commonwealth Policy, 1957-1964.

Paper Precis: "The 'Commonwealth' has proved to be a myth and a liability in Britain's external relations. And that is because the imperial illusion remained although the Empire itself had gone."

Critique: "Having lost an Empire Britain acquired a Commonwealth which has given her a new international role on the world stage."

Seminar Six: (concl'd.)

> Northedge, pp. 205-237.
> Frankel, pp. 221-233.
> Bernard Porter, The Lion's Share, A Short History of British
>   Imperialism, 1850-1970, pp. 303-354 (R)
>   Harold Macmillan, Memoirs, vol. 5, extracts (R)
>   C. E. Carrington, The Liquidation of the British Empire (R),
>   extracts.
>   Woodhouse, pp. 140-164.

Seminar Seven: The European Connection, 1945-1973.

Paper Precis: "Taking into account Britain's pre-1939 world status and
Empire commitments, the 'long road to Europe' was inevitable,
natural and possibly beneficial."

Critique: "The 'long road to Europe' was a disaster which left Britain
as an appendix rather than a leader of the E.E.C. It was a
fundamental post-war miscalculation."

> Northedge, pp. 142-172, 328-362.
> Frankel, pp. 233-244.
>   David Calleo, "Britain in Transit: the Postwar Muddle",
>   in H. R. Winkler, Twentieth Century Britain, pp. 216-237.
>   Miriam Camps, Britain and the European Community,
>   1945-1963, pp. 1-53, 274-366, 455-519 (R).
>   Fitzsimons, pp. 112-130, 140-143, 149-159.
>   Uwe Kitzinger, Diplomacy and Persuasion, How Britain
>   Joined the Common Market, extracts (R).
>   Woodhouse, pp. 215-246.

Seminar Ten: April 10: End of Term Test.

Commentaries on given and identified extracts from documents
studied in Seminars.

History 280F/103C
Fall 1975
Berkeley

University of California

Thomas Laqueur
Thomas Metcalf

EMPIRE AND IMPERIALISM

Reading assignments and location of material - The assignments
for each of the first four weeks have been divided into two
sections. The first lists essential reading for all members
of the seminar; books or articles in this section are available
on two hour reserve in Moffitt and in the history department
library. The second gives a selection of recommended books and
articles relevant to the week's topic. Graduate students will
be expected to do a reasonable amount of reading among these
works and to share what they have earned with the seminar.
Books and articles listed in section 2 will be available in
HGS. For Parts II and III of the course required readings will
be available in Moffitt and the South Asia Library Service
(Room 438, Doe Library); suggested readings will be in SSEALS
only.

Books ordered at the ASUC store:

    E.M. Forster - Passage to India
    K. Masselos - Nationalism on the Indian Subcontinent
    H. Wright - The New Imperialism

In addition a xerox copy of the first weeks reading and a few
selected articles will be available for purchase.

Part I - How was Rule Achieved: Capital, Trade, and Politics

October 7 - Motives of imperial expansion 1830-80

    Required Reading:
        R. Robinson and Gallagher- "Imperial of Free Trade"
                        Econ. Hist. Rev. VI, No. 1
                        (1953)

        O. McDonough- "Anti-Imperialism of Free Trade" Econ.
                Hist. Rev. XIV, no. 3(1962)

        D.C.M. Platt- "The Imperialism of Free Trade: Some
                Reservations" Econ. Hist. Rev. XXI (1968)

        "   " - "Further Objections to an 'Imperial of
                Free Trade" Econ. Hist. Rev. XXVI, no. 1
                (1973)

        Wright- selections from Lenin and Hobson, pp. 4-38
                (Lenin available for .50 from Yenan Bookshop)

Suggested Reading:
   J.A. Hobson -Imperialism. A Study

   V.I. Lenin -Imperialism. The Highest Stage of Capitalism

   E. Stokes, "Late Nineteenth Century Colonial Expansion
          and the Attack on the Theory of Economic
          Imperialism: A Case of Mistaken Identity?"
          Hist. Jour. XII, 2(1969)

   D.C.M. Platt -Finance, Trade and Politics in British
          Foreign Policy, 1815-1914 (1968)

   Albert H. Imlah -Economic Elements in the Pax
          Britannica (1958)

   L.H. Jenks -The Migration of British Capital to 1875
          (1927)

   R.L. Schuyler -The Fall of the Old Colonial System,
          1770-1870 (1945)

          of Gladstone and Disraeli (1973)

   W.P. Morrell -British Colonial Policy in the Age of
          Peel and Russell (1930)

   Klaus E. Knorr -British Colonial Theories, 1570-
          1850 (1944)

   Bernard Semmel -The Rise of Free Trade Imperialism
          (1972)

   D.K. Fieldhouse -The Colonial Empires from the
          Eighteenth Century (1965)

October 14- Motives of Imperial Expansion 1880-1900

   Required Reading:

      Review the reading from last week, especially Lenin
      and Hobson
      David Fieldhouse -Economics and Empire 1830-1914
                (1973) pp. 3-87, 260-68, 312-93,
                459-77

      Eric Stokes -"Uneconomic Imperialism" Hist. Jour.
                XVIII, 2(1975) pp. 409-416

      R. Robinson and J. Gallaghar -Africa and the Victorians (1961),
                pp. 410-472

Suggested Reading:

    Robert Collins -The Partition of Africa (1969) a book
              of readings

    R.F. Betts -Causes and Dimensions of Empire (1972)
           a book of readings

    William Langer -The Diplomacy of Imperialism (2nd ed. 1960)

    P. Duignan and L.H. Gann eds. The History and Politics
                          of Colonialism 1870-
                          1914 (vol. 1 of 5 vol.
                          History of Colonialism
                          in Africa 1870-1960)

    P. Gifford and W.R. Lewis, eds. -British and Germany
                             in Africa (1967)

    "   "   "   -France and Britain
                           in Africa (1971)

    P. Duignan and L.H. Gann -Burden of Empire: An
                         Appraisal of Western
                         Colonialism in Africa South
                         of Sahara (1968)

    J.D. Hargreaves -Prelude to the Partition of Africa
                (1963)

    G.N. Sanderson -England, Europe and the Upper Nile,
             1882-1899 (1965)

October 21- Jingoism and Domestic British Politics

Required Reading:

    Elie Halevy -Imperialism and the Rise of Labour, pp. 69-
           136

    Richard Price -An Imperial War and the British Working
             Class (1972) introduction and conclusion

    A.P. Thornton -The Imperial Idea and its Enemies Chaps 2
            and 3
    Schumpeter -extract in Wright, pp. 47-61

    Kipling - selected poems (xeroxes)

- 4 -

Henry Pelling -"British Labour and British Imperialism"
from Popular Politics and Society in
Late Victorian England (1968) pp. 82-100

Suggested Reading:

Bernard Semmel -Imperialism and Social Reform:
English Social Imperial Thought 1895-
1914 (1960)

H.V. Emy -Liberals, Radicals and Social Politics,
1892-1914 (1973)

Jeffrey Butler -The Liberal Party and the Jameson
Raid (1968)

Bernard Porter -Critics of Empire (1968)

H.C.G. Mathew -The Liberal Imperialists (1973)

Stephen Koss, ed. -The Pro-Boers: The Anatomy of an
Antiwar Movement (1973)

John W. Auld -"The Liberal Pro Boers" -J. Br. S. XIV,
2, May 1975

Louis L. Cornell -Kipling in India (1966)

Jonah Raskin -The Mythology of Imperialism

Philip Mason -The Glass, the Shadow and the Fire
(1975)

J.S. Galbraith -Reluctant Empire: British Policy on
the South African Frontier (1963)

J.S. Marais -The Fall of Kruger's Republic

October 28 - Colonialism/ British attitudes to Rule and Race

Required Reading:

Selections from Fritz Fanon -The Wretched of the Earth

G. Orwell -"Shooting an Elephant"

E.M. Forster -Passage to India

Philip Mason -Prospero's Magic, chaps. 2 and 4

- 5 -

Suggested Reading:

A. Memmi -The Colonizer and The Colonized

O. Mannoni -Prospero and Caliban

Philip Curtin -Imperialism (Harper and Row Reader on
            Racism)

V.G. Kiernan -The Lords of Creation

George Orwell -Burma Days

Part II -HOW RULE WAS ORGANIZED, AND WHO BENEFITTED

November 4: Politics and the Organization of Empire

Required Reading:

D.A. Low, Lion Rampant, pp. 8-112

T.R. Metcalf, The Aftermath of Revolt, pp. 3-45

T.R. Metcalf, "The British Indian Empire" (mimeo)

J. Beames, Memoirs of a Bengal Civil Servant, pp. 92-
        108 and 125-45;
                or
P. Woodruff (Mason), Rulers of India: Guardians
            (Vol. II), pp. 75-97

Suggested Reading:

I.T. Prichard, Chronicles of Budgepore (satire of
        British life in India)

P. Woodruff (Mason), Call the Next Witness (satirical
            novel)

Francis Hutchins, The Illusion of Permanence

Bernard Cohen, "Recruitment and Training of British
            Civil Servants in India", in R. Braibanti,
            ed., Asian Bureaucratic Systems
            Emergent from the British Imperial
            Tradition

B. Spangenberg, "The Problem of Recruitment for the
            Indian Civil Service during the late
            Nineteenth Century", Journal of Asian
            Studies, Vol. XXX (1970), pp. 341-60

E.M. Forster, The Hill of Devi (his life as minister to a maharaja)

November 11: Economics and the Beneficiaries of Empire (I) India

Required Reading:

        M.D. Morris, T. Raychaudhuri, et al., debate on 19th c. Indian economic history, in Indian Economic and Social History Review, Vol. V (1968), pp. 1-100 and 319-88

        A.K. Bagchi, "European and Indian Entrepreneurship in India", in E. Leach and S.N. Mukherjee, Elites in South Asia, pp. 223-56

        R.E. Frykenberg, "Elites in a South Indian District", Journal of Asian Studies, Vol. XXIV (1965), pp. 261-82

        Rajat Ray, "The Dynamics of Continuity in Rural Bengal", Indian Economic and Social History Review, Vol. X (1973), pp. 103-28; and "The Crisis of Bengal Agriculture", ibid. pp. 244-79 (highly recommended, but not required).

Suggested Reading:

        W.J. MacPherson, "Investment in Indian Railways", Economic History Review, Vol. VIII (1955/56) pp. 177-86

        D. Thorner, Investment in Empire: British Railway Enterprise in India

        John McLane, "The Drain of Wealth and Indian Nationalism, in T. Raychaudhuri, ed., Contributions to Indian Economic History II (1963), pp. 21-40

        Peter Harnetty, Imperialism and Free Trade: cashire and India in the mid-Nineteenth Century

        A.K. Bagchi, Private Investment in India 1900-1939

        D.H. Buchanan, Development of Capitalistic Enterprise in India

Elizabeth Whitcombe, Agrarian Conditions in Northern
India (Vol. I)

Prakash Tandon, Beyond Punjab (memoirs of an Indian
employed by a British firm).

November 18: Economics and the Beneficiaries of Empire(II):
Indonesia and West Africa

Required Reading:

J.S. Furnivall, Colonial Policy and Practice,pp. 219-
75.

Clifford Geertz, Agricultural Involution, pp. 47-123

Michael Crowder, West Africa Under Colonial Rule,
pp. 165-238, 273-307, 345-55, and
372-81

Suggested Reading:

Margery Perham, Life of Lord Lugard: the Years of Authority

Cyril Ehrlich, "Building and Caretaking: Economic
Policy in British Tropical Africa",
Economic History Review, Vol. (1973),
pp. 649-67

I.H. Gann and Peter Duignan, ed., Colonialism in
Africa (5 vols)

Gann and Peter Duignan, Burden of Empire (chs. XV,
XVI, and XXII)

Chinua Achebe, Things Fall Apart (West African novel)

November 25: The View from Below: Resistance Movements

Required Reading:

T. Metcalf, The Aftermath of Revolt, pp. 46-92

Eric Stokes, "Traditional Resistance Movements",
Past and Present, No. 48 (August 1970),
pp. 100-18

T.O. Ranger, "Connections Between Primary Resistance
Movements and Modern Nationalism", Journal of African History, Vol. IX (1968),
pp. 437-53 and 631-64

John Iliffe, "The Organization of the Maji Maji
Rebellion", Journal of African History,

Vol. VIII (1967), pp. 496-512

Barrington Moore, Social Origins of Dictatorship and
Democracy, pp. 330-41 and 353-85

Suggested Reading:

S.B. Chaudhuri, Civil Rebellion in the Indian
Mutinies

Stephen Fuchs, Rebellious Prophets: Messianic Movements
in India

M.H. Siddiqi, "The Peasant Movement in Pratapgarch,
1920" Indian Economic and Social History
Review, Vol. IX (1972), pp. 3-26

K.K. Sen-Gupta, "Agrarian Disturbances in Eastern and
Central Bengal in the later 19th
Century", IESHR, Vol. VIII (1971),
pp. 192-212

Muin-ud-din Ahmad Khan, Faraidi Movement

J. Iliffe, The Maji Maji Rebellion

Part III- THE END OF EMPIRE: HOW POWER WAS HANDED OVER, AND TO
WHOM

December 2: Nationalism and Imperialism-Confrontation and
Accomodation

Required Reading:

J. Masselos, Nationalism on the Indian Subcontinent,
pp. 30-182

M.K. Gandhi, An Autobiography (Beacon paperback ed.),
pp. 204-16, 313-32, and 454-96

J. Nehru, A Bunch of Old Letters, pp. 130-54

S. Rudolph, "The New Courage: an Essay in Gandhi's
Psychology", in T. Metcalf, ed.,
Modern India Anthology, pp.240-56;

132

or L. S. Rudolph, Modernity of
Tradition, pp. 160-92

Suggested Reading:

Judith M. Brown, Gandhi's Rise to Power

Ravinder Kumar, ed., Essays on Gandhian Politics

Anil Seal, The Emergence of Indian Nationalism

D.A. Low, ed., Soundings in Modern South Asian
History

J. Gallagher, G. Johnson, and A. Seal, Locality,
Province, and
Nation

Michael Brecher, Nehru- A Political Biography

B.R. Nanda, Mahatma Gandhi

Gopal Krishna, "Development of Indian National Congress
as a Mass Organization 1918-1923", in
T. Metcalf, ed., Modern India Anthology,
pp. 257-72; or Journal of Asian Studies,
Vol XXV (1966), pp. 413-30

December 9: The Transfer of Power

Required Reading:

D.A. Low, Lion Rampant, pp. 148-217

A.P. Thornton, The Imperial Idea and Its Enemies,
chs. VI and VII (pp. 300-406)

Gann and Duignan, Burden of Empire, pp. 320-59

Suggested Reading:

R.J. Moore, The Crisis of Indian Unity 1917-1940

C.H. Philips, ed., The Partition of India

Wavell, The Viceroys Journal (1944-47)

Paul Brass, "Muslim Separatism in the United Provinces",
Economic and Political Weekly Vol. V (1970),
nos. 3, 4, 5.

Carl Rosberg, Myth of Mau Mau (Kenya)

J. Coleman, Nigeria: Background to Nationalism

Philip Mason, Year of Decision: Rhodesia and Nyasaland
in 1960

HSTEU 423   FRANCE SINCE 1814

Spring quarter 1983   Professor Pinkney

I. BOOKS

   Readings will be assigned in the books listed below and in one book on reserve
for this course in the Odegaard Undergraduate Library. The books are listed here
in the order in which they will be used in the course.

   Gordon Wright, France in Modern Times. . . . W.W. Norton & Co., 3d. edition
   1981.

   Gordon Wright, Insiders and Outliers: The Individual in History. W.H.
   Freeman & Co., 1981.

   David H. Pinkney, Napoleon III and the Rebuilding of Paris. Princeton
   University Press, 1972.

   Theodore Zeldin, France, 1848-1945: Anxiety and Hypocrisy. Oxford
   University Press, 1981.

   Roger Martin du Gard, Jean Barois, Bobbs-Merrill, 1969.

   Lawrence Wylie, Village in the Vaucluse. Harvard University Press, 1981.

All members of the course should own copies of these books. They are available in
paperback editions.

II. READING ASSIGNMENTS

   First period, 1814-1899

   Wright, France in Modern Times, pp. 3-7. 99-262.

       Students who have not taken a course on the French Revolution and
       Napoleon would benefit from reading pages 14-82.

   Wright, Insiders and Outliers, pp. 1-27.

   David H. Pinkney, The French Revolution of 1830 (Princeton, 1972), Ch. IX,
   "Purge and Replacement." On reserve OUGL.

   Wright, Insiders and Outliers, pp. 43-63.

   Pinkney, Napoleon III and the Rebuilding of Paris, pp. 3-221.

   Zeldin, France, 1848-1945, Chs. 4 and 5.

Second Period, 1899 to the present

Wright, France in Modern Times, pp. 263-490.

Zeldin, France, 1848-1945, Ch. 6.

Wright, Insiders and Outliers, pp. 65-85.

Martin du Gard, Jean Barois, pp. vii-xxiii, 2-365.

Zeldin, France, 1848-1945, Ch. 8.

Wright, Insiders and Outliers, pp. 87-109, 111-33.

Wylie, Village in the Vaucluse, pp. v-xvii, 3-383.

Zeldin, France, 1848-1945, "Conclusion," pp. 390-409.

III. EXAMINATIONS

Mid-term examination, early May

Final examination, Monday, June 7, 8:30-10:20 AM.

IV. UNDERGRADUATE PAPERS

Each undergraduate member of the course will write one paper. It may be a report on a historical monograph, a report on a novel, or a commentary on one or more paintings. The paper will be due on Friday, May 28.

1. Report on a historical monograph.

Titles of acceptable books may be found in the bibliographical chapters of Wright, France in Modern Times (Chs. 17, 26, 37). Get the instructor's approval of the book you select before you read it.

Book reports should be about five double-spaced, typed pages in length (about 1,250 words) and should include the following items in the order given here. Please number the sections of your report corresponding to these items.

1. Author, title, publisher, publication date, number of pages.

2. Identification of the author. (See, Who's Who in America, British Who's Who, Qui est qui, Directory of American Scholars, or Contemporary Authors.)

3. Description of the content of the book. (This should take up about half of the report.)

4. Major thesis or theses of the book. (Webster defines "thesis" as "a position or proposition that a person advances and proposes to defend.")

5. Principal sources used by the author. (See bibliography and footnotes. Note particularly whether he or she has used primary sources [e.g., archives, memoirs, published collections of documents] or secondary sources [i.e., books and articles].)

6. Effectiveness of presentation -- organization, literary style, maps, graphs, charts.

7. Your personal judgment of the book. What does it contribute to your knowledge and understanding? Would you recommend it to another student? (Do not slight this item. I want to know what you think the importance of the book is.)

2. Report on a novel

Any novel by a French author and set in France of the nineteenth century or the twentieth century is acceptable. The report, five to seven pages in length, should include:

1. Identification of the author.

2. Summary of the plot of the novel.

3. Statement of how the novel depicts or reflects significant social, economic, political, or cultural developments in France.

4. Your judgment of what the book contributes to your knowledge and understanding of France and the French.

The following titles are offered as suggestions of acceptable novels to read. Other titles may be found in the bibliographical chapters of Wright, France in Modern Times. Get the instructor's approval of any novel you select before you read it.

Stendhal, The Red and the Black
Honoré de Balzac, Le Père Goriot. César Birotteau. The Elector of Arcis
Gustave Flaubert, A Sentimental Education. Madame Bovary.
Victor Hugo, Les Misérables
Emile Zola, Germinal. The Human Beast.
Anatole France, Penguin Island. The Revolt of the Angels.
Roger Martin du Gard, Les Thibaults, Parts 1 & 2.
L.F. Céline, Journey to the End of the Night
Jules Romains, Verdun
Henri Barbusse, Under Fire
Georges Bernanos, The Diary of a Country Priest
Gabriel Chevalier, Clochmerle
Albert Camus, The Plague
Jean Dutourd, The Best Butter

3. Commentary on a painting (or paintings)

The commentary may be on any work -- or more than one, if you prefer -- painted after 1814 by a French artist or by a French-based artist. It should be about five pages (1,250) words) in length and should include a brief identification of the artist, some lines on his or her importance in the development of French painting, and especially an explanation of how the painting reflects the times in which it was painted.

The following paintings would be appropriate subjects. There are many others.

> Théodore Géricault, "Le Radeau de la Méduse"
> Eugène Delacroix, "Liberté sur les barricades"
> Gustave Courbet, "L'Enterrement à Ornans"
> Francois Millet, "Les Glaneuses"   "L'Angelus"
> Honoré Daumier, two or more lithographs
> Edgar Degas, "A la Bourse"
> Edouard Manet, "Au Café Concert"   "Le Chemin de Fer" "Bar aux Folies Bergère"
> Claude Monet, "Gare Saint-Lazare, Paris"
> Auguste Renoir, "Le Moulin de la Galette" "Le Déjeuner des Canotiers"
> Pablo Picasso, "Les Demoiselles d'Avignon"
> Georges Seurat, "Un Dimanche d'Eté à la Grande Jatte"
> Henri de Toulouse-Lautrec, "La Danse du Moulin Rouge"
> Vincent Van Gogh, "Café du Nuit"

V. GRADUATE STUDENT LECTURES

Every graduate member of the course must prepare and deliver a lecture to the class on a subject agreed upon by him or her and the instructor. Before the end of the second week of the quarter graduate students should arrange with the instructor for a subject and a date of presentation.

****

MAKE-UP EXAMINATIONS AND WITHDRAWALS

I. A make-up examination will be given if a student misses a regularly scheduled examination because of personal illness, serious illness or death in his/her family, unavoidable transportation breakdown, or absence from campus on a recognized university activity. If a student knows in advance that he/she must miss an examination, he/she should notify the instructor. If a student misses an examination for an unacceptable reason, he/she fails the examination.

II. On dropping a course and withdrawals, see Time Schedule, Spring Quarter 1982, pp. 4, 6. A student who never attends class and does not withdraw must be given a grade of 0.0.

Yale University
HISTORY 633: PEASANTS, WORKERS, AND
REVOLUTION IN NINETEENTH-CENTURY FRANCE

John Merriman
Fall, 1981

Date	General Topic	Reading
September 9	INTRODUCTION	
September 16	APPROACHES TO REVOLUTION	Charles Tilly, The Vendee Richard Cobb, Reactions to the French Revolution
September 23	THE REVOLUTION OF 1830	David Pinkney, The French Revolution of 1830 John Merriman, ed., 1830 in France Merriman, "Fire and Fear in Rural Society"; and "Restoration Town, Bourgeois City," in Merriman, ed., French Cities in the Nineteenth-Century.
September 30	THE BOURGEOISIE	A. Daumard, Les bourgeois de Paris
October 7	THE ARTISANS AND REVOLUTION (No Class)	William Sewell, Jr., Work and Revolution in France Bernard Moss, The Origins of the French Labor Movement
October 14	ARTISANS AND PROLATARIANIZATION	Christopher Johnson, Utopian Communism in France Johnson, "Patterns of Proletarianization," Ronald Aminzade, "The Transformation of Social Solidarities in Nineteenth-Century Toulouse," Michelle Perrot, "The Three Ages of Industrial Discipline in Nineteenth-Century France" and Merriman, "Incident at the Statue of the Virgin Mary," in Merriman, ed., Consciousness and Class Experience

October 21	1848: FEBRUARY AND JUNE	Georges Duveau, 1848, Making of a Revolution Tilly and Lynn Lees, "The People of June, 1848," in R.D. Price, ed., Revolution and Reaction Remi Gossez, "Diversité des antagonismes sociaux vers le milieu du XIXe siècle," Revue économique, 1 (1956) Karl Marx, Class Struggles in France, 1848-50 Albert Soboul, "La question paysanne en 1848," La Pensée 18-19-20 (1948)
October 28	THE REPUBLIC AND THE VILLAGE	Maurice Agulhon, La République au village Robert Bezucha, "Masks of Revolution" in R.D. Price, Revolution and Reaction William Sewell, Kr., "La classe ouvrière de Marseille sous la Second République: structure sociale et comportement politique," Mouvement social, 76 (juillet-september, 1971)
November 4	THE REPRESSION OF ORDINARY PEOPLE	John Merriman, Agony of the Republic Karl Marx, The Eighteenth Brumaire of Louis Napoleon Bonaparte
November 11	THE COUP D'ETAT	Ted W. Margadant, French Peasants in Revolt Vincent Wright, "The Coup d'etat: Repression and the Limits to Repression"
November 18	IMAGES OF THE REPUBLIC	T.J. Clark, The Absolute Bourgeois Maurice Agulhon, Marianne au combat

140

December 2   THE COMMUNE

Stewart Edwards, The Paris
Commune, 1871
J. Rougerie, "Composision d'une
population insurgee,"
Mouvement Social 48
(juillet-september, 1964)
Louis Greenberg, "The Commune
of 1871 as a Decentralized
Reaction," Journal of
Modern History, 41, 3
(September, 1969)
Eugene W. Schulkind, "The
Activity of Popular Organi-
zation during the Paris
Commune of 1871," French
Historical Studies, 1, 4
(December, 1960)
Susanna Barrows, "After the
Commune," in Consciousness
and Class Experience

December 9   SOCIAL CHANGE IN THE
              NINETEENTH CENTURY

Eugen Weber, Peasants into
Frenchmen
Charles Tilly, "Did the Cake
of Custom Break?" in
Consciousness and Class
Experience
Charles Tilly, "France," in
Tilly's The Rebellious
Century.

Professor Stanley Hoffmann

POLITICAL DOCTRINES AND SOCIETY: MODERN FRANCE

COURSE OUTLINE

FALL TERM: FROM THE FALL OF THE OLD REGIME TO THE RULE OF THE THIRD REPUBLIC

Part I - Doctrines in discord
    A. The crucible
    B. French political doctrines (1815-1875)
Part II -The Stalemate Society
    A. Two dreams that failed
    B. French social classes: structure, values, attitudes
Part III-Almost a synthesis: The Third Republic ascendant (1875-1900)
    A. The "national allegory": politics
    B. The "national allegory": society

SPRING TERM: DECLINE AND RENEWAL IN THE 20th CENTURY

Part I - The Fall
    A. The challenge
    B. From Republican mystique to the politics of defeat (1900-1940)
Part II- Turmoil
    A. The lame revolutions (1940-1945)
    B. Trouble and immobility (1946-1958)
Part III-The ordeal of renovation: The Fifth Republic
    A. Grandeur and after: politics
    B. The dilemmas of modernization: society

SPRING TERM

DECLINE AND RENEWAL IN THE 20th CENTURY

OUTLINE OF LECTURES

Introduction - The synthesis challenged (Feb. 3)

Part I - The fall (Feb. 5-Feb. 26)
    A. The challenge
      1. The intellectual revolt
      2. The political problem
    Sections: Feb. 12

    B. From Republican mystique to the politics of defeat (1900-1940)
      1. From diffidence to decadence: the decline of the Left
      2. From conservatism to crack-up: the rise of the Right
    Sections: Feb. 26

Part II - Turmoil (March 1 - March 26)
    A. The lame revolutions (1940-1945)
       1. The fiasco of the Right: Vichy and back
       2. The fiasco of the Left: from Resistance to restoration
    Sections: March 12

    B. Trouble and immobility (1946-1958)
       1. Fiddlers on fire
       2. Intellectuals between escape and Communism
    Sections: March 26

Part III- The ordeal of renovation: the Fifth Republic (April 5 - April 26)
    A. Grandeur and after: politics
       1. France vs. the world: decline or grandeur?
       2. The regime and its fate
    Sections: April 16
    B. The dilemmas of modernization: society
       1. A new society?
       2. A cultural revolution?

Conclusion - France as a political community (April 28)
    Sections: April 30

REQUIREMENTS

1. Sections will be held on alternate Fridays at 10, instead of lectures. Students who take this course to meet the requirements of the Foreign Cultures area of the Core must take sections in which a substantial part of the readings will be in French.

2. Exams and papers

    Graduate students have the choice between - either writing a term paper of 4000-6000 words on a topic chosen in consultation with the instructor, as well as taking the final exam

        or

    writing a seminar-type paper (12,000 words) without taking the final exam. Papers are due May 12.

    Undergraduates - can take this course pass-fail
        - must write a paper of 4000-6000 words due May 12,
    on a topic chosen in consultation with the instructor or the course assistants, and take the final exam. There is no hour exam. The final exam is on May 19.

    Students interested in writing a paper on the period 1940-1944 should read the two volumes of "Fall of France: Causes" and "Fall of France: Results" published by the Center for European Studies for its Monographs on Europe series. Available at the Center for European Studies.

3. Books
    Books should be read in French by students who take this course to meet the requirements of the Core Curriculum; they can be read in French by those who read French without too much difficulty. The French title is given in parenthesis.

Books recommended for purchase

Alfred Cobban, A History of Modern France, vol 3, Pelican paperback
Stanley Hoffmann, Decline or Renewal? Viking
A. de Tocqueville, The Old Regime and the French Revolution, Anchor paperback,
   (L'ancien Régime et la Révolution, French paperback)
René Rémond, The Right Wing in France, U. of Penn. Press (La droite en France, Aubier)
Suzanne Berger, The French Political System, Random House paperback
de Gaulle, War Memoirs, Simon and Schuster (Mémoires de Guerre,Plon) and
de Gaulle, Memoirs of Hope, Simon and Schuster (Mémoires d'Espoir, Plon)
Theodore Zeldin, Anxiety and Hypocrisy (Oxford Press paperback)
William Andrews and Stanley Hoffmann (eds.) The Impact of the Fifth Republic on France
   (SUNY paperback)

Required readings

Part I

A. (1) Soltau, French Political Thought in the 19th Century (1959 ed.) Ch. XI
         (3-5), XII, XIII
    (2) Rémond, Ch. VI-VII
    (3) Charles Péguy, Basic Verities (bilingual), pp. 54-119, 150-153
         and Men and Saints (bilingual), pp. 35-39, 53-77, 86-117, 143-159
    (4) Roger Martin du Gard, Jean Barois (in English or in French)
             or
         for students who read French: Maurice Barrès, Les Déracinés
    (5) Georges Sorel, Reflections on Violence (Réflexions sur la Violence)
    (6) J.S. McClelland (ed.), The French Right, pp. 143-304
             or
         Charles Maurras, Oeuvres Capitales, III, V

B. (1) Cobban, Vol. 3, II and III, 1-2
    (2) Thomson, Democracy in France, Ch. V
    (3) Theodore Zeldin, Anxiety and Hypocrisy, Ch. 4, 6-9
    (4) Paul Valéry, Reflections on the World Today, pp. 28-112, 131-156
             Students who read French should read instead:
         Alain, Propos de Politique
    (5) Jean Jaurès, Studies in Socialism, I-IV, X-XIII, XVI
             or
         for students who read French, L'Armée Nouvelle, Ch. X
    (6) Léon Blum, For All Mankind (A l'échelle humaine)
    (7) Rémond, Ch. VIII
    (8) Ernst Nolte, Three Faces of Fascism (Holt, Rinehart paperback), part two
    (9) Robert Soucy, "The Nature of Fascism in France," Journal of Contemporary
             History , Vol. I, no. 1, 1966
   (10) A choice of either Marcel Aymé, The Miraculous Barber (Travelingue)
             or
         Jules Romains, Men of Good Will (Les hommes de bonne volonté):
             either Vol. 11, book 21, Mountain Days
                                     (Jours dans la montagne)
             or   Vol. 12, book 23, The Gathering of the Gangs
                                     (Naissance de la bande)
             or   Vol. 14, book 27, The Seventh of October
                                     (Le sept octobre)
             or

for students who read French, Drieu la Rochelle, Gilles
(11) Marc Bloch, Strange Defeat (L'étrange défaite)
(12) Charles de Gaulle, The Call to Honor (L'Appel), Chs. 1-3

The sections of Feb. 12 will deal with A (3), (4), (5), (6).
The sections of Feb. 26 will deal with B (3), (6).

Part II

A.   (1) Cobban, Vol. 3, III (3-4)
      (2) Robert Paxton, Vichy France, Prologue, Ch. II, III, V
      (3) S. Hoffmann, Decline or Renewal? Ch. 1-3
      (4) Jean Dutourd, The Best Butter (Au bon beurre)
      (5) de Gaulle, Unity (L'Unité), Chs. 5, 8 and
               Salvation (Le Salut), Chs. 3, 5-6

B.   (1) Cobban, Vol. 3, III (5-7)
      (2) Thomson, Ch. VII
      (3) Philip Williams, Crisis and Compromise (Anchor paperback), Chs. 5-12, 27-31
      (4) Rémond, Ch. IX
      (5) Roy Pierce, Contemporary French Political Thought (Oxford paperback),
               Chs. 1-4
      (6) H. Stuart Hughes, The Obstructed Path, Ch. 4-6
      (7) Two of the following authors:

               Georges Bernanos, Tradition of Freedom (La France contre les robots)
               Albert Camus, either The Rebel (L'Homme révolté)
                       or State of Siege in Caligula and Other Plays
                       (Vintage Paperback) (L'Etat de Siège)
                       or Rebellion, Resistance and Death
                       or, for students who read French, Actuelles II
               Andre Malraux, The Conquerors (Les Conquérants)
                       or Man's Fate (La Condition humaine)
             Jean-Paul Sartre, What is Literature (Qu'est-ce que la littérature,
                       in Situations II)
                    .or The Condemned of Altona (Les Séquestrés d'Altona)
             Simone Weil, The Need for Roots (L'enracinement)
    (8) Raymond Aron, The Opium of the Intellectuals (L'Opium des intellectuels)
               part I

The sections of March 12 will deal with Part I B (11), (12) and Part II A (3) and (5).
The sections of March 16 will deal with Part II B (3), (7) and (8).

Part III

A.   (1) Cobban, Vol. 3, III (8)
      (2) S. Hoffmann and J.B. Duroselle, in In Search of France
      (3) George Kelly, Lost Soldiers, Parts three to six
          or
          Tony Smith, The French Stake in Algeria, 1945-62, Ch. 5-8
      (4) de Gaulle, Memoirs of Hope: Renewal (Le Renouveau), chs. on Institutions,
               Overseas, Algeria, Europe, and Head of State; and Endeavor (L'Effort),
               Ch. 1-2
      (5) Philip Williams and Martin Harrison, Politics and Society in de Gaulle's
               Republic, Part I
               or

Jacques Chapsal, La vie politique sous la Ve République, Ch. I-III

(6) Suzanne Berger, The French Political System, 1-3,5

or

Jacques Chapsal, La vie politique sous la Ve République, Ch. IV (1-2), V,
    VI (1,3), VIII, X-XI, XII (3), XIII-XV

(7) S. Hoffmann, Decline or Renewal? ch. 4-6, 8, 10

(8) Annie Kriegel, The French Communists (Les Communistes)

(9) Andrews and Hoffmann (eds.), The Impact of the Fifth Republic on France, 1-4,
    6, 14

The sections of April 16 will deal with A (2), (5),(6), (7), and (9).

B. (1) Wylie, Kindleberger and Goguel in In Search of France

(2) A choice of either Laurence Wylie, Village in the Vaucluse
        (Harper paperback), Ch. 1-10, 17

    or

    Edgar Morin, The Red and the White (Commune en France)

(3) Andrews and Hoffmann (eds.), The Impact of the Fifth Republic on France, 7-9, 11-13

(4) Robert Gilpin, France in the Age of the Scientific State, Ch. 4, 9-11

(5) Ezra Suleiman, Elites in French Society, 1-3, 8-9

(6) Michel Crozier, The Bureaucratic Phenomenon, Ch. XI

The sections of April 30 will deal with B (1), (3), (5).

READING PERIOD: A. de Tocqueville, The Old Regime and the French Revolution
                Malraux, Antimemoirs, pp. 1-9, 71-174, 381-end (Antimémoires, pp. 9-18,
                    109-259, 475-fin)
                S. Hoffmann, Decline or Renewal?, Ch. 13-14, (Sur la France, 2-3), and
                    Ch. 16 of Andrews and Hoffmann (eds.), The Impact of the Fifth
                    Republic on France

There will be a meeting of sections during Reading Period to discuss the reading period
    assignments.

ORGANIZATION OF THE COURSE

The first week of the course will be devoted to a rapid survey
of the history of France, the second week to study of the geography
and peoples of France. Each of the succeeding weeks will be devoted
to a problem of contemporary French society, economy, or government.
Lectures will not duplicate reading assignments; examination will
draw on both. Regular attencance is necesssary.

Ordinarily, the course will meet on Mondays, Tuesdays, and Wednesdays
for lectures and on Thursdays and Fridays for discussions of the
subjects raised in lectures and readings of the week. On Mondays
through Wednesdays and occasionally on other days, the course will
meet jointly with FRENCH 378, and it will be taught by both
Professors Pinkney and Nostrand, Department of Romance Languages.
FRENCH 378 discussion sessions will be conducted in French.

READINGS

Readings will be assigned in:

> J. Hampden Jackson, ed., A Short History of France from Early
> Times to 1972 (Cambridge University Press, 2nd ed., 1974)

> Alfred Cobban, A History of France, vol. 3, France of the Republics
> (Penguin Books, 1965)

> Roy Pierce, French Politics and Political Institutions (Harper & Row,
> 2nd ed., 1973)

All members of HSTEU 378 and FRENCH 378 should own copies of these
books. They are available at the University Book Store.

Additional readings will be assigned in books and articles on reserve
in Odegaard Undergraduate Library.

French originals or translations of books listed in this syllabus
are starred, and are on reserve, along with other sources in French,
catalogued in the Reserve Area under French 378.

Students should keep notes on readings as well as on lectures and
should bring questions to the discussion meetings.

PAPERS AND EXAMINATIONS

Each student in the course will be required to write two papers
of five (or more) pages each: exercises in relating and integrating
major topics that will have been presented separately in lectures
and readings.

There will be one mid-term examination - on February 13 - and a two-
hour final examination.

REFERENCE BOOKS. BOOKS AND JOURNALS FOR OPTIONAL READING

History

> Alfred Cobban, A History of Modern France (Baltimore, 1963),
> 3 vols. (Covers 1715-1963).
>
> *Georges Duby and Robert Mandrou, Histoire de la civilisation
> francaise (Nouvelle ed., Paris, 1968), 2 vols. English translation:
> A History of French Civilization from the Year 1000 to the Present
> (N.Y., 1964).
>
> Paul Gagnon, France since 1789 (N.Y., 1972)
>
> Ernest J. Knapton, France: An Interpretive History (N.Y., 1971)
>
> Eugen Weber, Peasants into Frenchmen: The Modernization of Rural
> France, 1870-1914 (Stanford University Press, 1976)
>
> Gordon Wright, France in Modern Times, from the Enlightenment to
> the Present (2nd ed., Chicago, 1974)

Contemporary Problems

> Sanche de Gramont, The French: Portrait of a People (N.Y., 1969)
>
> Edward Tannenbaum, The New France (Chicago, 1961)
>
> Crane Brinton, The Americans and the French (Cambridge, 1968)

Current Affairs

> L'Express (Paris) - A weekly news magazine (centrist point of view)
>
> Le Nouvel Observateur (Paris) - A weekly news magazine (socialist
> point of view)

The numbers of these magazines most recently received by the
library are on the display shelves of the Periodicals Department,
2nd floor, Suzzallo Library. Delivery of both is erratic.

In the newspaper room (basement, Northwest corner of Suzzallo),
are Le Monde, received by air mail, and the more conservative
Le Figaro, received by surface mail.

READING ASSIGNMENTS

Reading is assigned in weekly segments corresponding with the
weekly topics. It should be completed each week before the discussion
meetings on Thursdays and Fridays.

---

* The * indicates a French version available on reserve under
FRENCH 378.

1. **History: The Living Past of France**   Week of January 5
   Jackson, A Short History of France, pp. 1-158

2. **Georgraphy, Peoples, and Politics**   Week of January 12
   Cobban, A History of Modern France,
   vol. III, pp. 8-157

   * Valerie Giscard d'Estaing, French Democracy or Towards a New
   Democracy or Democratie en France, Ch. I

        (Note: These three titles are all different editions
        of the same book)

3. **Centralization of Political and Economic Power**   Week of January 19
   Cobban, A History of Modern France, III, pp. 199-248

   Pierce, French Politics and Political Institutions

        Ch. I   "The French Political Tradition"
        Ch. II "From the Third Republic to the Fifth Republic"
        Ch. III "Presidential Government"
        Ch. IV "The Government and Parliament," pp. 79-87, 99-103,
                107-118 only

   *Michel Crozier, The Stalled Society or La Société bloquée
        Ch. 5 "The French Bureaucratic Style"

4. **Class Structure and the Changing Roles of Classes**   Week of Jan. 26

   *Ardagh, The New France
        Pp. 337-348 "A Slow Dismantling of the Barricades of Class"
        Pp. 375-383 "Towards an Americanized Affluence"
        Pp. 384-392 "Leisure"

   OR Ardagh, The New French Revolution, pp. 213-239, 258-265, 265-271

   Gordon Wright, Rural Revolution in France
        Ch. 8 "Rural Revolution: The Rise of a New Generation"
        (See also intersting but not required reading, pp. 185-208,
         "Six Village Sketches")

   *Hoffmann et al., In Search of France, pp. 159-234
        (Wylie on "Social Change at the Grass Roots."

5. **The Educational System**   Week of February 2

   W.D. Halls, Education, Culture and Politics in Modern France
        Pp. 3-19   "Historical Background"
        Pp. 21-34   "Education, National Sentiment and Culture"
        Pp. 221-231 "The Grandes Ecoles"

   Ezra Suleiman, Elites in French Society, pp. 13-74, 80-92

   *Crozier, Stalled Society or Société bloquée, Ch. 6 "The
   Collapse of the University"

First term paper due Friday, February 6. Five or more pages
on the relations or interactions between any two of the four
topics treated thus far in the course, numbers 2 through 5 on this
syllabus. You may confine your discussion to particular parts of
the topics that you select.

6. The Status of Women. The Family. Population Policy   Week of Feb. 9

    **Philippe Aries, "La Famille: A Report from France,"
      in: Encounter, XIX (August 1975), pp. 7-12

    *John Ardagh, The New France
      Pp. 348-366, "Families and Women: Feminity not Feminism"

OR John Ardagh, The New French Revolution, Pp. 239-253

    **C.B. Silver, "Salon, Foyer, Bureau: Women in the Professions
      in France," in: American Journal of Sociology, LXXVIII,
      (January 1973), pp. 836-851

MID-TERM EXAMINATION, FRIDAY, FEBRUARY L#

7. The Revolutionary Tradition   Week of February 17
                          (no class Monday, Feb. 16)

    Pierce, French Politics and Political Institutions

      Ch. V   "Political Conflicts and Social Crisis"
      Ch. VI "The Political Parties" to p. 177 only

    *Crozier, Stalled Society or Societe bloquee

      Ch. 7 "The Meaning of the Crisis of May 1968"

    W.D. Halls, Education, Culture and Politics in Modern
    France, Pp. 173-201

8. National Security, Nationalism, Colonies   Week of February 23

    *Hoffmann, In Search of France, pp. 305-318, 337-358
      (J.B. Duroselle on "Changes in French Foreign Policy since
      1945")

    William Pfaff, "U.S.-European Relations: The French Exception,"
      in: European Community, July-Aug. 1977, pp. 27-30

    Hannah Arendt, The Origins of Totalitarianism, pp. 45-50, 89-120

    Raymond Betts, Tricoleur: The French Overseas Empire

      Ch. 1   "Planting the Flag"
      Ch. 6   "From the Other Side"
      Ch. 7   "The Retreat from Empire"

** Photocopy on reserve, OUGL

9. <u>Industrialization</u>   Week of March 2

    **Rondo E. Cameron, "Economic Growth and Stagnation
    in France, 1815-1914," in: <u>Journal of Modern History</u>,
    XXX (March 1958), 1-13

    *Hoffmann, <u>In Search of France</u>, pp. 118-121, 147-158
    (Charles Kindleberger on "The Post-War Resurgence of the
    French Economy")

    *Ardagh, <u>The New France</u>, pp. 28-45 "The Economy: Precarious
    Miracle"

10. <u>Urbanization and the Rural Exodus: Conclusions</u>   Week of March 9

    *Ardagh, <u>The New France</u>, pp. 262-300, "Paris: The Beloved
    Monster"

<u>OR</u> Ardagh, <u>The New French Revolution</u>, pp. 175-202

    Pierce, <u>French Politics and Political Institutions</u>

      Ch. 10 "Problems of French Politics"

    Giscard d'Estaing, <u>French Democracy</u> or <u>Towards a New Democracy</u>
    or <u>Democratie en France</u>

      Conclusion, "An Ambition for France"

SECOND TERM PAPER DUE MONDAY, MARCH 9.

The directions are the same as those for the first paper except
that this time one of the two topics is to be selected from among
numbers 3, 4, 5, and 6 listed on this syllabus, the other from
the last four.

FINAL EXAMINATION, WEDNESDAY, MARCH 18, 8:30 - 10:20 a.m.

POLICY ON MAKE-UP EXAMS AND WITHDRAWALS

1. A make-up examination will be given if a student misses the
regularly scheduled examination because of personal illness, serious
illness or death in his/her family, unavoidable transportation breakdown, or absence from campus on a recognized university activity.
If a student knows in advance that he/she must miss an examination,
he/she should notify the instructor. If a student misses an
examination for an unacceptable reason, he/she fails the
examination.

2. On dropping a course and withdrawals, see <u>Time Schedule</u>, Winter
quarter 1981, pp. 4, 6. A student who never attends class and does
not withdraw must be given a grade of 0.0.

History 409 (History of Central Europe, 1648-1871)   Mr. Hamerow

Textbooks: K. S. Pinson, Modern Germany
           H. Holborn, A History of Modern Germany, 2 vols.

  I. The Origins of Modern Germany
     Textbook: Holborn, vol. I, chap. 1.
     Readings:
     G. Barraclough, The Origins of Modern Germany, chap. 10.
     L. von Ranke, History of the Latin and Teutonic Nations (London, 1909),
         pp. 1-19, 96-108.
     C. V. Wedgwood, The Thirty Years' War, chap. 12.

 II. The Age of Absolutism in Central Europe
     Textbook: Holborn, vol. II, chap. 3
     Readings:
     F. Schevill, The Great Elector, chap. 17.
     F. L. Carsten, Princes and Parliaments in Germany, chap. 6.
     S. Pufendorf, An Introduction to the History of the Principal Kingdoms
         and States of Europe, chap. 8.

III. The Rise of the German Dualism
     Textbook: Holborn, vol. II, chap. 8.
     Readings:
     W. L. Dorn, Competition for Empire, pp. 318-342.
     G. Ritter, Frederick the Great, Chap. 9.
     Frederick the Great, Posthumous Works, Vol. I (The History of My Own
         Times), chap. 2.

 IV. The Era of Enlightened Despotism
     Textbook: Holborn, vol. II, chap. 10.
     Readings:
     W. H. Bruford, Germany in the Eighteenth Century, Part IV, chap. 2.
     H. Rosenberg, Bureaucracy, Aristocracy, and Autocracy, chap. 5.
     G. E. Lessing, Education of the Human Race.

  V. The Years of French Hegemony
     Textbook: Pinson, pp. 23-33.
     Readings:
     G. P. Gooch, Germany and the French Revolution, chap. 22.
     F. Meinecke, Cosmopolitanism and the National State, bk. I, chap. 8.
     F. M. Anderson, Constitutions and Other Select Documents, pp. 206-209,
         261-267, 339-341, 397-416.

 VI. Reform and Liberation
     Textbook: Pinson, pp. 33-49.
     Readings:
     R. Aris, History of Political Thought in Germany, chap. 13.
     E. N. Anderson, Nationalism and the Cultural Crisis in Prussia, chap. 7.
     J. G. Fichte, Addresses to the German Nation, chap. 14.

VII. The Reconstruction of Central Europe
Textbook: Pinson, pp. 50-63.
Readings:
E. L. Woodward, Three Studies in European Conservatism, pp. 15-43.
H. Nicolson, The Congress of Vienna, chaps. 15-16.
E. Hertslet, The Map of Europe by Treaty, vol. I, pp. 200-207, 221-248.

VIII. The Period of the Restoration
Textbook: Pinson, pp. 63-74.
Readings:
H. von Treitschke, History of Germany in the Nineteenth Century,
   vol. III, pp. 206-233.
W. O. Henderson, The Zollverein, chap. 3.
J. C. Legge, Rhyme and Revolution in Germany, pp. 124-153.

IX. The Emergence of a New Social Order
Textbook: Pinson, pp. 75-79.
Readings:
T. S. Hamerow, Restoration, Revolution, Reaction, chaps. 2-3.
E. Kohn-Bramstedt, Aristocracy and the Middle-Classes in Germany,
   chap. 4.
F. List, The National System of Political Economy (1904 ed.), chaps. 34
   and 36.

X. The Revolution of 1848
Textbook: Pinson, pp. 80-108.
Readings:
V. Valentin, 1848: Chapters of German History, chap. 8.
W. E. Mosse, The European Powers and the German Question, chap. 1.
K. Marx, Revolution and Counter Revolution, chaps. 5-8.

XI. The Triumph of Reaction
Textbook: Pinson, pp. 109-121
Readings:
A. W. Ward, Germany, 1815-1890, vol. I, chap. 7.
G. A. Craig, The Politics of the Prussian Army, pp. 120-148.
E. Hertslet, The Map of Europe by Treaty, vol. II, pp. 1106-1108,
   1129-1138, 1143-1145, 1148-1155.

XII. The New Era and the Constitutional Conflict
Textbook: Pinson, pp. 121-131.
Readings:
O. Pflanze, Bismarck and the Development of Germany, chap. 6.
E. Eyck, Bismarck and the German Empire, pp. 58-88.
O. von Bismarck, The Man and the Statesman, vol. I, chap. 11.

XIII. The Struggle for Supremacy in Central Europe
Textbook: Pinson, pp. 132-141.
Readings:
H. Friedjung, The Struggle for Supremacy in Germany, chap. 5.
H. von Sybel, The Founding of the German Empire, vol. V, pp. 479-506.
Wilhelm I, The Correspondence of William I and Bismarck, vol. I,
   pp. 50-85.

XIV. The Achievement of National Unification
Textbook: Pinson, pp. 141-155.
Readings:
W. H. Dawson, The German Empire, vol. I, chap. 7.
J. Redlich, Emperor Francis Joseph of Austria, chap. 11.
E. Ollivier, The Franco-Prussian War and Its Hidden Causes, pp. 468-494.

History 410   History of Central Europe, 1871 to the Present   Mr. Hamerow

TEXTBOOK: K. S. Pinson, Modern Germany

I. The Bismarckian Era: Domestic Affairs

   Textbook: pp. 156-218

   Readings:

      E. Eyck, Bismarck and the German Empire, pp. 202-243
      F. Stern, Gold and Iron, chap. 9
      M. Busch, Bismarck: Some Secret Pages of His History, vol. III, chap. 3

II. The Bismarckian Era: Foreign Policy

   Textbook: pp. 291-312

   Readings:

      G. A. Craig, Germany, 1866-1945, chap. 4
      W. L. Langer, European Alliances and Alignments, chap. 13
      W. T. S., Dugdale, German Diplomatic Documents, vol. I, chaps. 4-7

III. The Age of Wilhelm II

   Textbook: pp. 274-291

   Readings:

      E. L. Woodward, Great Britain and the German Navy, chap. 1
      G. P. Gooch, Before the War, vol. II, pp. 203-238
      B. von Bulow, Memoirs, vol. II, chaps. 6 and 23

IV. German Thought and Society

   Textbook: pp. 219-273

   Readings:

      G. Stolper, German Economy, pp. 36-77
      H. S. Hughes, Consciousness and Society, pp. 183-200, 229-248
      E. Bernstein, Evolutionary Socialism, chap. 1

V. The Dual Monarchy in Decline

   Readings:

      A. J. May, The Hapsburg Monarchy, chaps. 14-15
      H. C. Meyer, Mitteleuropa in German Thought and Action, chap. 3
      F. F. von Beust, Memoirs, vol. II, chaps. 1, 24-30

VI. Central Europe and the First World War

   Textbook: pp. 313-349

   Readings:

      F. Fischer, Germany's Aims in the First World War, chap. 6
      A. Rosenberg, The Birth of the German Republic, chap. 5
      R. H. Lutz, Fall of the German Empire, vol. I, chap. 16

VII. The Establishment of a New Order

Textbook: pp. 350-410

Readings:

H. Nicolson, Peacemaking 1919, chap. 8
K. Epstein, Matthias Erzberger, chaps. 13-14
P. Scheidemann, The Making of a New Germany, chaps. 7-8

VIII. The Republican Experiment

Textbook: pp. 411-466

Readings:

S. W. Halperin, Germany Tried Democracy, chaps. 22-24
A. Wolfers, Britain and France between the Wars, chaps. 5, 15-16
G. Stresemann, Diaries, Letters and Papers, vol. II, pp. 404-438

IX. The Decline of Weimar Germany

Textbook: pp. 467-478

Readings:

K. D. Bracher, The German Dictatorship, pp. 168-198
J. W. Wheeler-Bennett, The Nemesis of Power, pp. 210-244
F. von Papen, Memoirs, chaps. 12-13

X. The Succession States of Central Europe

Readings:

C. A. Gulick, Austria from Habsburg to Hitler, vol. II, pp. 1266-1308
H. Seton-Watson, Eastern Europe between the Wars, pp. 171-198 & 268-288
K. Schuschnigg, My Austria, chaps. 5-7

XI. The Political System of the Third Reich

Textbook: pp. 479-521

Readings:

F. Neumann, Behemoth, part III, chap. 1
E. Wiskemann, The Rome-Berlin Axis, chaps. 3-5
A. Hitler, Mein Kampf, vol. I, chap. II

XII. Central Europe and the Second World War

Textbook: pp. 521-531

Readings:

H. Holborn, The Political Collapse of Europe, chap. 6
H. R. Trevor-Roper, The Last Days of Hitler, chap. 1
J. Goebbels, Diaries, pp. 33-62

XIII. The Reconstruction of Germany

Textbook: pp. 532-562

Readings:

    F. Meinecke, The German Catastrophe, chaps. 13-15
    E. Davidson, The Death and Life of Germany, chaps. 9-10
    L. D. Clay, Decision in Germany, chaps. 19-20

XIV.   Central Europe Today

Textbook: pp. 563-600

Readings:

    H. W. Gatzke, Germany and the United States, chap. 8
    R. Dahrendorf, Society and Democracy in Germany, chaps. 26-27
    W. Brandt, A Peace Policy for Europe, chaps. 13-14

PRINCETON UNIVERSITY

Department of History

HISTORY 366

Politics and Society in Germany Since 1848

Fall Term 1979-80   Professor Abraham

All books have been placed on reserve and, to the extent possible,
are available in paperback at the U-Store. Note that not all books
are required. Lecture topics and readings are tentative and subject
to revision.

Berghahn, V., Germany and the Approach of War
Bracher, K. D.,The German Dictatorship
Dahrendorf, R.,Society and Democracy in Germany
Engels, F.,The Role of Force in History
Halperin, S. W.,Germany Tried Democracy
Hamerow, T.,Restoration, Revolution, Reaction
Henderson, W. O.,The Rise of German Industrial Power
Krieger, L.,The German Idea of Freedom
Lichtheim, G.,Marxism: Historical and Critical Study
Lipset, S. M.,Political Man
Moore, B,Social Origins of Dictatorship and Democracy
Nicholls, A. J.,Weimar Germany and the Rise of Hitler
Schoenbaum, D.,Hitler's Social Revolution
Sheehan, J. ed.,Imperial Germany
Steele, J.,Inside East Germany

The following books are on reserve only and may be used either
as substitutes, where appropriate, or in developing paper topics.

Anchor, R., Germany Confronts Modernization
Craig, G., Politics of the Prussian Army
Joll, J., The Second International
Kent, G., Bismarck and His Times
Massing, P., Rehearsal for Destruction
Neumann, F., Behemoth: Structure and Practice of National Socialism
Nicholls, A. J., ed., German Democracy and the Triumph of Hitler
Pascal, R., From Naturalism to Expressionism
Pflanze, O., Bismarck and the Development of Germany
Poulantzas, N., Fascism and Dictatorship
Pulzer, P. G. J., Rise of Political Anti-Semitism
Rosenberg, A., Imperial Germany and the Birth of the German Republic
Schorske, C., German Social Democracy

*   *   *

Week	Lecture Topics	Readings
1A	Introd: The "German Question"	Dahrendorf, Chs. 1-4 Krieger, Intro. & ch. 1
B	Germany, the French Revolution and Napoleonic Reforms	Lichtheim, Pt. III, ch. 1 Krieger, Chs. 4, 5

157

Week	Lecture Topics	Readings
2A	Revolutions of 1848	Hamerow, pp. 1-195
B	Restoration	Hamerow, pp. 199-262
3A	Unification: Political + Diplomatic	catch up
B	Bismarck	Engels, pp. 11-108
4A	Marriage of Rye and Iron	Moore, pp. 433-452, 460-467 Sheehan, ed. pp. 15-60
B	Industrialization	Henderson, pp. 31-242
5A	German Liberalism: Nature and Limits	Krieger, Chs. C, C, Epil. Sheehan, ed. pp. 61-151
B	Neo-Conservativism and Anti-Semitism	Pulzer or Massing
6A	General Review and Discussion	catch up
B	MID-TERM EXAM	
7A	Rise of the Socialist Movement	Lichtheim, III: 3-8
B	Marxism, Labor and Negative Integration	Lichtheim, Pts. IV & V or Schorske (entire)
8A	Imperialism	Sheehan, pp. 153-268
B	Domestic Politics and WWI	Berghahn, pp. 1-214
9A	1918-1919: Another Revolutionary Failure	Rosenberg, pp. 73-276
B	Weimar Republic: What Was It	Nicholls, pp. 1-177 or Halperin, pp. 79-201, 280-321, 347-460
10A	Rise of Nazism and Collapse of the Republic	Bracher, pp. 142-214 Dahrendorf, Ch. 24 Lipset, pp. 127-154
B	The Nazis in Power	Bracher, pp. 214-370, 400-468 or Neumann or Schoenbaum
11A	Revolution, Reconstruction or Another Restoration	Dahrendorf, Ch. 25
B	The Cold War and the Division of Germany	Catch up and move ahead
12A	East Germany or the German Democratic Republic	Steele, entire Dahrendorf, Ch. 26
B	West Germany or Germany	Dahrendorf, Ch. 5-23, 27

Fall Term 1979

COURSE REQUIREMENTS

I.   All students will write an in-class mid-term examination.
     (Approximately 20% of grade).

II. Participation in precepts is essential; you get out only when
     you put in. (Approximately 25% of grade).

III. There will be two options for a final exercise, A or B.

     A. A 12-15 page paper which develops in greater detail one
         of the topics discussed in the course. This may take the
         form of a review essay or a meaningful research paper.
         Topics and books should be selected in consultation with
         your preceptor. The paper will be due no later than
         December 18.

                              or

     B. A take-home type exam in which synthetic and critical
         abilities along with knowledge of the readings and
         lectures will be tested. Overall length will be approxi-
         mately the same as in choice A. Format and due date to
         be specified later.

History 5-744   University of Minnesota   Mary Jo Maynes
Fall, 1983   523 Social Sciences
Course Syllabus

Topics in Modern German History: Society and Politics in Imperial Germany, 1871-1918

The purpose of this proseminar is to introduce students to some of the central questions concerning the history of Germany during the Second Empire. We will focus
on subjects of current interest among historians of Germany, particularly among
social historians. The following reading list is not meant to be exhaustive, but
does include major works which will introduce you to the issues at hand. I have
attempted to include as many works in English as possible to make the topics accesi-
ble to non-readers of German.

Weekly Topics and Readings

September 29 - Introduction to the Course

October 6 - The History and Historiography of the Second Empire

CORE READINGS: The appropriate chapters of one of the following general works:
H. Böhme, Social and Economic History of Germany (London, 1978).
G.A.Craig, Germany, 1866-1945(Oxford, 1980).
H.Holborn, A History of Modern Germany, Vol. III (New York, 1965).
E. Sagarra, A Social History of Germany
H.-U. Wehler, Das deutsche Kaiserreich (Göttingen, 1973).

SUPPLEMENTARY READINGS:
R.Braun, "Historische Demographie in Rahmen einer integrierten Geschichtsbeschreib-
ung," G&G, 3(1977), 5-25.
G.Eley, "Memories of Underdevelopment:Social History in Germany," SH, 2(1977), 785-
791.
R.J.Evans, "Feminism and Female Emancipation in Germany, 1870-1945: Sources, Problems
and Methods of Research," CEH 9(1976), 323-351.
K.Hausen, "Familie als Gegenstand historischer Sozialwissenschaft,"G&G, 1(1975),
171-209.
G.Iggers, The German Conception of History (Middletown, Conn., 1968).
     New Directions in European Historiography (Middletown, Conn., 1975),
especially Chapters I, "The Crisis of the Conventional Conception of Scientific
History," and IV, "Marxism and Modern Social History."
J.A.Moses, The Politics of Illusion (London, 1975).
V.Lidtke, "The Formation of the Working Classes in Germany," CEH, 13(1980), 393-400.
W.Mommsen, "The Debate on German War Aims," JCH, 3(1966)
     "Gegenwärtige Tendenzen der Geschichtsschreibung der Bundesrepublik,"
G&G, 7(1981), 149-188..
J.J.Sheehan, "Germany, 1890-1918: A Survey of Recent Research," CEH 1(1967), 345-372.
R.H.Tilly, "Soll und Haben: Recent German Economic History and the Problems of Econ-
omic Development," JEH, 29(1969), 300-319.
Plus the following special issues:
"Historische Forschung in der DDR, 1960-1970," ZfG Sonderbund 18(1970)
"Kontroversien über Historiographie," G&G 7(1981)
"Wege der neuen Sozial-und Wirtshaftsgeschichte," G&G, 6(1980)

October 13 - Economic Development: Its Pace and Impact

CORE READINGS:
K.Borchardt,"The Industrial Revolution in Germany, 1700-1914," in C.M.Cipolla, ed.,
The Fontana Economic History of Europe, vol. 4 (London, 1973), 76-161.
H.Rosenberg, "Political and Social Consequences of the Great Depression, 1873-
1896," EHR(1943), 58-73.

SUPPLEMENTARY READINGS:
P.Aycoberry, Cologne entre Napoleon et Bismarck (Paris, 1981).
W.Abel, Geschichte der deutschen Landwirtschaft (Stuttgart, 1962).
K.D.Barkin, The Controversy over German Industrialization, 1890-1902 (Chicago, 1970).
H.Böhme, "Bankenkonzentration und Schwerindustrie, 1873-1896," in H.-U. Wehler, ed.,
Sozialgeschichte Heute.
K.Borchardt, The Industrial Revolution in Germany (London, 1972).
J.H.Clapham, The Economic Development of France and Germany, 1871-1913 (Cambridge,
1961).
D.Crew, Town in the Ruhr: A Social History of Bochum, 1860-1914 (New York, 1979).
A.V.Desaï, Real Wages in Germany, 1871-1913 (Oxford, 1968).
G.D. Feldman, "The Collapse of the Steel Works Association, 1912-1929: A Case Study
of the Operation of German 'Collectivist Capitalism'" in H.-U. Wehler, ed., Sozial-
geschichte Heute.
W.Fischer, "Government Activity and Industrialization in Germany, 1815-1870," in
W.W.Rostow, ed., The Economics of Take-off and Sustained Growth (New York, 1963).
G.Franz, ed., Deutsche Agrargeschichte (Frankfurt, 1967-70).
W.O. Henderson, The Rise of German Industrial Power, 1834-1914 (London, 1975).
        The Zollverein (New York, 1939).
V. Hentschel, Wirtschaft und Wirtschaftspolitik in wilhelminischen Deutschland
(Stuttgart, 1978).
W.G.Hoffmann, Das Wachstum der deutsche Wirtschafts seit der Mitte des 19. Jahr-
hunderts (Berlin, 1965).
W.Köllmann, Bevölkerung in der Industriellen Revolution (Göttingen, 1974).
        "The Process of Urbanization in Germany at the Height of Industrializa-
tion,"JCH, 4(1969), 59-76.
H.Kaeble and H. Volkmann, "Konjunktur und Streik in Deutschland während des Uber-
gangs zum organisierten Kapitalismus," ZWSg, 92(   ), 513-544.
E.Maschke, "Outline of the History of German Cartels from 1873 to 1914," in E.
Crouzet, ed., Essays in European Economic History (London, 1969)
H.H.Liang, "Lower-class Immigrants in Wilhelmine Berlin," CEH, 3(1970), 94-111.
P.Lundgreen, "Educational Expansion and Economic Growth in Nineteenth-Century
Germany: A Quantitative Study," in L. Stone, ed., Schooling and Society (Baltimore,
1976).
        Bildung und Wirtschaftswachstum (Berlin, 1973).
H.Mottek, "Die Gründerkrise," Jahrbuch für Wirtschaftsgeschichte, 1(1966), 51-128.
        et al, Studien zur Geschichte der industriellen Revolution in Deutschland
(Berlin, 1960).
H.Rosenberg, Grosse Depression und Bismarckzeit (Berlin, 1967).
R.Spree, Wachstumstrends und Konjunkturzyklen der deutschenWirtschaft von 1820
bis 1913 (Göttingen, 1978).
A.Sutcliffe, Towards the Planned City: Germany, Britain, France and the United States,
1780-1914 (New York, 1981).

History 5-744, page 3.

R.Tilly, _Financial Institutions and Industrialization in the Rhineland, 1850-1870_
(Madison, Wi., 1966).
  "German Banks and German Industry," JEH (1976), 180-188.
F.Tipton, Jr., _Regional Variation in the Economic Development of Germany during the_
Nineteenth Century (Middletown, Conn., 1976).
M.Walker, _Germany and the Emigration, 1816-1885_ (Cambridge, Ma., 1964).
F.Wunderlich, _Farm Labor in Germany, 1810-1945_ (Princeton, 1961).
G.Zang, ed., _Provinzialisierung einer Region: Zur Enstehung der bürgerlichen Gesell-_
in der Provinz (Frankfurt/M., 1978).

October 20 - The Working-Class Movement

CORE READINGS:
V.L.Lidtke, "German Social Democracy and German State Socialism, 1876-1884," IRSH,
91(1964), 202-225.
R.Dominick, "Democracy or Socialism? A Case Study of Vorwärts," CEH, 10(1977), 286-
311.
J.H.Quataert, "Unequal Partners in an Uneasy Alliance: Women and the Working-Class
in Imperial Germany," in J.H.Quataert and M.Boxer, eds., _Socialist Women_ (New York,
1978).

SUPPLEMENTARY READINGS:
P. Angel, _Eduard Bernstein et l'evolution du socialisme allemand_ (Paris, 1961).
R.Breitman, "Negative Integration and Parliamentary Politics. Literature on German
Social Democracy, 1890-1933," CEH, 13(1980), 175-197.
G.D.H. Cole, _A History of Socialist Thought_ (London, 1953).
W.Conze and D.Groh, _Die Arbeiterbewegung in der nationalen Bewegung_ (Stuttgart, 1966).
W.Denzsch, _Handwerker und Lohnarbeiter in der frühen Arbeiterbewegung_ (Göttingen, 1980).
R.J.Evans, "German Social Democracy and Women's Suffrage, 1891-1918," JCH, 15(1980).
W.Fischer and G.Bajor, eds., _Die Soziale Frage. Neuere Studien zur Lage der Fabrik-_
arbeiter am Vorabend des ersten Weltkriegs (Frankfurt, 1973)
D.Fricke, _Bismarcks Pratorianer. Die Berliner politische Polizei gegen die deutsche_
Arbeiterbewegung (Berlin, 1962).
P. Frölich, _Rosa Luxemburg: Ideas in Action_ (London, 1967).
P. Gay, _The Dilemma of Democratic Socialism: Eduard Bernstein's Challenge to Marx_
(New York, 1962).
D.Geary, _European Labour Protests, 1848-1939_ (London, 1981).
D.Groh, _Negative Integration und revolutionärer Attentismus: die deutsche Sozial-_
ismus am Vorabend des ersten Weltkriegs (Frankfurt, 1973).
Institut für Marxismus-Leninismus beim Zentralkommittee der SED, _Geschichte der_
deutschen Arbeiterbewegung (Berlin, 1966) 8 vols.
V.L.Lidtke, _The Outlawed Party: Social Cemocracy in Germany, 1878-1890_ (Princeton,
1966).
W.H.Maehl, _August Bebel: Emperor of the German Worker_ (Philadelphia 1980).
  "Recent Literature on the German Socialists, 1891-1932,"
J. A. Moses, _Trade Unionism in Germany from Bismarck to Hitler, 1869-1933_ (London,
1982).
S. Na'amen _Die Konstituierung der deutschen Arbeiterbewegung, 1862-1863._
  Von der Arbeiterbewegung zur Arbeiterpartei

162

J.P.Nettl, Rosa Luxemburg (London, 1966).
M. Nolan, Social Democracy and Society: Working-Class Radicalism in Düsseldorf, 1890-1920(New York, 1980).
P.H.Noyes, Organization and Revolution: Working-Class Associations in the German Revolutions of 1848-49 (Princeton, 1966).
T.Offermann, Arbeiterbewegung und liberales Bürgertum in Deutschland, 1850-1863 (Bonn, 1979).
J.H.Quataert, Reluctant Feminists in German Social Democracy (Princeton, 1979).
G.Ritter, Die Arbeiterbewegung in wilhelminischen Reich (Berlin, 1963). Arbeiterbewegung, Parteien und Parlamentarismus
G. Roth, Social Democrats in Imperial Germany (Totowa, N.J., 1967).
C.W.Schorske, German Social Democracy, 1905-1917 (Cambridge, Ma., 1955).
K.Tenfelde and H.Volkmann eds., Streik: Zur Geschichte des Arbeitskampfes in Deutsch-während der Industrialisierung
W.Thönessen, Die Frauenemanzipation in Politik und Literatur der deutschen Sozial-demokratie (Berlin, 1960)..
H.-U. Wehler, Sozialdemokratie und Nationalstaat, 1840-1914 (Göttingen, 1971).

October 27 - "New Social History" of the German Working Class

CORE READINGS:
D.Crew, "Definitions of Modernity: Social Mobility in a German Town, 1880-1901," in P.Stearns and D. Walkowitz- eds., Workers and the Industrial Revolution
R.Dasey, "Women's Work and the Family: WomenGarment Workers in Berlin and Hamburg before the First World War," in R. Evans and W.R. Lee, eds., The German Family
D.Geary, "Radicalism and the Workers," in R.Evans, ed., Society and Politics in Wilhelmine Germany

SUPPLEMENTARY READINGS:
P.Borscheid, Textilarbeiterschaft in der Industrialisierung (Stuttgart, 1978).
D.F.Crew, "Steel, Sabotage and Socialism: The Strike at the Dortmund 'Union' Steel Works in 1911," in R.J.Evans, ed., The German Working Class, 1888-1933
R.J.Evans, "Introduction: the Sociological Interpretation of German Labour History," in R.J.E-vans, ed., The German Working Class, 1888-1933 (london, 1981)
       "Red Wednesday in Hamburg: Social Democrats, Police and Lumpenproletariat in the Suffrage Disturbances of 17 January, 1906," SH, 4(1979), 1-32.
M.Grüttner, "Working-class Crime and the Labour Movement: Pilfering on the Hamburg Docks, 1888-1923," in R.J.Evans, ed., The German Working Class, 1888-1933.
J.Kocha, ed., Arbeiterkultur im 19.Jahrhundert. Special Issue of G&G, 5(1979).
J.Kuczynski, A Short History of Labour Conditions Under Industrial Capitalism: Germany, 1800 to the Present (London, 1945).
J.S.Roberts, "Drink and the Labour Movement," in R.J.Evans, ed.,, The German Working Class, 1888-1933
L.Schofer, The Formation of a Modern Labor Force, Upper Silesia, 1865-1914.(Berkeley, 1975),
H.Schomerus, Die Arbeiter der Maschinenfabrik Esslingen
K.Tenfelde, Sozialgeschichte der Bergarbeiterschaft in der Ruhr im 19. Jahrhundert (Bonn, 1977).

History 5-744, page 5.

November 3 - Ruling Classes and Mittelstände

CORE READINGS:
S. Angel-Volkov, "The Decline of German Handicrafts - Another Reappraisal," VSWg, (1974), 165-184.
J.J.Sheehan, "Conflict and Cohesion among German Elites in the Nineteenth Century," in R,Bezucha, ed., Modern European Social History.
E.Spencer, "Employer Response to Unionism: Ruhr Coal Industrialists before 1914," JMH, 48(1976), 397-412.

SUPPLEMENTARY READINGS:
P.Aycoberry, "Der Strukturwandel in Kölner Mittelstand, 1820-1860," G&G, 1(1975), 78-98.
L.Cecil, Albert Ballin: Business and Politics in Imperial Germany, 1888-1914, (Princeton, 1967).
          "The Creation of Nobles in Prussia, 1871-1918," AHR, 75(1970), 757-795.
J.M.Diefendorf, "Businessmen and Politics in the Rhineland, 1789-1834
  Engelsing, Zur Sozialgeschichte der Mittel- und Unterschichten (Göttingen, 1973).
J.R.Gillis, "Aristocracy and Bureaucracy in Nineteenth-Century Prussia," P&P (1968).
H.J.Hennings, Das westphalische Bürgetuum in der Epoche der Hochindustrialisierung (1972).
H.Jaeger, Unternehmer in der deutschen Politik (Bonn, 1967).
 H.Kaeble, "Long=Term Changes in the Recruitment of the Business Elite: Germany Compared to the U.S., Breat Britain and France Since the Industrial Revolution," JSH, 13(1980), 404-421.
H.Herwig, The German Naval Officer Corps (Oxford, 1973).
J.Kocka, Die Angestellten in der deutschen Geschichte (Göttingen, 1981).
          Entrepreneurship in a Late-comer Country. Socio-economic and Socio-cultural determinants of German Entrepreneurship in the Late 19th and Early 20th Centuries.
          Unternehmer in der deutschen Industrialisierung (Göttingen, 1975).
E.Kohn-Bramsted, Aristocracy and the Middle Classes in Germany (London, 1937).
L.W.Muncy, "The Prussian Landräte in the Last Years of the Monarchy," CEH, 4(1973) 299-338.
H.Reif, Westphalische Adel, 1770-1860
H.Rosenberg, "Die Pseudodemokratisierung der Rittergutsbesitzklass," in H.-U. Wehler, ed., Moderne deutsche Sozialgeschichte.
K.Saul, Staat, Industrie und Arbeiterbewegung im Kaiserreich (Düsseldorf, 1974).
E.G.Spencer, "Businessmen, Bureaucrats and Social Control ib the Ruhr, 1896-1914," in H.U. Wehler, ed., Sozialgeschichte Heute.
D.Visser, The German Captains of Enterprise, "European Economic History, 6(1969), 309-328.
F.Zunkel, Das Rheinsiche-Westphalische Unternehmertum, 1834-1879 (Köln, 1962).
F.Stern Gold and Iron

November 10 - Family and Gender

CORE READINGS:
S.Bajohr, "Illegitimacy and the Working Class: Illegitimate Mothers in Brunswick, 1900-1933," in R.J.Evans, ed., The German Working Class, 1888-1933.
R.J.Evans, "Prostitution, State and Society in Imperial Germany," P&P, 70(1976), 106=129.
K.Hausen, "Family and Role Division: The Polarization of Sexual Stereotypes in the Nineteenth Century - an Aspect of the Dissociation of Work and Family Life," in R.J.Evans and W.R.Lee eds., The German Family

164

SUPPLEMENTARY READINGS:
R.J.Evans,"Politics and the Family: Social Democracy and the Working-Class Family in Theory and Practice before 1914," in R.J.Evans and W.R.Lee, eds., The German Family.
W.H.Hubbard, Familiengeschichte: Materialen zur deutschen Familie seit dem Ende des 18.Jahrhunderts(Munich, 1983).
A.E.Imhof, "Women, Family and Death: Excess Mortality of Women of Childbearing Age in Four Communities in Nineteenth-Century Germany," in R.J. Evans and W.R.Lee, eds., The German Family.
J.H.Jackson, "Overcrowding and Family Life: Working-Class Families and the Housing Crisis in Late Nineteenth-Century Duisberg," in R.J.Evans and W.R,Lee, eds., The German Family.
W.R.Lee, "Family and Modernisation: The Peasant Family and Social Change in Nine-teenth-Century Bavaria," in R.J. Evans and W.R. Lee, eds., The German Family.
J. Knodel, The Decline of Fertility in Germany (Princeton, 1974).
J.Kocka, "Family and Bureaucracy in German Industrial Management," Business History Review (1971), 133-356.
W.R.Lee, "The German Family: A Critical Survey of the Current State of Historical Research," in R.J.Evans and W.R.Lee, eds., The German Family/

H.Medick et al,Industrialization before Industrialization, especially Medick's essay "The Structural Function of Household and Familie in the Transition from Traditional Agrarian Society to Industrial Capitalism,"
M.Mitterauer and R.Sieder, Vom Patriarchat zur Partnerschaft: Zum Strukturwandel der Familie(Munich, 1977).
R.P.Neuman, "Industrialization and Sexual Behavior: Some Aspects of Working-Class Life in Imperial Germany," in R. Bezucha, ed., Modern European Social History
A.R.Neumann, "The Influence of Family and Friends in German Internal Migration," JSH (1979), 277-288.
D.Sabean, Small Peasant Agriculture in Germany," Peasant Studies, 7(1978), 218-224.
H.Schomerus, "The Family Life-Cycle: A Study of Factory Workers in Nineteenth-Century Württemberg," in R.J.Evans and W.R.Lee, eds., The German Family.
R.Spree, Soziale Ungleichheit vor Krankheit und Tod.
I.Weber-Kellermann, 'Die Deutsche Familie: Versuch einer Sozialgeschichte (Frankfurt, 1974).
See also: "Frauen in der Geschichte des 19. und 20. Jahrhundert" Special Issue of G&G 7(1981).

November 17 - Ideas, Culture, Education and Ideology

CORE READINGS:
S.Angel-Volkov, "The Social and Political Functions of Late 19th-Century Anti-Semitism: The CAse of Small Handicraft Masters, in H.-U. Wehler, ed., Sozial-geschichte Heute.
A.Hall, "The War of Words: Anti-Socialist Offensives and Counterpropaganda in Wil-helmine Germany, 1890-1914," JCH, 11(1976), 11-42.
K.H.Jarausch, "Liberal Education as Illiberal Socialization: The Case of Students in Imperial Germany," JMH, 5(1978), 609-638.
H.Lebovics, "Agrarians vs. Industrializers: Social Conservative Resistance to Industrialism and Capitalism in Late-Nineteenth-Century Germany," IRSH(1967), 31-65.

SUPPLEMENTARY READINGS:

J.C.Albisetti, Secondary School Reform in Imperial Germany (Princeton, 1983).
A.Ascher, "Professors as Propagandists: The Politics of Kathedersozialismus," JCEA (1963).
R,M.Berdahl, "New Thoughts on German Nationalism," AHR (1972), 65-80.
K.Bergmann, Agrarromantik und Grossstadtfeindschaft (Mersenheim, 1970).
W.H.Bruförd, The German Tradition of Self-Cultivation: "Bildung" from Humboldt to Thomas Mann. (London, New York, 1975).

S.Fishman, The Struggle for German Youth: The Search for Educational Reform in Imperial Germany (New York, 1976).
D.Fricke, Zur Militisierung des deutschen Geisteslebens in wilhelminischen Kaiserreich," ZfG, 8(1960), 1069-1107.
P.Gay, Freud, Jews and Other Germans (New Haven, 1977).
J.E.Groh, Nineteenth-Centurt German Protestantism: The Church as a Social Model= (Washington, D.C., 1982).
A.Hall, Scandal, Sensation and Social Democracy: The SPD Press in Wilhelmine Germany
K.Hartmann et al, Schule und Staat im 18. und 19. Jahrhundert (Frankfurt, 1974).
H.S.Hughes, Consciousness and Society: The Reorientation of European Thought, 1890-1930 (New York, 1958).
N.Jacobs, "The German Social Democratic Party School in Berlin, 1906-1914," HW,5 (1978), 179-187.
K.H.Jarausch, Students, Society and Politics in Imperial Germany (Princeton, 1982).

A.Kelly, The Descent of Darwin: The Popularization of Darwin in Germany, 1860-1914 (Chapel Hill, 1981).
W. Laqueur, Young Germany: A History of the German Youth Movement (New York, 1962).
G.Lukacs, Deutsche Literatur im Zeitalter des Imperialismus. (Berlin, 1947).
C.E.McClelland, State, Soci ety and University in Germany, 1700-1914.
F.Meyer, Schule der Untertanen: Lehrer und Politik in Preussen, 1848-1900.
G.L.Mosse, The Crisis of German Ideology (New York, 1964).
_____, Germans and Jews (New York, 1970).
_____, The Nationalization of the Masses (New York, 1975).
P. Paret, The Berlin Secession: Modernism and Its Enemies in Imperial Germany (Cambrideg, Ma., 1980).
F.Ringer, The Dec line of the German Mandarins: The German Academic Community, 1890-1933(Cambridge, 1969).
S.Ragins, Jewish Responses to Anti=Semitism in Germany, 1870-1914 (Cinncinnati, 1980).
R.Rürup, "Kontinuität und Diskontinuität der Judenfrage im 19. Jahrhundert," in H.-U. Wehler, ed., Sozialgeschichte Heute.
E.Schmidt-Volkman, Der Kulturkampf in Deutschland (Göttingen, 1962).
N.Schwarte, Schulpolitik und Pädagogik der deutschen Sozialdemokratie an der Wende vom 19. zum 20. Jahrhundert (Cologne, 1980).
J.Sperber, "Roman Catholic Identity in Rhineland=Westphalia, 1800-1890," SH,7(1982), 305-318.
G.D.Stark, "Pornography, Society and Law in Imperial Germany," CEH, 14(1981), 200-227.
F.Stern, The Politics of Cultural Despair (Berkeley, 1961).
K.Vondung, ed., Das Wilhelminische Bildungsburgertum (Göttingen, 1976).
G.Wiegelmann, ed., Kultureller Wandel im 19. Jahrhundert (Göttingem, 1975)
H.G.Zmarzlik,"Der Sozialdarwinismus in Deutschland als geschichtliche Probleme," VfZ, 11(1963), 246-273.

December 1 - Parties, Pressure Groups and Politics

CORE READINGS:
R.J.Evans, "Liberalism and Society: The Feminist Movement and Social Change,"
  in R.J.Evans, ed., Society and Politics in Wilhelmine Germany.
G.Eley, "Defining Social Imperialism: Use and Abuse of An Idea," SH, 3(1976),
  265-290.
H.-U. Wehler, "Bismarck's Imperialism," P&P, 48(1970), 119-155.

SUPPLEMENTARY READINGS:
N.J.Alden, Germany After Bismarck: The Caprivi Era (Cambridge, 1955).
M.Balfour, The Kaiser and His Times (Hammondsworth, 1965).
L.Bergstrasser and W. Mommsen, Geschichte der politischen Parteien in Deutschland
  (Munich, 1965).
D.Blackbourn, "The Mittelstand in German Society and Politics, 1871-1914," SH.
  4(1977),409-434.
          "Class and Politics in Wilhelmine Germany: The Center Party and the
  Social Democrats in Württemberg," CEH, 9(1976), 220-250.

H.Böhme, "Bismarcks Schutzzollpolitik und die Festigung des konservativen Staates,"
  in H.Böhme. ed., Probleme.
L. Cecil, A. Ballin: Business and Politics in Imperial Germany (Princeton, 1967).
G.Eley, Reshaping the German Right:Radical Nationalism and Political Change after
  Bismarck
R.J.Evans, The Feminist Movement in Germany (London, 1976)
          Society and Politics in Wilhelmine Germany (London, 1978). Any article.
D.Fricke et al, Die bürgerliche Parteien in Deutschland, 1830-1945 (Leipsig, 1968).
R.Gellately, The Politics of Economic Despair: Shopkeepers and German Politics
  1890-1914 (London, 1974).
L. Gall, Bismarck, Der Weisse Revolutionär (Frankfurt/M., 1980).
A.Hackett, "The German Women's Movement and Suffrage, 1890-1914," in R. Bezucha,
  ed., Modern European Social History.
          The Politics of Feminism in Wilhelmine Germany, 1890-1918 (New York, 1979).
J.C.Hunt, "The bourgeois Middle in German POlitics, 1871-1933: Recent Literature,"
  CEH‡ 11(1978), 107-112.
          "Peasants, Grain Tariffs and Meat Quotas: Imperial German Protectionism
  Revisited," CEH, 7(1974), 311-331.
H.Kaeble, Industrielle Interessenpolitik in der Wilhelmischen Gesellschaft: Zentral-
  bund deutscher Industrieller (Berlin, 1965).
E. Kehr, Economic Interest, Militarism and Foreign Policy (Berkeley, 1977[2])
I. Lambi, "Die Organization der industriellen Schutzzollinteressen," in E.Born, ed.,
  Moderne deutsche Wirtschaftsgeschichte.
.Müller-Link. Industrialisierung und Aussenpolitik: Preussen-Deutschland und das
  Zarenreich von 1860 bis 1890 (Göttingen, 1977).
L. O'Boyle, "Liberal Leadership in Germany, 1867-1884," JMH (1956).
H.J.Puhle, Agrarische Interessenpolitik und Preussischer Konservatismus(Hanover, 1966).
          "Aspekte der Agrarpolitik im organisierten Kapitalismus," in H.-U. Wehler,
  ed., Sozialgeschichte Heute.
J.C.G.Röhl, Germany Without Bismarck: The Crisis of Government in the Second Reich
  (Berkeley, 1967).
          "Staatsstreichpläne oder Staatsstreichbereitschaft? Bismarcks Politik
  in der Entlassungskrise," HZ, 203 (1966).

K.Saul, "Staatsintervention und Arbeitskampf in Wilhelminischen Reich, 1904-1914,"
in B.-U., Wehler, Sozialgeschichte Heute .
D.Schoenbaum, Zabern 1913: Consensus Politics in Imperial Germany (Boston, 1982).
J.J.Sheehan, Liberalism in an Unliberal Society: A History of Liberalism in Nine-
teenth-Century Germany (Princeton, 1976).
J.L.Snell, The Democratic Movement in Germany, 1789-1914 (Chapel Hill, 1976).
D.Stegmann, Die Erbern Bismarcks ((Cologne, 1970).
F.Stern Gold and Iron(New York, 1977).
M.Stürmer, "Staatsstreichgedanken im Bismarckreich," HZ, 209(1969).
F.Ternstedt, Sozialgeschichte der Sozialpolitik in Deutschland vom 18. Jahrhundert
bis zum ersten Weltkrieg (Göttingen, 1981).
F.B.Tipton, "Farm Labor and Power Politics in Germany, 1850-1914," JEH, (1974).
H.A.Winkler, "Bürgerliche Emanzipation unf National Einigung. Zur Entstehung des
Nationalliberalismus in Deutschland,' in H.Böhmen. ed., Probleme .

December 8 - The Social and Political History of the First World War

CORE READINGS:
K.Jarausch, "World Power or Tragic Fate?" CEH 5(1972), 72-92.
J.Kocka, "The First World War and the Mittelstände: German Artisans and White-
Collar Workers," JCH, (1973), 101-123).
R.G.Moeller, "Dimensions of Social Conflict in the Great War: The View from the
German Countryside," CEH, 14(1981), 142-168.

SUPPLEMENTARYRREADINGS:
V.Berghahn, Der Tirpitz Plan: Genesis und Verfall der innenpolitischen Krisenstrategie
unter Wilhelm II (Düsseldorf, 1971).
V.Berghahn and M.Kitchen, eds., Germany in the Age of Total War (London, 1981)/
K.J.Bieber, Die deutschen Gewerkschaften im ersten Weltkrieg (1970).
G,Craig, The Politics of the Prussian Army, 1640-1945 (Oxford, 1955).
G.D.Feldman, Army, Industry and Labor, 1914-1918 (Princeton, 1966).
F.Fischer, Germany's Aims in the First World War (New York, 1967).
              War of Illusions (New York, 1975).
I.Geiss and H.Pogge v. Strandmann, Die Erforderlichkeit des Unmöglichen (Frankfurt,
1965).
K. Jarausch, The Enigmatic Chancellor: Bethmann-Hollweg and the Hubris of Imperial
Germany (New Haven, 1973).
E. Kehr, Economic Interest, Militarism and Foreign Policy (Berkeley, 1977[2])
M. Kitchen- The · German Officer Corps (London, 1968).
              The Silent Dictatorship: The Politics of the German High Command Under
Hindenburg and Ludendorff (New York, 1976).
J.Kocka, Klassengesellschaft im Krieg (Berlin, 1968).
H.C.Meyer, Mitteleuropa in German Thought and Action, 1815-1945 (The HAgue, 1955).
A. Mendelssohn-Bartholdy, The War and German Society=-(New York, 1971).
G.Ritter, The Sword and the Sceptre: the Problem of Militarism in Germany 4 vols.,
K. Schwabe, "Zur politischen Haltung der deutschen Professoren im ersten Weltkrieg,"
HZ, (1961). 193-
H.-U.Wehler, Imperialismus (Cologne, 1975).

History 5-744, page 10.

Additional Bibliography

Students desiring to delve more deeply into topics relating to the history of
Imperial Germany may find the following guides useful:
Dahlmann-Waitz, Quellenkunde der deutschen Geschichte (10th ed., Stuttgart, 1965).
The American Historical Association's Guide to Historical Literature, and also
published by the AHA, N.Rich's Germany, 1815-1914 (Washington, D.C., 1968) J.
C.Fout's German History and Civilization, 1806-1914: A Bibliography of Scholarly
Periodical Literature (Metuchen,N.J., 1974) is very useful. There are a number
of important German guides, including B.Gebhardt's Handbuch der deutschen Geschichte
(9th ed., Stuttgart, 1970) and W.Zorn's Handbuch der deutschen Wirtschafts- und
Sozialgeschichte (Stuttgart, 1976). For the topics of interest in this course,
there are a number of important bibliographies by H.-U. Wehler on Imperialismus,
Moderne Sozialgeschichte and Moderne deutsche Wirtschaftsgeschichte
For a handy introduction to the libraries and archives of Germany, see E.K.
Welsch, Research Resources in Germany: Libraries and Archives (published by the
Council for European Studies in 1975).

Coll ections of Articles

H.Böhme, Probleme der Reichsgrundungszeit, 1848-1879 (Cologne, Berlin, 1968).
K.E.Born, ed., Moderne deutsche Wirtschaftsgeschichte (Colognem Berlin, 1966).
W.Conze, ed., Sozialgeschichte der Familie in der Neuzeit Europas (Stuttgart,
1977).
R.J.Evans, ed., Society and Politics in Wilhelmine Germany (London, New York,
1978).
          The German Working Class, 1888-1933 (London and Totowa, N.J.,
1982).
R.J.Evans and W.R.Lee, eds., The German Family:Essays on the Social History
 of the Family in Nineteenth and Twentieth-Century Germany (London and Totowa,
N.J., 1981).
I.Geiss and B.Wendt, eds., Deutschland in der Weltpolitik der 19. und 20.
Jahrhundert (Düsseldorf, 1973).
H.Helczmanovski, ed., Beiträge zur Bevölkerungs- und Sozialgeschichte (Munich,
1973),
H. Kaeble, ed., Probleme der Modernisierung in Deutschland (Wiesbaden, 1978).
W.J.Mommsen and G.Hirschfeld, eds., Social Protest, Violence and Terror in
Nineteenth and Twentieth-Century Europe (London, 1982).
F.Oeter. ed., Familie und Gesellschaft (Tübingen, 1966).
G.A.Ritter, ed., Entstehung und Wandel der modernen Gesellschaft (Berlin, 1970).
G.A.Ritter and J.Kocka, eds., Deutsche Sozialgeschichte (Munich, 1974),
H.Rosenbaum, ed., Familie und Gesellschaftsstruktur (Frankfurt, 1974).
T.Schieder, ed., Erster Weltkrieg (Cologne and Berlin, 1969).
M.Stürmer. ed., Das kaiserliche Deutschland (Düsseldorf, 1970).
H.-U.Wehler,ed., Krisenherde des Kaiserreichs (Göttingen, 1970).
          Moderne deutsche Sozialgeschichte (Cologne, Berlin, 1968).
          Sozialgeschichte Heute (Göttingen, 1974).
G.Ziebura, ed., Grundfragen der deutsche Aussenpolitik seit 1871 (Darmstadt, 1975).

Abbreviations of Journals Cited

AHR	American Historical Review
CEH	Central European History
EHR	Economic History Review
G&G	Geschichte und Gesellschaft
HW	History Workshop
HZ	Historische Zeitschrift
IRSH	International Review of Social History
JCEA	Journal of Central European Affairs
JCH	Journal of Contemporary History
JEH	Journal of Economic History
JMH	Journal of Modern History
P&P	Past and Present
SH	Social History
VfZ	Vierteljahreshefte für Zeitgeschichte
VSWg	Vierteljahresschrift für Sozial- und Wirtschaftsgeschichte
ZfG	Zeitschrift für Geschichte
ZWSg	Zeitschrift für Wirtschafts-und Sozialgeschichte

History 5-744
Course Requirements

Since students are enrolled in the seminar for a number of different reasons,
I have tried to establish requirements that have a degree of flexibility
built in. Please be sure to consult with me throughout the course to discuss
your progress, your plans and your response to the class.

Reading
All participants in the seminar are required to read all the core readings
and at least one selection each week from the supplementary reading list.
You should come to class each week prepared to discuss what you have read.

Class participation
The class will be structured around discussions of our readings. All students
should expect to participate in discussion every week. In addition, you will
choose one week when you will prepare a presentation to 'start off' the class.
Your presentation should be some kind of critical response to the core
readings and the supplementary readings you have chosen. It will be your role
to outline what you see as the basic issues or problems raised by the readings,
to discuss connections among them, to compare the various approaches to
answering historical questions they imply, to assess their effectiveness.
I will distribute a sign-up sheet for you to indicate your preference for the
week of your presentation on October 6.

Written Assignments
Weekly reaction papers: Every week you should turn in some kind of short,
informal reaction to your week's readings. In some fashion or other, this
paper should address the following points:
-how did the supplementary reading(s) pertain to problems or questions
 raised in the core readings or by the discussion question I distributed for
 that week?
-how effectively were these questions handled?
These papers will be turned in at the beginning of the class discussion so that
I can structure the class so as to include discussion of the supplementary
readings. They can be turned in in any form, as long as they are legible.

Short book reviews: During the coures of the quarter, you are to turn in
at least two reviews of books taken from the supplementary reading list.
These reviews should be about two pages, typed and single spaced
and are to be distributed to the whole class (hence you will all end up with
a good collection of book reviews as a by-product of the class!) Turn the
review in to me on the Tuesday of the week in question, and I will take care
of copying it for the rest of the class. I will also ask you to sign up for
book reviews to assure that we have no more than one review of a book. Check
on availability befôre signing up.

Long paper: There will be one major paper due at the end of the quarter, but
its form can be up to you. Each student will work out an option with me by
 the middle of the quarter. You might consider the following possibilities:

171

- (for undergraduates) senior paper or honors thesis
-(for graduate students) - a historiographic essay and research proposal
 that could be the first stage of a Plan B paper.
- (for anybody) - a journal review.

I will set up individual appointments for the week of October 17 to discuss plans with each of you.

History 5-745   University of Minnesota   Mary Jo Maynes
Topics in Modern German History: 1918-1945   523 Social Science Tower
Course Syllabus, Winter, 1981.   373-4430

The purpose of this proseminar is to introduce students to some of the central
problems of twentieth-century German History. The following outline is not meant
to be an exhaustive bibliography,   , but rather a presentation of
some of the more significant contributions to a select set of topics. For each
subject, there are listed CORE READINGS which all class members will be expected to
complete for each topic the class discusses. These have been selected from among
works available in English. In addition, class members will be responsible for
reading and reporting on works chosen from among the SUPPLEMENTARY READINGS as
well.

Bibliographic Guides

For the study of modern German history, some standard bibliographic references are:
Dahlmann-Waitz, Quellenkunde der deutschen Geschichte (Stuttgart, 1965 10); the
American Historical Association's Guide to Historical Literature; B.Gebhart,
Handbuch der deutschen Geschichte (Stuttgart, 1970 9); Deutsche Bibliographie;
Jahresverzeichnis für deutsche Hochschulschriften and Jahresberichte für deutsche
Geschichte. Perhaps most useful of all is the recently published critical bibliograp hy
by P. Stachura, The Weimar Era and Hitler (Oxford, 1977).

Collections of Articles

In addition to the historical journals which publish articles on this era, the
following collections of articles may be consulted:
H.Buchheim et al, Der Fü-hrer ins Nichts
*K.Bullivant, ed., Culture and Society in the Weimar Republic (Totowa, N.J., 1977).
G.A.Craig and F.Gilbert, eds., The Diplomats, 1919-1939 (Princeton, 1953).
I.FGeiss and B.J.Wendt, eds., Deutschland in der Weltpolitik des 19. und 20. Jahr-
hundert (Düsseldorf, 1973).
C.Gneuss, ed., Der Weg in die Diktatur (Munich, 1962).
A.Hermans and T. Schieder, eds., Staat, Wirtschaft und Politik in der Weimarer
Republik (Berlin, 1967).
*H.Holborn, ed., Republic to Reich (N.Y., 1972).
G.Jasper, ed., Von Weimer zu Hitler, 1930-1933 (Cologne, 1968).
E.Kolb, Von Kaiserreich zur Weimarer Republik. (Köln, 1972).
*H.Krausnick et al, The Anatomy of the SS State (N.Y., 1965).
I. Lederer, ed., The Versailles Settlement (Boston, 1960).
E.Matthias and R.Morsey, eds., Das Ende der Parteien (Düsseldorf, 1960).
H.Mommsen et al, eds., Industrielles System und politische Entwicklung in der
Weimarer Republik (Bochum, 1974).
*A.J.Nicholls and E.Matthias, eds., German Democracy and the Triumph of Hitler
(London, 1971).
W.Schieder, ed., Faschismus als Sozialbewegung (Hamburg, 1976).
*P.Stachura, ed., The Shaping of the Nazi State. (New York, 1978).
F.Stern, ed., The Path to Dictatorship (N.Y., 1966).
*H.A.Turner, ed., Nazism and the Third Reich (N.Y., 1972).
R.G.L.Waite, ed., Hitler and Nazi Germany (London, 1969).
G.Ziebura, ed., Grundfragen der deutschen Aussenpolitik zeit 1871 (Darmstadt, 1971).

* On reserve in Wilson Library

Genaral Interpretations
Students will be expected to read the appropriate sections of one of the following
generaly surveys of German history (or an equivalent text):
*G.A.Craig, Germany: 1860-1945
*H.Holborn, A History of Modern Germany, Vol. III
*A.J.Ryder, Twentieth-Century Germany

Section One - World War I and Revolution
Text: Holborn, pp. 414-533 or Craig, pp. 339-433 or Ryder, pp. 102-216.

CORE READINGS:
*R,Rürup, "Problems of the German Revolution, 1918-1919," JCH (1968), 109-135.
*D.K.Buse, "Ebert and the German Crisis, 1917-1920," CEH (1972), 234-256.

SUPPLEMENTARY READINGS:
F.L.Carsten, Revolution in Central Europe, 1918-1919 (London, 1972).
G.D.Feldman, Army, Industry and Labour, 1914-1918 (Princeton, 1966).
G.D.Feldman et al, "Die Massenbewegung der Arbeiterschaft am Ende der Ersten Welt-
krieg," Politische Vierteljahrschrift 13 (1972), 84-105.
F.Fischer, Germanys Aims in the First World War (N.Y., 1967).
H.H.Herwig, "The First German Congress of Workers and Soldiers' Councils and the
Problem of Military Reforms," CEH, 1 (1968).
R.Hunt, THe Creation of the Weimar Republic
V.Kluge, Soldatenräte und Revolution (Göttingen, 1975).
M.Kitchen, The Silent Dictatorship (New York, 1976).
J.Kocka, "The Fisrst World War and the Mittelstand," JCH (1973), 101-123.
———— Klassengesellschaft im Krieg.
S.Miller and K.Potthoff, eds., Die Regierung der Volksbeauftragten, 1918/19
(Düsseldorf, 1969).
A.Mitchel, Revolution in Bavaria, 1918/19.
D.W.Morgan, The Socialist Left and the German Revolution, 1917-1922
G.A.Ritter and S.Miller, eds., Die deutsche Revolution, 1918-19 (Frankfurt, 1968).
A.J.Ryder, The German Revolution of 1918 (Cambridge, 1967).
P. v. Oertzen, Betriebsräte in der Novemberrevolution.
E.Waldman, The Spartacist Uprising of 1919 (Milwaukee, 1958).
F.Zunkel. Industrie und Staatssozialismus (Tübingen, 1974).

Section Two - The Weimar Era
Text: Holborn, pp. 533-711 or Craig, pp. 434-565 or Ryder, pp. 216-282.

The Weimar Era: Economy and Society
CORE READINGS:
∗ G.R.Feldman, "The Social and Economic Policies of German Big Business, 1918-1929,"
AHR 75(1969), 47-55.
∗ H.A.Turner, "The Ruhrlade, Secret Cabinet of Heavy Industry in the Weimar Republic,"
CEH, 3 (1970), 195-228.
∗ B.Weisbrod, "Economic Power and political stability reconsidered: heavy industry
in ‘Weimar Germany, " SH, 4(1979), 241-264.

SUPPLEMENTARY READINGS:

R.A.Brady, The Rationalization Movement in Germany Industry
C.Bresciani-Turroni, The Economics of Inflation (London, 1937).

G.Feldman, "Big Business and the Kapp Putsch," CEH 4(1971), 99-130.
_____, Iron and Steel and the German Inflation
C.P.Kindleberger, The World in Depression (Berkeley, L.A., 1973).
P.Krieger, Deutschland und die Reparationen (Stuttgart, 1973).
D.Petzina, "Germany and the Great Depression," JCH, 41(1968), 59-74.
N.Reich, Labor Relations in Republican Germany
⨯ F.Ringer, ed., The German Inflation of 1923 (N.Y., 1969).
F.Wunderlich, Labor Under German Democracy.

The Weimar Era: Politics

CORE READINGS:
⨯ W.T.Angress, "Weimar Coalition and Ruhr Insurrection, March-April, 1920," JMH, 29(1957), 1-20.
⨯ A.Chanady, "The Dissolution of the German Democratic Party,"≌AHR, 73(1968), 1433-143.
⨯ D.Abraham, "Constituting Hegemony: the Bourgeois Crisis of Weimar Germany," JMH, 51 (1979), 417-433.

SUPPLEMENTARY READINGS:
W.Angress, The Stillborn Revolution: The Communist Bid for Power in Germany, 1921-1923 (Princeton, 1963).
R.Bridenthal and C.Koontz, "Beyond Kinder, Kirche, Küche: Weimar Women in Politics and Work," CEH, 6(1973), 148-66.
A.Chanady, "The Disintegration of the German National People's Party," JMH, 39 (1967).
A.Dorpalen, Hindenburg and the Weimar Republic.
K. Epstein, Matthias Erzberger and the Dilemma of German Democracy (Princeton, 1959).
J.Erger, Der Kapp-Lüttwitz Putsch (Düsseldorf. 1967).
D.Felix, Walther Rathenau and the Weimar Republic (Baltimore, 1971)
R.Fischer, Stalin and German Communism (Cambridge, Mass., 1948).
O.K.Flechtheim, Die KPD in der Weimarer Republik (Frankfurt, 1969).
B.Frye, "The German Democratic Party,"Western Political Quarterly, 16(1968).
R.A.Gates, "German Socialism and the Crisis of 1929-33," CEH, 7:4(1976), 332-59.
L.Hertzman, DNVP: Right-Wing Opposition in the Weimar Republic.
R.Hunt, German Social Democracy, 1918-1933 (New Haven, 1964).
W,Kreutzberger, Studenten und Politik, 1918-1933 (Göttingen, 1972).
L.E.Jones, "The Dying Middle: Weimar Germany and the Fragmentation of Bourgeois Politics," CEH, 5(1972), 23-54.
C.Maier, Recasting Bourgeois Europe: Stabilization in France, Germany and Italy in the Decade After World War I (Princeton, 1975).
B.Peterson, "The Politics of Working-Class Women in the Weimar republic," CEH, 10 (1977), 87-111.
W.Strube, Elites Against Democracy: Leadership Ideals in Bourgeois Political Thought in Germany, 1890-1933 (Princeton, 1973).
M.Stürmer, Koalition und Opposition in der Weimarer Republik (Düsseldorf, 1967).
K,Sontheimer, Anti-demokratisches Denken in der Weimarer Republik.
H.A.Turner, Jr., Stresemann and the Politics of the Weimar Republic (Princeton, 1963).
R.F.Wheeler, "German Women and the Communist International: The Case of the USPD," CEH, 8(1975), 113-139.
H.Weber, Die Wandlungen des deutschen Kommunismus (Frankfurt, 1969), 2 vols.
H.A.Winkler, Mittelstand, Demokratie und Nationalsozialismus.
W.Zorn, "Student Politics in the Weimar Republic," JCH (1970).

The Weimar Era: The Artist as Social Critic

CORE READINGS:

✗K.Bullivant, "Thomas Mann and Politics in the Weimar Republic," in K. Bullivant, ed., Culture and Society in the Weimar Republic
✗ G.Craig, "Engagement and Neutrality in Weimar Germany," JCH 2:2 (1967), 49-65.
W.Sauer, "Weimar Culture:Experiments in Modernism," Social Research, 39(1972), 254-84.

SUPPLEMENTARY READINGS:

W.Angress, "Pegasus and Insurrection: Die Linkskurve and Its Heritage," CEH, 1(1968), 35-55.
✗ R.Burns, "Theory and Organization of Revolutionary Working-Class Literature in the Weimar Republic," in K.Bullivant, ed., Culture and Society.
I.Deak, Weimar Germany's Left-Wing Intellectuals.
K.W.Epstein, The Genesis of German Conservatism (Princeton, 1966).
P.Gay, Weimar Culture (N.Y., 1968).
H.Stuart Hughes, Consciousness and Society (N.Y., 1958).
M.Jay, The Dialectical Imagination: A History of the Frankfurt School and the Institute of Social Research (Boston, 1973).
M.Kater, "Krisis des Frauenstudiums in der Weimar Republik," VSWg, 59(1972), 207-55.
_____, "The Work Student: A Socio-Economic Phenomenon of Early Weimar Germany," JCH, 10:1(1975), 71-94.
S.Kracauer, From Caligari to Hitler.
H.Lethen, Die Neue Sachlichkeit: Studien zur Literatur des "Weissen Sozialismus" (Stuttgart, 1977).
B.Lane, Architecture and Politics in Germany, 1918-1945.
W.Laqueur, Weimar: A Cultural History (N.Y., 1975).
G.L.Mosse, The Crisis of German Ideology (N.Y., 1964).
B.S.Myers, The German Expressionists: A Generation in Revolt (N.Y., 1966).
D.R.Richards, German Best-Sellers of the Twentieth Century (Berne, 1966).
F.Ringer, The Decline of the German Mandarins:The German Academic Community,1890-1933.
F.Stern, The Politics of Cultural Despair (Berkeley. 1961).
J.L.Willett, Art and Politics in the Weimar Era.
H.M.Wingler, The Bauhaus (N.Y., 1969).

The Weimar Era: The Early NSDAP

CORE READINGS:

✗ J.Noakes, "Conflict and Development in the NSDAP, 1924-1927," JCH, 1:4(9166), 3-36.
✗ B.Lane, "Nazi Ideology: Some Unfinished Business," CEH, 7(1974), 3-30.

SUPPLEMENTARY READINGS:

A.Bullock, Hitler: A Study in Tyranny.
J.Fest, Hitler: A Biography.
H.Gordon, Hitler and the Beer Hall Putsch (Princeton, 1972).
P.Honigsheim, "The Roots of the Nazi Concept of the Ideal Peasant," Rural Sociology 12(1947), 3-21.
P.Hüttenberger, Die Gauleiter (Stuttgart, 1969).
E.Jäckel, Hitler's Weltanschauung (Middletown, Conn., 1972).

J.MNoakes, The Nazi Party in Lower Saxony, 1921-1933 (London, 1972).
D.Orlow, The History of the Nazi Party (London, 1971/73), 2 vols.
G.Pridhem, Hitler's Rise to Power: The Nazi Movement in Bavaria (London, 1973).
✗ P. Stachura, "'Der Fall Strasser': Gregor Strasser, Hitler and National Socialism,"
in P. Stachura, ed., The Shaping of the Nazi State.
O.-E.Schüddekopf, Linke Leute von Rechts. Dis nationalrevolutionärer Minderheiten
und die Weimarer Republik (Stuttgart, 1960)/.
✗ G.Stankes, "The Evolution of Hitler's Ideas on Foreign Policy, 1919-1925," in P.
Stachura, ed., The Shaping of the Nazi State.
✗ R.G.L.Waite, Adolph Hitler's Anti-Semitism: A Study in History and Psychoanalysis,"
in B.B.Wolman, ed., The Psychoanalytic Interpretation of History.
_____, Adolph Hitler's Guilt Feelings: A Problem in History and Psychology,"
JIH, 1(9171).
_____, Vanguard of Nazism: The Free Corps Movement in Germany, 1918-1923.

The Weimar Era: Accounting for the Success of the Radical Right

CORE READINGS:

✓ R.Bessel, "Eastern Germany as a Structural Problem in the Weimar Republic," SH,
3(1978), 199-218.
✗ T.Childers, "The Social Bases of the National Socialist Vote," JCH, 11:4(1976),
17-42.
✗ C.Fischer, "The Occupational Background of the SA's Rank-and-File Membership during
the Depression Years, 1929 to mid-1934," in P.Stachura, ed., The Shaping of the Nazi
State. Also the critique in SH, 6(1979), 111-116.
✗ P. Loewenberg, "The Psychohistorical origins of the Nazi Youth Movement," AHR, 767
(1971), 1457-1502.

SUPPLEMENTARY READINGS:

H.P.Bleuel, Deutsche Studenten auf dem Weg ins Dritten Reich (Gütersloh, 1967).
R.J.Evans, "German Women and the Triumph of Hitler," JMH, 48(9176) (Unavailable).
H.Lebovics, Social Conservatism and the Middle Classes in Germany, 1914-1933
(Princeton, 1969).
R.Rogawski, "The Gauleiter and the Social Origins of Fascism," CSSH, 19 (19   ),399-430.
W.Schieder, Fascismus als Sozialbewegung .
P.D.Stachura, Nazi Youth in the Weimar Republic .
H.A.Winkler, "From Social Protectionism to National Sozialism: The German Small
Business Movement in Comparative Perspective," JMH, 48(9176), 1-18.

Section Three- The Nazi Era
Text: Holborn, pp. 711-818 or Craig, pp. 569-764 or, Ryder, pp. 283-452.

The Nazi Era: The Machtergreifung

CORE READINGS:

✗ H.Mommsen, The Reichstag Fire and Its Political Consequences," in H.A.Turner, ed.,
Nazism and the Third Reich .

H.A.Winkler, "German Society, Hitler, and the Illusion of Restoration, 1930-1933," JCH, 11(1976), 1-16.

SUPPLEMENTARY READINGS:

W.S.Allen, The Nazi Seizure of Power.
K.D.Bracher et al, Die nationalsozialistische Machtergreifung (Cologne, Opladen, 1960).
_____, "Parteinstaat, Präsidialsystem, Notstand: zum Problem der Weimarer Staatskrise," Politische Vierteljahresschrift, 3:3(9162), 212-224.
R.Breitman, "On German Social Democracy and General Schläicher, 1932-33," CEH, 9(1976), 352-378.
R.Heberle, From Democracy to Nazism (Baton Rouge, 1945).
_____, "Zum Soziologie der nationalsozialistischen Revolution," VjhZg (1965)
R.J.Pritchard, The Reichstag Fire(N.Y., 1972).
H.A.Turner, "Big Business and the Rise of Hitler," AHR, 75(1969), 54-69.
A.J.P. Taylor, "Hitler's Seizure of Power" in A.J.P Taylor Europe: Grandeur and Decline
The Nazi Era: The SS State

CORE READINGS:

⋆ H.Buchheim, "The SS - Instrument of Domination," in H.Krausnick et al, The Anatomy of the SS State.
⋆ H.S.Levine, "Local Authority and the SS State; The Conflict over Population Policy in Danzig - West Prussia, 1939-1945," CEH 4 (1969), 331-355.

SUPPLEMEMTARY READINGS:

⋆ M.Broszat, "The Concentration Camps, 1933-1945," in H.Krausnick et al, The Anatomy of the SS State.
K.Bracher, The German Dictatorship (N.Y., 1970).
M.Broszat, Der Staat Hitlers (Munich, 1969).
P.Diehl-Thiele, Partei und Staat im Dritten Reich (Munich, 1969).
H.Höhne, The Order of Death's Head.
E.Kogon, The Theory and Practice of Hell: The German Concentration Camps and the System Behind Them (N.Y., 1950).
H.Mommsen, Beamtentum im Dritten Reich (Stuttgart, 1966).
E.N.Peterson, The Limits of Hitler's Power (Princeton, 1969).
W.Schäfer, NSDAP: Entwicklung und Struktur der Staatspartei des Dritten Reichs (Marburg, 1957).
I.Staff, Justiz im Dritten Reich (Frankfurt, 1964).
G.Stein, The Waffen SS (Ithaca, 1966).
C.W.Snyder, "The History of the SS Totenkopfdividsion and the Postwar Mythology of the Waffen SS," CEH, 6(1973), 339-362,
T.Taylor, Sword and Swastika: Generals ans Nazis in the Third Reich (N.Y., 1952).

The Nazi Era: Society and Economy

ACORE READINGS:

⋆ A.S.Milward, "Fascism and the Economy," in W.Laqueur, ed., Fascism.
⋆ T.Mason, "Labour and the Third Reich, 1933-1939," P&P, 33 (1966), 113-141.
⋆ J.McIntyre, "Women and the Professions in Germany, 1930-1940," in A.Nicholls and E. Matthias, eds., German Democracy and the Triumph of Hitler.

SUPPLEMENTARY READINGS:

R.Armeson, Total Warf are and Compulsory Labor (The Hague, 1965).
T.DeWitt, "The Economics and Politics of Welfare in the Third Reich,"CEH, 11:3(1978), 256-278.
✦ G.J.Giles, "The Rise of the National Socialist Student Association and the Failure of Political Education in the Third Reich," in P.Stachura, ed., The Shaping of the Nazi State.
R.Grunberger, A Social History of the Third Reich (London, 1971).
D.Guerin, Fascism and Big Business (London, 1973).
G.Hallgarten, Hitler, Reichswehr und dir Industrie (Frankfort, 1965).
E.Hennig, Thesen zur deutschen Sozial-und Wirtschaftsgeschichte, 1933-38 (Frankfurt, 1973).
J.D.Heyl, "Hitler's Economic Thought: A Reappraisal," CEH, 6(1973), 83-96.
D.Horn,"Hitler Youth and the Educational Decline in the Third Reich," History of Education Quarterly (Winter, 1976).

R.L.Kaehl, RKFDV: German Resettlement and Population Policy, 1939-45 (Cambridge, Mass., 1957).
T.Mason, Arbeiterklasse und Volksgemeinschaft. Dokumente und Materialen zur deutschen Arbeiterpolitik, 1936-39 (Opladen, 1975).
✦ _____, "The Legacy of 1918 for National Socialism," in A.Nicholls and E.Matthias, eds., German Democracy and the Triumph of Hitler.
_____, "Women in Germany, 1925-1940: Family., Welfare and Work," History Workshop, 1(1976), 74-113 and 2(1977), 5-32.
A.S.Milward, Ther German Economy at War, 1939-45 (Berkeley, L.A!., 1977).
D.Schoenbaum, Hitler's Social Revolution (N.Y., 1966).
A.Schweitzer, Big Business and the Third Reich (Bloomington, 1964).
J.Stephenson, Girl's Higher Education in Germany in the 1930s," JCH, 10:1(1975), 41-70.
✦ _____, "Tha Nazi Organization of Women, 1933-39," in P.Stachura, ed., The Shaping of the Nazi State.
_____, Women in Nazi Society.
D.Winkler, Frauenarbeit im Dritten Reich.

The Nazi Era: Germans and Jews

CORE READINGS:

✦ H.Krausnick, "The Persecution of the Jews," in H.Krausnick et al, The Anatomy of the SS State.
✦ L.D.Stokes, "The German People and the Destruction of the European Jews," CEH, 6 (1973), 167-191.

SUPPLEMENTARY READINGS:

U.D.Aden, Judenpolitik im Dritten Reich (Düsseldorf, 1972).
C.R.Browning, The Final Solution and the German Foreign Office (N.Y., 1979).
L.S.Davidowicz, The War Against the Jews, 1933-1945 (N.Y., 1945).
H.M.Graupe, The Rise of Modern Judaism: An Intellectual History of German Jewry, 1650-1942 (HKrieger, 1979).
A.Hillgruber, "Die Endlösung und das deutsche Ostimperium als Kernstück des rassen-ideologischen Programms des Nationalsozialismus," VjhZg, 20(1972), 133-155.
G.L.Mosse, Germans and Jews: The Right, the Left and the Search for a "Third Force" in Pre-Nazi Germany (N.Y., 1970).

179

E.Reichmann, Hostages of Civilization: A Study of the Social Causes of Anti-Semitism in Germany.
G.Reitlinger, The Final Solution.
U.Tal, Christians and Jews in Germany (Ithaca, 1974).

The Nazi Era: Resistance

CORE READINGS:

✶ D.Horn, "Youth Resistance to in the Third Reich," JSH, 7(1973), 26-50,
✶ E.Matthias, "Resistance to National Socialism: The Example of Mannheim," P&P, 45 1969),

SUPPLEMENTARY READINGS:

H.C.Deutsch, The Conspiracy Against Hitler in the Twilight War.
P.Hoffmann, Widerstand, Staatsstreich, Attentat: Der Kampf der Opposition Gegen Hitler (munich, 1969).
T.Prittre, Germans Against Hitler (London, 1964).
G.Ritter, Carl Goerdeler und der deutsche Widerstand (Munich, 1964).
H.Rothfels, The German Opposition to Hitler.
K.Schabrod, Widerstand am Rhein und Ruhr, 1933-1945 (Düsseldorf, 1969).
W.Schmitthenner and H.Buchheim, eds., Der deutsche Widerstand gegen Hitler (Cologne, 1966). Translated?
B.Vollmer, Volksopposition im Polizeistaat,
F.v.Schlabrenndorf, The Secret War Against Hitler (London, 1966).

Section Four - Understanding Fascism

CORE READINGS:

✶ F.L.Carsten, "Interpretations of Fascism," in W.Laqueur, ed., Fascism.
✶ T.W.Mason, "The Primacy of Politics," in H.A.Turner, ed., Nazism and the Third Reich.
✶ G.Allardyce, "What Fascism Is Not: Thoughts on the Deflation of a Concept," AHR, 84(9179), 367-398.

SUPPLEMENTARY READINGS:

L.K.Adler and T.G.Peterson, "Red Fascism: The Merger of Nazi Germany and Soviet Russia in the American Image of Totalitarianism, 1930s to 1950s," AHR, 75(1969), 1046-1063.
✶ W.Laqueur, ed., Fascism (Berkeley, L.A., 1976).
E.Nolte, Three Faces of Fascism.
N.Poulantzas, Fascism and Dictatorship: The Third International and the Problem of Fascism (London, 1974).
W.Sauer, "National Socialism: Totalitarianism or Fascism?" AHR, 730(1967), 404-424.
H.A.Turner, Jr., ed., Reappraisals of Fascism (N.Y., 1975).
W.Wippermann, "The Postwar German Left and Fascism," JCH, 11:4(1976), 185-220.

Abbreviations of Commonly Cited Periodicals

AHR	American Historical Review
CEH	Central European History
HZ	Historische Zeitschrift
G&G	Geschichte und Gesellschaft
JCH	Journal of Contemporary History
JIH	Journal of Interdisciplinary History
JMH	Journal of Modern History
P&P	Past and Present
SH	Social History
VjhZg	Vierteljahresheft für Zeitgeschichte

PRINCETON UNIVERSITY
Department of History

History 557

Fall Term, 1981-1982

Prof. C.E. Black
Prof. R.S. Wortman

Tuesdays, 1:30-4:30
History Seminar Room - Firestone Library

History 557 - Modern and Contemporary Russian History

I. Introduction

   1. Organization Meeting
   2. Pre-Emancipation Russia

II. Social and Economic Change 1861-1905

   3. Emancipation and the Peasant Problem
   4. Economic Structure and Growth
   5. Social Structure and Change

III. State Institutions and Political Movements 1861-1905

   6. Institutional Reforms and the Revolutionary Movement, 1861-1881
   7. Bureaucracy, Estates and Politics, 1881-1905
   8. The Revolution of 1905

IV. Industrialization and Revolution 1905-1917

   9. Between Revolutions
  10. The February Revolution
  11. The October Revolution
  12. The Civil War and Lenin's Domestic Policies
  13. Interpretations of Modern Russian History

CB:1ah 8/11/81 (20)

PRINCETON UNIVERSITY
Department of History

History 557

Modern and Contemporary Russian History

General Histories and Reference Works

Academy of Sciences of the USSR, A Short History of the USSR, by A.
  Samsonov and others (2 vols., 1965) 1626.116.5.1965
Auty, Robert, and Dmitrii Obolensky, Companion to Russian Studies, I.
  An introduction to Russian history (1976). DK 40.I54
Black, C. E., ed. Rewriting Russian History: Soviet Interpretations
  of Russia's Past (rev. ed., 1962) 1626.183
  ____, The Transformation of Russian Society: Aspects of Social Change
  Since 1861 (1960) 1630.183
Carr, E.H., A History of Soviet Russia: The Bolshevik Revolution,1917–
  1923 (3 vols., 1951–53) 1627.191.239.02; The Interrignum, 1923–24
  (1954) 1627.2.239.3; Socialism in One Country, 1924–26 (2 vols.,
  1958–59) HX313.C3; (with R. W. Davies) Foundations of a Planned
  Economy, 1926–1929 (1971) HC335.C15
Chew, A.F., An Atlas of Russian History (rev.ed. 1967) SLAV 1624.252
Florinsky, M.T., Russia: A History and An Interpretation (2 vols.1953)
  1626.352
Gilbert, Martin, Russian history atlas (1972)
Girault, René, and Marc Ferro, De la Russie àl'URSS: l'histoire de la
  Russie de 1850 à nos jours (1974) 1627.178.3795
Grinsted, Patricia, Archives and Manuscript Repositories in the USRR:
  Moscow and Leningrad (1972)
Heer, Nancy W., Politics and History in the Soviet Union(1971) 1627.22.442
Horecky, P.L., ed., Basic Russian Publications: An Annotated Bibliography
  on Russia and the Soviet Union (1962) DRB0427.476
  ____, Russia and the Soviet Union: A Bibliographic Guide to Western-
  Language Publications (1965) DRB0427.47602
Istoriia Rossii v XIX veke (9 vols., 1907–11) 1627.178.465
Kornilov, A., Modern Russian History (2 vols., 1916–17) 1627.178.495
  ____, Kurs istorii Rossii XIX veka (2vols. 1918) 1627.175.53
Kovalchenko, I.D., ed., Istochnikovedeniie istorii SSSR(1973) 1927.2.4887
Marushkin, B.I., History and politics: American historiography on Soviet
  society (1975)
Mazour, A.G., The Writing of History in the Soviet Union (1971) 1626.626.2
Pushkarev, S.G., ed.,Dictionary of Russian Historical Terms from the
  Eleventh Century to 1917 (1970) SH
Shapiro, A.L., Bibliografiia istorii SSSR (1968) 1627.2.085
Yaney, George L., The systematization of Russian government: Social
  evolution and the domestic administration of imperial Russia, 1711–19
  (1973) 7575.984

Pre-Emancipation Russia

Pintner, Walter N., Russian economic policy under Nicholas I (1967) HC 334.
Raeff, Marc, Michael Speransky: statesman of imperial Russia, 1772-1839(19!

Recommended:

Blackwell, W.L., The beginnings of Russian industrialization, 1800-1860
    (1968) HC334.B5
Crisp, Olga, "The state peasants under Nicholas I," Slavonic and East
    European Review (June 1959), 387-412
Curtiss, John S., The Russian army under Nicholas I(1965) 1627.182.7
Druzhinin, N.M., ed., Absoliutizm v Rossi, XVII-XVIII vv.(1964) 1627.16.11
Jones, Robert E., The emancipation of the Russian nobility, 1762-1785(1973.
    HT647.J65
Gleason, Abbott, European and Muscovite: Ivan Kireevski and the origins of
    Slavophilism(1972) 1627.182.52.395
Haxthausen, August von, Studies of the interior of Russia, S.F. Starr, ed.
    (1972) 1621.441.2.1972
Kabuzan, V.M. Narodonaselenie Rossii v XVIII-pervoi polovine XIX v.(1963)
    HA1431.K11
    , Izmeneniia v razmechenii naseleniia Rossii v XVIII-pervoi polovine
    XIX v. (1971
Kizevetter, A.A., "Vnutrennaia politika v tsarstvovanie Nikolaia
    Pavlovicha," in Istoriia Rossii v XIX veke, I, 169-231.
Lincoln, W. Bruce, Nicholas I (1977).
Malia, M.E., Alexander Herzen and the birth of Russian socialism, 1812-185!
    (1961) 1627.178.455.61
Mazour, A.G., The first Russian revolution. 1825: the Decembrist movement
    (1937) 1627.182.765
McGrew, R.E., Russia and the cholera, 1823-1832 (1965) 8977.253.61
McNally, R.T., Chaadayev and his friends (1971) 6210.24.809
Monas, Sidney, The third section: police and society in Russia under
    Nicholas I (1961) HV8224.M74
Pitner, W.M., "The social characteristics of the early nineteenth-century
    Russian bureaucracy," Slavic Review, XXIX (Sept. 1970) 429-443
    , "The Russian civil service on the eve of the great reform," Journal
    of Social History (Spring 1975), 55-68.
Raeff, M., Plans for political reform in imperial Russia, 1730-1905(1966)
    1626.744
    , "The Russian autocracy and its officials," Harvard Slavic Studies,
    IV, 77-91. 3013.436
Riasanovsky, Nicholas V., Nicholas I and official nationality in Russia,
    1825-1855(1959) 1627.182.765
Rogger, H.J., National consciousness in eighteenth-century Russia(1960)
    1630.781
Squire, P.S., The third department: the establishment and practices of
    the political police in the Russia of Nicholas I (1968) HV8224.559
Torke, H.J., "Das russische Beamtentum in der ersten Hälfte des 19
    Jahrhunderts," Forschungen zur osteuropäischen Geschichte, XIII
    (1967) 1626.171

-3-

184

Emancipation and the Peasant Problem

Blum, Jerome, Lord and peasant in Russia (1961) HT807.B62
Field, Daniel, The end of serfdom: nobility and bureaucracy in Russia, 1855-1861 (1976)
Gerschenkron, A., "Russia: Agrarian policies and industrialization, 1861-1917," Cambridge Economic History, VI. pt.2; or his Continuity in History and Other Essays, 140-229. HC240.G465

Recommended:

Chernukha, V.G., Krestianskii vopros i pravitelstvennoi politike Rossii 60-70gg XIX v. (1972) HD715.C5.125
Confino, Michael, Domaines et seigneurs en Russie vers le fin du XVIII siècle:études de structures agraires et de mentalités économiques (1963) HD713.C76
_____, Systèmes agraires et progrès agricole: l'assolement triennal en Russie aux XVII-XIX siècles: études d'économie et de sociologie rurales(1969) 9427.264
Druzhinin, N.M., Gosudarstvennye krestiane i reforma P.D. Kiseleva (2 v. 1946-58) HD713.D83
_____, "Pomeshch‹e› khoziaisto posle reformy 1861 g.," Istoricheskie Zapiski, 89 (1972), 187-232. 1627.2.489
Emmons, Terence, The Russian landed gentry and the peasant emancipation of 1861 (1968) HT647.E6.1968
_____, "The peasant and the emancipation," in Wayne Vucinich, ed., The Peasant in Nineteenth Century Russia (1968), 41-71. HD1536.R9V8
Kabuzan, V.M., Narodonaselenie Rossii v XVIII- pervoi polovine XIX v. (1963) HA1431.K11
_____, Izmeneniia v razmeshchenii naseleniia Rossii v XVIII -pervoi polovine XIX v. (1971)
Litvak, B.G., Russkaia derevnia v reforme 1861 goda: chernozemnyi tsentr 1861-1895 gg. (1972) HD715.L57
Nechkina, M.V., ed., Revoliutsionnaia situatsiia v Rossii v 1859-1861 gg., I (1960) introductory essay. 1627.185.116Z
Portal, R., Le statut des paysans libérés du servage, 1861-1961 (1963) HT807.P6
Rieber, Alfred J., The politics of autocracy: letters of Alexander II to Prince A. I. Bariatinskii, 1857-1864 (1966) 1627.185.118.01
Scheibert, Peter, Die russische Agrarreform von 1861: ihre Probleme und der Stand ihrer Erforschung (1973) HD715.S383
Treadgold, Donald W., The great Siberian migration: government and peasant in resettlement from emanciaption to the First World War (1957) 1717.9.
Zaionchkovsky, P.A., Otmena krepostnoga prava v Rossii (3rd ed. 1968) HT807.Z2
_____, "Sovetskaia istoriografiia reformy 1861 goda," Voprosy istorii (Feb. 1961), 85-104; Eng. summary, 221-222

-4-

Kahan, A., "Government policies and the industrialization of Russia,"
    Journal of Economic History(1967), 460-477, 836-851
Portal, Roger, "The industrialization of Russia," Cambridge economic
    History of Russia, VI(I), 801-874
Von Laue, T.H., Serge Witte and the industrialization of Russia(1963)
    HC333.V89

Recommended:

Barel, Yves, Le dévelopment économique de la Russie tsariste(1968)
Barkai, Haim, "The macro-economics of Tsarist Russia in the industrial-
    ization period: monetary developments, the balance of payments and
    the gold standard," Journal of Economic History XXXIII(June 1973)
    339-371
Bater, James H., St. Petersburg: industrialization and change(1976)
Berlin, Pavel, Russkaia burzhuaziia v staroe i novoe vremia(1972)
    HT690.R9B4
Buryshkin, P.A., Moskva kupecheskaia(1954) 1631.655.22
Crisp, Olga, Studies in the Russian Economy Before 1914(1976),
    esp. pp. 96-219
Gerschenkron, A., "The rate of industrial growth in Russia since 1885,"
    Tasks of Economic History, VII(1947),144-174
Gindin, I.F., Gosudarstvennyi bank i ekonomicheskaia politika tsarskogo
    pravitelstva, 1861-1902 gody(1960) HG186.R8G5
Girault, René, Emprunts russes et investissements français en Russie,
    1887-1914(1973)
Goldsmith, R.W., "The economic growth of tsarist Russia since 1885,"
    Economic Development and Cultural Change,IX(April 1961), 441-475
Laverychev, V. Ia., Krupnaia burzhuaziia v poreformennoi Rossii,1861-1900
    (1974) HC335.L285
Lenin, V.I., The development of capitalism in Russia (1956) HC333.L54
Lyashchenko, P., History of the national economy of Russia (1949)
McKay, J.P., Pioneers for profit: foreign entrepreneurship and Russian
    industrialization, 1885-1913(1970) HG5572.M2
Metzer, J., "Railroad developments and market integration: the case of
    Tsarist Russia," Journal of Economic History,XXXIV(Sept.1974), 529-55
Michelson, Alexandre, L'essor économique de la Russie avant la guerre de
    1914(1965) HC334.5.M45
Robbins, R.G., Jr., Famine in Russia, 1891-1892: the imperial government
    responds to a crisis(1975) HC340.F3R6
Shepelev, L.E., Aktsionernye kompanii v Rossii(1973) HD2876.S53

-5-

SOCIAL STRUCTURE AND CHANGE, 1861-1905

Gindin, I.F., "The Russian bourgeoisie in the period of capitalism:
their development and distinctive features," Soviet Studies in
History, VI (Summer, 1967) 3-50
Von Laue, T.H., "Russian labor between field and factory, 1892-1903,"
California Slavic Studies, III (1964), 33-65
Zelnik, R.E., Labor and society in Tsarist Russia: the factory workers of
St. Petersburg, 1855-1870 (1971) HD8526.245

Recommended:

Anderson, Barbara A., Internal migration in a modernizing society: the
case of late nineteenth century European Russia (1974) P685.1974.123
Anderson, B., Coale, A., Harm, E., Human Fertility in Russia since the
Nineteenth Century (Princeton, 1979)
Brower, Daniel, "L'urbanization russe a la fin du XIX siecle,"
Annales, Economies, Societes, Civilizations, (Jan-Feb,1977) pp.
70-86. (Hl A5721)
Field, Daniel, Rebels in the name of the tsar (1976)
Guroff, G., and S.F. Starr, "A note on literacy in Russia, 1890-1914,"
Jahrbücher für Geschichte Osteuropas, XIX (1971) 520-531
Hamm, M.F., ed., The city in Russian history (1976)
Johnson, Robert, Peasant and Proletarian: The Working Class of Moscow in
the Late Nineteenth Century (1979)
Johnson, W.H.E., Russia's educational heritage (1950) 6863.501
Kerblay, B.H., L'isba d'hier et d'aujourd'hui (1963)
Korelin, A.P., Dvorianstvo v poreformennoi Rossii, 1861-1904 (1979)
Korkunov, N.M., Russko e gosudarstvennoe pravo (2 v. 1909) 7605.536.11
Lavrychev, V. Ia., Krupnaia burzhuazia v perforemennoi Rossii 1861-1900
(1974)
Leikina-Svirskaia, V.R., Intelligentsiia v Rossii vo vtoroi polovine XIX
veka (1971) HD9038.R9L43
Leroy-Beaulieu, A., The empire of the Tsars and the Russians (3rd ed. vols.
1621.575
Rashin, A.G., Naselenie Rossii za 100 let, 1811-1913 (1956) HB3604.R18
Rieber, A., "The Moscow entrepreneurial group: The emergence of a new
form of autocratic politics," Jahrbücher für Geschichte Osteuropas,
XXV (1977), 1-20, 174-99.
Sinel, Allan A., Classroom and chancellery: state and educational reform
in Russia under Count Dmitry Tolstoi (1973) LA831.7.S5
Smolitsch, Igor, Geschichte der russischen Kirche, 1700-1917 (1964)
5446.8637
Tugan-Baranovsky, M.I., The Russian factory in the nineteenth century
(3rd ed. 1970) HD2356.R9T8513.1970
Vucimich, A., Science in Russian culture, 1861-1917 (1970) 8014.947
, Social thought in Tsarist Russia: the quest for a general science
of society, 1861-1917 (1976)
Wallace, D.M., Russia (rev. ed. 1912 [1970]) 1621.953.12

Starr, S.F., Decentralization and self-government in Russia, 1830-1870
    (1972) 7575.875
Wortman, R.S., The development of Russian legal consciousness (1976)

Recommended:

Abbott, R.J., Police reform in Russia, 1858-1878(1970) P685.1971.111
Amburger, Erik, Geschichte der Behördenörganisation Russlands von Peter
    dem Grossen bis 1917 (1966) 7575.122
Balmuth, D., "Origins of the Russian press reform of 1865," Slavonic
    and East European Review, XLVII(July 1961), 369-388
Byrnes, R.F., Pobedonostsev: his life and thought(1968) 1627.178.727.231
Chernukha, V.G., Vnutrenniaia politika tsarizma s serediny 50kh do
    nachala 80 gg. XIX v. (1978)
Czap, P., "Peasant-class courts and peasant customary justice in Russia,
    1861-1912," Journal of Social History, I (Winter 1967), 149-178
Garmiza, V.V., Podgotovka zemskoi reformy 1864 goda (1957) HD713.G18
Kaiser, F.B., Die russische Justizreform von 1864 (1972) 7942.5087
Miller, Forrest A., Dmitrii Miliutin and the reform era in Russia(1968)
    1627.178.643.644
Petrovich, M.B., The emergence of Russian Panslavism, 1856-1870(1956)
    1627.185.712
Pomper, Philip, Peter Lavrov and the Russian revolutionary movement(1972)
    1627.185.568.729
    , The Russian revolutionary intelligentsia(1970) HA7523.P674
Ruud, D., "The Russian empire's new censorship law of 1865, "Canadian
    Slavic Studies III(1969), 235-245
Venturi, F., Roots of Revolution (1960) 1627.178.932.11
Vilenskii, B.V., Sudebnaia reforma i kontrreforma v Rossii(1969) 7942.936
Walicki, A., The Controversy over Capitalism(1969) HX312.W28
Weeks, Albert L., The first Bolshevik: a political biography of Peter
    Tkachev(1968) HX312.T55W4
Woehrlin, William F., Chernyshevski: the man and the journalist
    1627.185.25.981
Wortman, R.S., The crisis of Russian populism(1967) HX312.W6.1967
Zaionchkovskii, P.A., Krizis samoderzhaviia na rubezhe 1870-1880 godov
    (1964) 1627.185.991.2

_7_

Haimson, L., The Russian Marxists and the origins of Bolshevism (1955)
1627.178.426
Radkey, O.H., The agrarian foes of Bolshevism (1958), Chaps. I-III
1627.191.744.2
Timberlake, C.E., ed., Essays on Russian liberalism (1972) 1627.178.331

Recommended:

Ascher, Abraham, Pavel Axelrod and the development of Menshevism (1972)1627.189.
Baron, Samuel H., Plekhanov: the father of Russian Marxism (1963) 1136.133.
HX311.P72B2
Besançon, Alain, Le tsarévitch immolé: la symbolisme de la loi dans la
culture russe (1967) 1630.172
Billington, James H., Mikhailovsky and Russian populism (1958) 1627.178.642.1
Byrnes, R.F., Pobedonostev: his life and thought (1968) 1627.178.727.231
Eroshkin, N.P., Istoriia gosudarstvennykh uchrezhdenii dorevoliutsionnoi
Rossii (1968) 7575.331
Frieden, Nancy M., "The Russian cholera epidemic, 1892-93, and medical
professionalization," Journal of Social History, X(1973) 1627.189.375
Galai, S., The liberation movement in Russia, 1900-1905 (1973)
Kazakevich, R.A. and F.M. Suslova, Mister Paips falsifitsiruet istoriiu
(1966) HX311.P66K3
Keep, J., The rise of social democracy in Russia (1963) 1627.189.515
Lane, David, The roots of Russian communism: a social and historical study
of Russian social democracy 1898-1907 (1969) HX312.L17
Pipes, Richard, Social democracy and the St. Petersburg labor movement
1885-1897 (1963) HX311.P66
_____, "Russian conservatism in the second half of the nineteenth century,"
Slavic Review, XXX(March 1971)
_____, Struve: liberal on the left (1970) 1627.189.887.722
Pirumova, N.M., Zemskoe liberalnoe dvizhenie: sotsialnye korni i
evoliutsiia do nachala XX veka (1977)
Robbins, R.G., Famine in Russia, 1891-1892: the imperial government
responds to a crisis (1975)
Rogger, Hans, "Russia," The European right: a historical profile, H. Rogger
and E. Weber, eds. (1965), 443-500 7560.781
_____, "Reflections on Russian conservatism 1861-1905," Jahrbücher für
Geschichte Osteuropas (1966), 195-212
Sakharova, L.G., Zemskaia kontreeforma 1890g (1968) 7592.991
Sidel'nikov,S.M. Agrarnaia politika samoderzhaviia v period imperializma(1980)
Solovev, Iu.B., Samoderzhavie i dvorianstvo v konste XIX veka (1973)
1627.178.865
Stites, Richard, The Women's Liberation Movement in Russia (1978)
Tvardovskaia, V.A. Ideologiia poreformennogo samoderzhaviia; M.N.
Katkov i ego izdaniia (Moscow, 1978)
Venturi, F., Roots of revolution: a history of the populist and socialist
movements in nineteenth century Russia (1960) 1627.178.932.11
Wildman, Allan K., The making of a workers' revolution: Russian social
democracy, 1891-1903 (1967) 1627.189.9475
Zaionchkovskii, P.A., Rossiiskoe samoderzhavie v kontse XIX stoletie:
politicheskaia reaktsia 80kh--nachala 90kh godov (1970) 7575.992
_____, Pravitelstvennyi apparat samoderzhavnoi Rossii v XIX v. (1978)

The Revolution of 1905

Melinger, Howard, and John M. Thompson, Count Witte and the Tsarist government in the 1905 revolution (1972) 1627.189.95.628

Scharz, Solomon, The Russian revolution of 1905: the workers' movement and the formation of Bolshevism and Menschevism (1967) 1627.189.84

Recommended:

Chermenskii, E.D., Burzhuaziia i tsarizm v pervoi russkoi revoliutsii (2nd ed. 1970) 1627.189.2545

Demochkin, N.N., Sovety 1905 goda--organy revoliutsionnoi vlasti (1963) 1627.189.292

Dubrovskii, S.M., Krestianskoe dvizhenie v revoliutsii 1905-1907 gg. (1956) 1627.189.313

Fischer, A., Russische Sozialdemokratie und bewaffnete Aufstand im Jahre 1905 (1963) 1627.189.345

Harcave, Sidney, First blood: the Russian revolution of 1905 (1964) 1627.189.432

Hildermeier, Manfred, Die Sozialrevolutionare Partei Russlands (1979)

Kindersley, Richard, The first Russian revisionists: a study of "legal Marxism" in Russia (1962) HX311.K57

Larsson, R., Theories of revolution: from Marx to the first Russian revolution (1970) 7532.564

Macey, David, A.C., "The peasantry, the agrarian problem, and the revolution of 1905-1907," Columbia Essays in International Affairs, VII (1971), 1-35 PITN 451.261

Mendel, Arthur P., Dilemmas of progress in tsarist Russia: legal Marxism and legal populism (1961) HX311.M52

Perrie, Maureen, "The Russian peasant movement of 1905-1907; its social composition and revolutionary significance," Past and Present, No. 57 (Nov. 1972), 123-155

_____, The Agrarian Policy of the Russian Socialist-Revolutionary Party, (1976)

Sablinsky, Walter N., The road to Bloody Sunday: Father Gapon and the St. Petersburg massacre of 1905 (1976)

Schneiderman, Jeremiah, Sergei Zubatov and revolutionary Marxism: the struggle for the working class in tsarist Russia (1976)

Sodorov, A.L., ed., Vyshii podem revoliutsii 1905-1907 gg. (3 v.1955-56) 1627.189.113.2

Treadgold, D. W., Lenin and his rivals: the struggle for Russia's future, 1898-1906 (1975) 1627.189.912

Tobias, Henry J., The Jewish Bund in Russia from its origins to 1905 (1972) HD8537.042T6

Trotsky, L., 1905 (1971) 1627.189.913.1971

-9-

Between Revolutions, 1905-1917

Black, C. E., "The nature of imperial Russian society," The development
  of the USSR (1964), 173-208
Hosking, G.A., The Russian constitutional experiment: government and Duma
  1907-1914 (1973) 7575.475

Recommended:

Anfimov, A.M., Rossiiskaia derevnia v gody pervoi mirovoi voiny (1914-
  fevral ' 1917 g. (1962) HD 1992.A65
Atkinson, Dorothy, "The statistics on the Russian land commune 1905-1917,"
  Slavic Review, XXXII (1973), 773-787
Avrekh, Aron Ia., Stolypin i tretia Duma (1968) 1627.189.883.186
Diakin, V.S., Samoderzhavie, burhauziia, i dvorianstvo (1978)
____, "Stolypin i dvorianstvo," Problemy krestianskogo zemlevladeniia
  i vnutrennii politiki Rossii (1972), 231-274. (xerox)
FitzLyon, K., and T. Browning, Before the Revolution: A View of Russia
  under the Last Tsar (1977).
Haimson, L., Ed. The Politics of Rural Russia, 1905-1914 (1979), "The
  problem of social stability in urban Russia, 1905-1917," Slavic Review,
  XXIII (Dec. 1964), 619-642; XXIV (March 1965), 1-56; XXIV (Sept. 1965)
  552-527.
Hamm, Michael R., "Liberal politics in wartime Russia: an analysis of the
  Progressive Bloc," Slavic Review, XXXIII (Sept. 1974), 453-468
Hennessy, Richard, The Agrarian Question in Russia, 1905-1917
Kokovtsov, V.N., Out of my past (1935) 1627.189.523
Laverychev, V. Ia., Po tu storonu barrikad: iz istorii borby moskovskoi
  burzhuazii s revoliutsiei (1967) 1627.191.645
Levin, Alfred, The second Duma (1940) 1627.189.582
____, The third Duma: election and profile (1973) 7575.5819
Maklakov, V.A., The First State Duma (1964) 1627.189.612.11
Miller, Margaret, The economic development of Russia, 1905-1914 (2nd ed.
  1967) HC334.5M5.1967
Milyukov, P. Political memories, 1905-1915 (1967) 1627.189.643.03
Nötzold, Jürgen, Wirschaftspolitische Alternativen der Entwicklung Russlands
  in der Ära Witte und Stolypin (1966) HC334.5.N6
Oberlaender, Erwin, ed., Russia enters the twentieth century, 1894-1917
  (1971) 1627.189.79597.1971
Owen, L.A., The Russian peasant movement, 1906-1917 (1937)1627.189.643.692
Pinchuk, B.C., The Octobrists and the third Duma, 1907-1912 (1974)
  1627.189.717
Roosa, R., "Russian industrialists look to the future: thoughts on
  economic development, 1905-1917," Essays in Russian and Soviet History,
  J.S. Curtiss, ed., (1963) 1627.189.7965
Shanin, T., The awkward class: Political sociology of peasantry in a
  developing society: Russia 1910-1925(1972), Chapters 1-7 HN523.545
Stavrou, T.D., ed., Russia under the last tsar (1969) 1627.189.7965
Stone, Norman, The eastern front, 1914-1917 (1976)

-10-

James T. Shotwell, gen. ed., <u>Economic and Social History of the World War.</u>

<u>Russian Series</u>, Carnegie Endowment for International Peace

*   *   *   *   *

Antsyferov, A. N., <u>Russian agriculture during the war</u> (1930) HD713. R89

Florinsky, M. T., <u>The end of the Russian empire</u> (1931) 1627. 2. 351

Golovin, N. N., <u>The Russian army in the world war</u> (1931) 14094. 16. 04. 399

Gronsky, P., et al., <u>The war and the Russian government</u> (1929) 1627.189. 947

Kayden, M., et al., <u>The cooperative movement in Russia during the war</u> (1929) HD3512. K18

Kon, S., et al., <u>The cost of the war to Russia</u> (1932) HB3604. C82

Mikhelson, A., <u>Russian public finances during the war</u> (1928) HJ1207. R92

Nolde, B. E., <u>Russia in the economic war</u> (1928) HC333. N7

Odinetz, D. M., et al., <u>Russian schools and universities in the world war</u> (1929) 14094. 58. 795

Polner, T. I., <u>Russian local government during the war and the union of zemstvos</u> (1930) 7592. 731

Struve, P. B., et al., <u>Food supply in Russia during the world war</u> (1930) HD9015. R9S9

Zagorskii, S. O., <u>State control of industry in Russia during the war</u> (1928) HD3616. R9Z2

-11-

The February Revolution

Ferro, Marc, The Russian revolution of February 1917 (1972)1627.191.3457
Rabinowitch, A., Prelude to revolution: the Petrograd Bolsheviks and the July 1917 uprising (1968) 1631.577.72

Recommended:

Anweiler, Oskar, The soviets: the Russian workers, peasants and soldiers councils 1905-1921 (1975) HX313.A713.1975
Bonwetsch, Bernd, Kriegsallianz und Wirtschaftsinteressen: Russland in den Wirtschaftsplänen Englands und Frankreichs, 1914-1917 (1973) HF3495.364.1973
Burdzhalov, E.N., Vtoraia russkaia revoliutsiia: vosstanie v Petrograde (1967) 1627.191.226.2
_____, Vtoraia russkaia revoliutsiia: Moskva, front, periferiia (1971) 1627.191.226.03
Chamberlin, W.H., The Russian revolution (2 vols., 1935) 1627.2.249.3.1954
Diakin, V.S., Russkaia burzhuaziia i tsarizm v gody pervoi mirovoi voiny, 1914-1917 (1967) 1627.189.298
Hasegawa, Tsuyoshi, "The formation of the militia in the February revolution: an aspect of the origins of dual power," Slavic Review, XXXII (June 1973), 303-322
Katkov, George, Russia, 1917: the February revolution (1967) 1627.191.515
Kerensky, A.F., Russia and history's turning point (1965) 1627.2.519.2
_____, and P.R. Browder, The Russian provisional government of 1917: documents (3v. 1961) 1627.191.214
Mints, I.I., Istoriia velikogo oktabria (2 v. 1967) 1627.191.645
_____, ed., Sverzhenie samoderzhaviia (1970) 1627.191.8935
Pipes, Richard, ed., Revolutionary Russia (1968) 1627.191.264
Riha, Thomas, A Russian European: Paul Milyukov in Russian politics (1969) 1627.189.643.77
Rosenberg, William G., Liberals in the Russian revolution: the Constitutional Democratic party, 1917-1921 (1974) 7575.7826
Sukhanov, N.N. The Russian Revolution, 1917; a personal record 1627.191.744.2
Volobuev, P.B., Ekonomicheskaia politika vremennogo pravitelstva (1962) HC333.V88
Wildman, Allan, The End of the Russian Imperial Army, I, (1980) DK265.9.A6W54

-12-

The October Revolution

Rabinowitch, Alexander, The Bolsheviks come to power: the Russian
revolution of 1917 in Petrograd (1976)
Sobolev, P.M., ed., History of the October revolution
(1966) 1627.191.116.2
Keep, John, The Russian Revolution: A Study of Mass Mobilization
(1976). DK265.K36

Recommended:

Avdeev, N., ed., Revoliutsiia 1917 goda: khronika sobytii
(6 vols. 1923-30) DK265.13.R47
Carr, E.H., The Bolshevik revolution, 1917-1923 (3v., 1951-53)
1627.191.239.02
Daniels, Robert V., Red October: the Bolshevik revolution of 1917
(1967) 1627.2.283.2
Deutscher, Isaac, The prophet armed: Trotsky, 1879-1921
(1954) 1627.2.577.34
Fischer, Louis, The life of Lenin (1964) 1627.2.577.34
Golikov, G.N., and M.I. Kuznetsov, eds., Velikaia Oktiabrskaia
sotialisticheskaia revoliutsiia: Entsiklopediia (1977)
Istoriia kommunisticheskoi partii sovetskogo soiuza (I-III, 1964-68,
covers 1883-1920) 7575.654
Lenin, V.I., State and revolution (1932) 1627.2.577.06.11
Melgunov, S.P., The Bolshevik seizure of power (1972)
1627.191.632.1972
Mints, I.I., Istoriia velikago oktabria. II. Sverzhenie
vremennogo pravitelstva. Ustanovlenie diktatury proletariata
(1968) 1627.191.645
Radkey, O.H., The election of the Russian constitutent assembly
of 1917 (1958) 1627.191.744
_____, The agrarian foes of Bolshevism: promise and default
of the Russian Socialist Revolutionaries, February to October.
1917 (1958) 1627.191.744.2
Reed, John, Ten days that shook the world (1919) 1627.191.753
Reiman, Mikhail, Russkaia revoliutsiia, 23 fevralia-25 oktabria
1917 (2 v., Prague 1968)
Sukhanov, N.N., The Russian revolution, 1917: a personal record
(1955) 1627.191.891
Tucker, Robert C., ed., The Lenin anthology (1975) 1621.2.577.0914
_____, Stalin as revolutionary, 1879-1929: a study in history and
personality (1973) 1627.2.874.916
Ulricks, Teddy, "The 'crowd' in the Russian revolution: towards
reassessing the nature of revolutionary leadership," Politics
and Society, IV (Spring 1974), 397-413
Wade, Rex, "The rajonnye sovety of Petrograd: the role of local
political bodies in the Russian revolution," Jahrbücher für
Geschichte Osteuropas, XX(1972), 227-240
_____, The Russian search for peace, February-October 1917
(1969), 1627.2.951

-13-

Civil War and Intervention

Kenez, Peter, Civil war in South Russia, 1918 (1971) 1627.191.517
Luckett, R., The White generals: an account of the White movement
   and the Russian civil war (1971) 1627.191.529

Recommended:

Boersner, D., The Bolsheviks and the national and colonial
   question, 1917-1928 (1957) 7558.191
Bradley, John, Allied intervention in Russia (1968) 1627.191.206
Brinkley, G.A., The volunteer army and the Allied intervention in
   South Russia, 1917-1921 (1966) 1627.191.211
Chamberlin, W.. The Russian revolution (1935), V. 1, 335-427;
   V. 2 1627.2.249.3
Deutscher, Isaac, The prophet armed: Trotsky, 1879-1921 (1954),
   325-522 1627.2.914.9925
Ellis, C.H., The British "intervention" in Transcaspia, 1918-1919
   (1963) 1627.191.323
Footman, David, Civil war in Russia (1961) 1627.191.206
Haimson, Leopold H., ed., The Mensheviks from the revolution of
   1917 to the second World War (1975)
Kazemzadeh, Firuz, The struggle for Transcaucasia, 1917-1921
   (1951) 1711.514
Kennan, George F., Russia leaves the war (1956) 1627.2.5185
Kritsman, L., Geroicreskii period velikoi russkoi revoliutsii (1924)
   1627.191.5435
Lerner, Warren, Karl Radek: the last internationalist (1970)
   HX312.R364.1970
Lindemann, Albert S., The 'red years': European socialism versus
   Bolshevism. 1919-1921 (1974)
Pipes, Richard, ed., Revolutionary Russia (1968), articles by Keep,
   Erickson, Meyer, 180-281. 1627.191.264
Radkey, O.H., The unknown civil war in Soviet Russia: a study of
   the Green movement in the Tambov region, 1920-1921 (1976)
Reshetar, John S., Jr., The Ukrainian revolution, 1917-1920 (1952)
   16386.761
Ritter, G., Das Kommunemodell und die Begründung der Roten Armee
   im Jahre 1918 (1965) 1627.2.775
Silverlight, John, The victors' dilemma: allied intervention in
   the Russian civil war. 1917-1920 (1970) 1627.191.8565
Strakhovsky, L.I., Intervention in Archangel (1944) 14094.93.883
Suny, R.G., The Baku commune, 1917-1918: class and nationality in
   the Russian revolution (1972) 1711.41.891
Thompson, John M., Russia, Bolshevism, and the Versailles Peace
   (1966) 14094.28.904
Ullman, Richard H., Anglo-Soviet relations, 1917-1921 (3 v. 1962-72)
   1457.794.92

Lenin's Domestic Policies

Carr, E.H., The Bolshevik revolution, 1917-1923 (3v. 1951-53)
I and II. 1627.191.239.02
Daniels, R.V., The conscience of the revolution: Communist
opposition in Soviet Russia (1960) 1627.2.283

Recommended:

Avrich, Paul, The Russian anarchists (1967) HX914.A9
_____, ed., The anarchists in the Russian revolution (1973)
1627.191.1365
_____, Kronstadt 1921 (1973) 1627.2.137
Bettelheim, Charles, Les Luttes des classes en URSS: première
période 1917-1923 (1974) 1627.2.1773
Carrère d'Encausse, H. L'Union soviétique de Lénine à Staline,
1917-1953 (1972) 1627.2.2393
Cohen, Stephen F., Bukharin and the Bolshevik revolution: a
political biography, 1888-1938 (1973) 1627.2.224.261
Fitzpatrick, Sheila, The commissariat of enlightenment: Soviet
organization of education and the arts under Lunacharsky,
October 1917-1921 (1970) 6863.351
Gorodetsky, E.N., Rozhdenie sovetskogo gosudarstva 1917-1918 (1965)
7575.402
Iroshnikov, M.P., Predsedatel soveta narodnykh kommisarov
Vladimir Ulianov: ocherki gosudarstvennoi deiatelnosti
1917-1918 (1974) 7575.4915.2
Lewin, Moshe, Lenin's last struggle (1968) 1627.2.5828
Liebman, Marcel, Leninism under Lenin (1975) French ed. HX312.643653)
Lorenz, Richard, Die Anfänge der bolschewistischen Industriepolitik
(1965) HC335.2.L6
Male, D.J., Russian peasant organization before collectivization
(1971) HD715.M2243
Pietsch, Walter, Revolution Und Staat: Institutionen als Träger
der Macht in Sowjetrassland (1917-1922) (1969) 7575.719
Pipes, Richard, The formation of the Soviet Union: communism and
nationalism 1917-1923 (rev. ed. 1964) 1627.2.722.11
Radkey, O.H., The sickle under the hammer: the Russian socialist
revolutionaries in the early months of Soviet rule (1963)1627.191.744.3
Rigby, T.H., Lenin's Government; Sovnarkom 1917-1922
Schapiro, Leonard, The origin of Communist autocracy: political
opposition in the Soviet State. First phase, 1917-1922 (1965)
1627.101.811
Venediktov, A.V., Organizatsia gosudarstvennoi promyshlennosti v SSSR
1917-1920 (1957) V. I HC335.V4

-15-

Interpretations

Billington, J. H., "Six views of the Russian revolution," World Politics,
(April 1966), 452-473.   XVIII
Black, C. E., ed., The transformation of Russian society (1960),
661-680.
Carr, E. H., "The Russian revolution: its place in history,"
The October revolution (1969), 1-33, 1627.191.239.01
Krupina, T. D., "The theory of 'modernization' and certain problems
in the development of Russia in the late nineteenth and early
twentieth centuries," trans. from Istoriia SSSR, No. 1
(1971), 191-205.
"50th anniversary of the great October socialist revolution:
theses of the central committee of the C.P.S.U.,"
Current Digest of the Soviet Press (July 12, 19, 1976).

Recommended:

Istoriia   Kommunisticheskoi partii Sovetskogo Soluza (Moscow:
Izd. Politicheskaia Literatura, 1973 [Izd. 4-oe, dop.]),
225-230, 7575.49204.1973.
Iz glabiny: sbornik statei o russkoi revoliutsii (Moscow 1918;
reprint Paris 1968) 1627.191.753.
Keep, J. H. L., "The achievements of the Russian revolution,"
R. H. B. Lockhart, The two revolutions: an eyewitness study
of Russia, 1917 (1967) 1627.191.572.
McNeal, Robert H., ed., The Russian revolution: why did the Bolsheviks
win? (1969).
Medvedev, Roy, On socialist democracy (1975) 7549.627.1975.
Moscow, Institut Marksizma-Leninizma pri TsK KPSS. Istoriia
Kommunisticheskoi partii Sovetskogo Soluza (mart 1917-
mart 1918 gg.), Tom 3-ii, kinga 1-aia, 7575.654.
Poltoratzky, Nikolai P., "The Vekhi dispute and the significance
of Vekhi," Canadian Slavonic Papers, IX (1967), 86-106.
Schapiro, Leonard, "The Vekhi group and the mystique of revolution,"
Slavonic and East European Review, XXXIV (Dec. 1955),
56-76, 0901.S362.
Solzhenitsyn, A., ed., From under the rubble (1975) 1627.22.368.
Uldricks, Teddy, "Petrograd revisited: new views of the Russian
revolution," The History Teacher, VIII (August 1975),
611-623.
Vekhi (Rn. ed., 1912) 3024.9313
Vekhi (Signposts) DK32.7xV4 Eng. trans. with commentaries by
Schapiro and Poltoratzky.

THE RUSSIAN INTELLIGENTSIA

History 201
Fall Semester 1976

M. A. Miller
207 E. Duke University

Requirement: research paper due at end of the semester

Topics and Readings

I. The Intelligentsia: Origins
    Raeff, Origins of the Russian Intelligentsia
    Recommended: M. Confino, "Apropos de la noblesse russe,"
                 Annales (Nov.-Dec., 1967), pp. 1163-1205.

II. The Intelligentsia: Development, Evolution and Dynamics
    Pomper, Russian Revolutionary Intelligentsia

III. The First Generation: The Fathers
    Raeff (ed.), Russian Intellectual History
        Chaadaev, pp. 159-173
        Kireevsky, pp. 174-207
        Belinsky, pp. 252-261
    Recommended: R. McNally's biography of Chaadaev;
                 A. Gleason's biography of Kireevsky; and
                 H. Bowman's biography of Belinsky.

IV. Literature of the First Generation
    Turgenev, "Rudin" and "On the Eve" (in separate editions
        or Vintage Turgenev, vol. II)
    Recommended: Dobroliubov, "When Will the Real Day Come?,"
                 R. Matlaw (ed.), Belinsky, Chernyshevsky,
                 Dobroliubov: Selected Criticism.

V. The Second Generation: The Sons
    Dobroliubov, "The Organic Development of Man," Raeff (ed.),
        Russian Intellectual History, pp. 262-287.
    Kropotkin, "Must We Occupy Ourselves" (pp. 46-116) and
        "The Russian Revolutionary Party" (pp. 134-159) in
        Selected Writings on Anarchism and Revolution.
    Recommended: Venturi, Roots of Revolution; Lampert,
                 Sons Against Fathers; Miller, Kropotkin

VI. Literature of the Second Generation (I)
    Turgenev, Fathers and Sons. Also, Pisarev's review
        "Bazarov" (195-218) and "Apropos of Fathers and Sons"
        (169-177).
    Recommended: Chernyshevsky, What is to be Done?;
                 Dostoevsky, Notes from Underground.

VII. Literature of the Second Generation (II)
    Dostoevsky, The Possessed.

2

VIII. The Third Generation: Marxism in Russia
Haimson, The Russian Marxists, pp. 3-114.

IX. Literature of the Third Generation
M. Gorky, Mother

X. Revolt from Within
"Vekhi," Canadian Slavic Studies,
II, 2 (Summer 1968), 151-174
II, 3 (Fall 1968), 291-310
II, 4 (Winter 1968), 447-463
III, 1 (Spring 1969), 1-21
III, 3 (Fall 1969), 494-515
Trotsky, "Concerning the Intelligentsia," Partisan Review,
Fall, 1968

XI. Literature of the Inter-Revolutionary Period (1905-1917)
Belyi, St. Petersburg

XII. The Dilemma of the Soviet Intelligentsia
Daedalus, 1960 (Summer), pp. 487-502 (Pipes), 503-519
(Labedz), 648-666 (letter to Pasternak from editors
of Novyi Mir on Dr. Zhivago).

XIII. Theory of the Russian Intelligentsia
Nahirny, "The Russian Intelligentsia," Comparative Studies
in Society and History, IV, 4 (July, 1962), 403-435.
Malia, "What is the Intelligentsia?," Daedalus, Summer,
1960, pp. 441-458.
Confino, "On Intellectuals," Daedalus, Spring, 1972.

XIV. Intellectuals and Intelligentsia
Shils, "Intellectuals and the Powers," Rieff (ed.), On
Intellectuals, pp. 25-48.
Mannheim, Ideology and Utopia, pp. 153-164 (hardback,
pp. 136-146).
Geertz, "Ideology as a Cultural System," Apter (ed.),
Ideology and Discontent, pp. 47-76. Reprinted in
C. Geertz, The Interpretation of Cultures, pp. 193-233.
Eisenstadt, "Intellectuals and Tradition," Daedalus,
Spring, 1972, pp. 1-20.

SELECTED BIBLIOGRAPHY

I. Studies on Intellectuals

J. Agree, "Religion and the Intellectuals." Partisan Review, February, 1950, 106´113 (a symposium).

R. Aron, The Opium of the Intellectuals.

J. Barzun, House of Intellect.

M. Beloff, The Intellectual in Politics.

J. Benda, Treason of the Intellectuals.

Randolf S. Bourne, War and Intellectuals, Collected Essays, 1915-19/

V. Brombert, "Toward a Portrait of the French Intellectual," Partisan Review, Summer, 1960, 480-502. (This article also forms chapter 2 of Brombert's book, The Intellectual Hero, 20-40. See also his bibliography in this book, 239-250, dealing mainly with the treatment of intellectuals in French literature).

D. Caute, Communism and the French Intellectuals.

L. Coser, Men of Ideas (pp. 157-170 on Bolshevik intellectuals as professional revolutionaries).

M. Cunliffe, "The Intellectuals: The U.S.," Encounter, May, 1955, 23-33.

Lewis S. Feuer, "The Political Linguistics of 'Intellectual,' 1898-1918," Survey. Winter 1971. Vol. 16, No. 1, 156-183.

J. Fischer, "Intellectual with a Gun," Harper's Magazine, February, 1956, 10-18. (See also in the same issue R. L. Bruckberger, "An Assignment for Intellectuals," 68-72.)

N. Glazer, "Revolutionism and The Jews: The Role of the Intellectuals," Commentary. February, 1971, pp. 55-61.

Cesar Grana, Modernity and its Discontents.

John Harrison, The Reactionaries: A Study of the Anti-Democratic Intelligentsia (Yeats, Pound, Lawrence, etc.)

R. Hofstadter, Anti-Intellectualism in American Life.

H. S. Hughes, Consciousness and Society (espec. Chapt. 10).

J. Huizinga, Homo Ludens (see also Dahrendorf's essay in Rieff, On Intellectuals).

G. B. de Huszar (ed.), The Intellectuals [espec. articles by Lafargue (322-327), Gorky (233-238), Stalin (407-410), Kautsky (328-337), Noman (338-345).

A. Koestler, "The Intelligentsia," The Yogi and the Commissar.

L. Krieger, "The Intellectuals and European Society," Political Science Quarterly, June, 1952; (Reprinted in R. J. Scally (ed.), Forces of Order and Movement in Europe Since 1815.)

C. Lasch, The New Radicalism in America, 1889-1963: The Intellectual as a Social Type.

S. M. Lipset, Political Man (espec. "American Intellectuals: Their Politics and Status," pp. 332-371).

K. Mannheim, Ideology and Utopia (espec. pp. 153-164).

R. K. Merton, "Role of the Intellectual in Public Bureaucracy," Social Theory and Social Structure.

R. Michels, "Intellectuals," Encyclopedia of the Soc. Sci. (1932 ed.) VIII, 118-126 (with full bibliography).

T. Molnar, The Decline of the Intellectual.
L. Namier, Revolution of the Intellectuals (the 1848 Revolutions).
C. Cruise O'Brien (ed.), Power and Consciousness (essays by Nettl, Chomsky, Kolko, and others on intellectuals and political power, primarily in context of recent American history).
P. Rieff, (ed.), On Intellectuals (Parsons, Shils, Nettl).
D. Riesman, T. Parsons, et al., "Comments on American Intellectuals," Daedalus, Summer, 1959.
F. K. Ringer, The Decline of the German Mandarins: The German Academic Community, 1890-1933 (espec. the introduction, pp. 1-13, for theoretical discussion of the mandarin and his ideology).
E. Shils, "Intellectuals," International Encyclopedia of the Social Sciences (1968 ed.), VII, 399-415 (see also in the same volume this author's related article, "The Concept and Function of Ideology," pp. 66-76).
_____, "Ideology and Civility: On the Politics of the Intellectual," Sewanee Review, 66, 450-480.
_____, "The Intellectuals and the Powers: Some Perspectives for Comparative Analysis," Comparative Studies in Society and History, I, No. 1, 1958 (also included in Rieff, On Intellectuals, pp. 25-48) (Reprinted in Selected Papers of Edward Shils, vol. I).
K. von Beyme, "Intellectuals, Intelligentsia," Marxism, Communism and Western Society, IV, 301-312 (with bibliography).
M. Weber, "Intellectualism, Intellectuals and the History of Religion," The Sociology of Religion.
_____, "The Litearti," The Religion of China (also in From Max Weber, ed., by Gerth and Mills, as "The Chinese Literati").
F. Znaniecki, The Social Role of the Man of Knowledge.

II. Studies on the Russian Intelligentsia (in English)

P. Avrich, "Anti-Intellectualism and Anarchism," The Russian Anarchists, 91-119.
N. Berdiaev, Origin of Russian Communism (espec. chapt. 1: "Formation of the Russian Intelligentsia and its Character").
I. Berlin, Introduction to F. Venturi, Roots of Revolution [also in A. E. Adams (ed.), Imperial Russia after 1861 (Heath), 1-181].
_____, "The Marvellous Decade," Encounter, June, Nov., Dec. (1955), May (1956).
J. Billington, "The Intelligentsia and the Religion of Humanity," American Historical Review, 1960, 807-821.
A. Blok, "The People and the Intelligentsia"; "The Intelligentsia and the Revolution," Raeff (ed.), Russian Intellectual History, 358-371.
P. Boborykin, "Nihilism in Russia," Fortnightly Review, 1868, No. 20, 117-138.
H. Bowman, "The Intelligentsia in 19th Century Russia," Slavic and East European Journal, 1957, 5-21.
D. Brower, "The Problem of the Russian Intelligentsia," Slavic Review, Dec. 1967, 638-647.
_____, "Fathers, Sons and Grandfathers: Social Origins of Radical Intellectuals in 19th Century Russia," Journal of Social History, Vol. 2, No. 4, Summer, 1969, 333-355.

_____, Training the Nihilists.
M. Confino, "Histoire et psychologie," Annales, Nov.-Dec., 1967, 1163-1205 (review of Raeff's Origins).
A. Gershenkron, "The Problem of Economic Development in Russian Intellectual History of the 19th Century," E. J. Simmons (ed.), Continuity and Change in Russian and Soviet Thought.
G. Fischer, "The Intelligentsia and Russia," C. Black (ed.), The Transformation of Russian Society, 253-274.
_____, Russian Liberalism: From Gentry to Intelligentsia.
_____, "The Russian Intelligentsia and Liberalism," Harvard Slavic Studies, IV (1957), 317-336.
A. McConnell, "Origin of the Russian Intelligentsia," Slavic and East European Journal, VIII, Spring, 1964.
J. Maynard, "The Intellectuals and the Worship of the Plain Folk," Russia in Flux.
M. Miller, "Ideological Conflicts in Russian Populism," Slavic Review, March, 1970, 1-21.
V. Nahirny, "The Russian Intelligentsia: From Men of Ideas to Men of Convictions," Comparative Studies in Society and History, July, 1962, vol. IV, No. 4, 403-435.
R. Pipes (ed.), The Russian Intelligentsia (espec. M. Malia, "What is the Intelligentsia?") (reprinting of Daedalus, summer, 1960).
A. Petrunkevich, "The Role of the Intellectuals in the Liberating Movement in Russia," The Russian Revolution (Harvard, 1918), 3-21.
A. Pollard, "The Russian Intelligentsia," California Slavic Studies, III, 1964, 1-32.
P. Pomper, The Russian Revolutionary Intelligentsia.
M. Raeff, Origins of the Russian Intelligentsia.
B. G. Rosenthal, "Nietzsche in Russia: The Case of Merezhkovsky," Slavic Review, Sept., 1974, 429-452.
F. Seeley, "The Heyday of 'The Superfluous Man' in Russia," Slavonic and East European Review, December, 1952, 92-112.
H. Seton-Watson, "The Russian Intellectuals," G. B. de Huszar (ed.), The Intellectuals, 41-50.
F. Stepun, "The Russian Intelligentsia and Bolshevism," Russian Review, 1958.
S. R. Tompkins, The Russian Intelligentsia.
L. Trotsky, "Concerning the Intelligentsia," Partisan Review, Fall, 1968, 585-598.
A. Wildman, "The Russian Intelligentsia of the 1890's," American Slavic and East European Review, 1960.

III. Studies on the Russian Intelligentsia (in Russian)

1. N. Cherevanin, "Dvizhenie intelligentsii," L. Martov, et.al.. (eds.), Obshchestvennoe dvizhenie v. Rossii v nachala XX veka (St. P., 1909-1911, 3 vols.), vol. I.

2. "Intelligentsiia," Bol'shaia sovetskaia entsiklopediia (2nd edition), vol. 18, pp. 270-272 (includes bibliography)

3. D. Ivanov-Razumnik, Istoriia Russkoi obshchestvennoi mysli (2 vols., St. P., 1910).

4. V. R. Leikina-Svirskaia, "Formirovanie raznochinskoi intelligentsii," Istorria SSSR, 1958, No. 1, 83-104.

5. V. R. Leikina-Svirskaia, Intelligentsiia v. Rossii vo vtoroi polovine XIX veka (Moscow, 1971).

6. D. Osvianiko-Kulikovskii, Istoriia Russkoi intelligentsii (9 vols., St. P., 1908-1910) (see espec. vols. 7, 8, 9).

7. N. A. Rubakin, Sredi Knig (Moscow: Nauka, 1911-1913, 2 vols.) I, 393-400. (This section, entitled "Vopros ob intelligentsii" contains an excellent bibliography of pre-revolutionary writings on the intelligentsia in Russia.)

8. G. I. Shchetina, "Intelligentsiia, revoliutsiia, samoderzhavie," Istoriia SSSR, 1970, No. 6, 153-172.

9. A. Volskii (Makhaiskii), Umstvennyi rabochii (St. P., 1906).

10. S. M. Troitskii, "Russkoe dvorianstvo XVIII veka v izobrazhenii amerikanskogo istorika," Istoriia SSSR, No. 5, 1970, 205-212.

IV. Bibliographies of Related Areas

L. J. Edinger (ed.), "Leadership: An Interdisciplinary Bibliography," Political Leadership in Industrialized Societies, 348-366.

N. J. Smelser, Theory of Collective Behavior, 388-427.

J. W. Thibaut and H. H. Kelly, The Social Psychology of Groups, 292-304.

ORIGINS OF THE RUSSIAN REVOLUTION

I. Introduction

II. Marxism, Revolution and Russia

A. Ulam, The Unfinished Revolution
R. Tucker, The Marxian Revolutionary Idea
R. Pipes, Russia under the Old Regime

III. The Intelligentsia and the Student Movement

P. Pomper, Russian Revolutionary Intelligentsia
L. Feuer, "The Russian Student Movement," Conflict of Generations
D. Brower, Training the Nihilists

IV. From Populism to Marxism

"To Define Populism," Government and Opposition, III, 2 (Spring, 1968),
    137-42, 173-79
M. Miller, Ideological Conflicts in Russian Populism," Slavic Review,
    March, 1970, 1-22
I. Berlin, "Introduction," Roots of Revolution by Franco Venturi
R. Pipes, "Russian Marxism and its Populist Background," Russian Review,
    October, 1960, 316-37
_____, "Narodnichestvo: A Semantic Inquiry," Slavic Review, September,
    1964, 441-58.
A. Walicki, Controversy over Capitalism

V. Formation of the Proletariat

F. Venturi, Roots of Revolution, 507-57
T. von Laue, "Russian Peasants in the Factory," Journal of Economic
    History, March, 1961, 61-80
_____, "Russian Labor between Field and Factory," California Slavic
    Studies, III, 1964, 33-65
J. Schneiderman, Sergei Zubatov and Revolutionary Marxism, chap. 1
D. Pospielovsky, Russian Police Trade Unionism, chap. 1
R. Zelnik, "Populists and Workers," Soviet Studies, Oct., 1972, 251-69
_____, "Russian Rebels," Russian Review, July, 1976, 249-89, and
    October, 1976, 417-47

VI. The Revolution of 1905

S. Harcave, Russian Revolution of 1905 (also called: First Blood)
O. Anweiler, The Soviets, 1-96
S. Schwarz, Russian Revolution, 1905
W. Sablinsky, The Road to Bloody Sunday

VII. Constitutional Autocracy

    A. Hosking, The Russian Constitutional Experiment
    P. Miliukov, Political Memoirs
    V. Maklakov, The First State Duma
    A. Levin, The Second Duma
    W. Walsh, "Political Parties in the Russian Dumas," Journal of Modern
       History, June, 1950, 144-50

VIII. War and Social Polarization

    M. Cherniavsky, Prologue to Revolution
    L. Haimson, "Problem of Social Stability," Slavic Review, Dec. 1964,
       619-42 and March, 1965, 1-22. Also reprinted in M. Cherniavsky (ed.),
       Structure of Russian History, 341-80
    Landmarks (ed. by B. Shagrin and A. Todd)
    "Vekhi," (ed. by M. Shatz and J. Zimmerman), Canadian Slavic Studies, II,
       2 (Summer, 1968), 151-74

IX. The Revolution of 1917

    A. Rabinowitch, The Bolsheviks Come to Power
    J. Keep, The Russian Revolution
    R. Daniels, Red October
    M. Ferro, The Russian Revolution
    L. Trotsky, History of the Russian Revolution
    A. Ulam, The Bolsheviks

X. The Post-Revolutionary Crisis

    A. Solshenitsyn, From under the Rubble
    R. Medvedev, On Socialist Democracy
    A. Sakharov, Sakharov Speaks
    S. Fedyukin, The Great October Revolution and the Intelligentsia

SOVIET POLITICS AND SOCIETY SINCE 1917
History 558/Politics 537

Princeton University
Spring Term 1979-80   Stephen F. Cohen

Most courses deal mainly with what is known and agreed upon
about major historical events. This seminar is somewhat different.
The main purpose of the seminar is to familiarize participants with
a variety of Western and Soviet materials on the important subjects
and periods in Soviet history; but it is also to examine critically
the adequacy of existing Western scholarship and to explore the
need for new research and different interpretations.

Course requirements are: reading of assigned materials each
week; full participation in the weekly discussions; and, at the
end of the term, a paper, which may be of the basic research, bibliographical, or thematic kind, on a topic chosen in consultation
with me.

It should be understood that the schedule of weekly topics
and readings is tentative and flexible. I hope that all participants will contribute to deciding what should be read and discussed.
Two sessions at the end have been left open so that time given to
assigned topics may be increased and/or other topics added. In
addition, the readings allow for a considerable choice (which may
be further enlarged by your own suggestions) and take into account
the circumstance that participants' familiarity with the literature
will vary. Whatever your choice of readings, however, all partici-
pants--indeed, anyone working in Soviet history and politics--
should become generally familiar with the following works because
of their scholarly value or point of view:

        Medvedev, Let History Judge
        Chamberlin, The Russian Revolution (2 vols.) (op)
        Schapiro, Communist Party of the Soviet Union
        Conquest, The Great Terror (op)
        Lewin, Russian Peasants and Soviet Power
        Fainsod, Smolensk Under Soviet Rule
        Deutscher, Stalin (rev. ed.)
        Deutscher, The Prophet Armed and The Prophet Unarmed (op)
        Tucker, Stalin as Revolutionary
        Tucker (ed.), Stalinism
        Cohen, Bukharin and the Bolshevik Revolution
        Carr, A History of Soviet Russia (op)
        Hough and Fainsod, How the Soviet Union is Governed
        Rabinowitch, The Bolsheviks Come to Power

These titles (except the Hough-Fainsod book) are in paperback
editions and available, under the listing of this course, at the
University Store. In addition, I have asked the University Store
to have available the following paperback titles:

Heer, Politics and History in the Soviet Union
Nove, Economic History of the USSR
Daniels, Conscience of the Revolution
Cohen, et al. (eds.), The Soviet Union Since Stalin
Schapiro, Origins of the Communist Autocracy
Tucker, Soviet Political Mind
Tucker, (ed.), Lenin Anthology
Medvedev, On Socialist Democracy (os)
Trotsky, The Revolution Betrayed
Linden, Khrushchev and the Soviet Leadership

All purchases are, of course, optional. And all of the above titles, as well as titles marked with an asterisk in the syllabus, are on reserve for this course in the library.

SCHEDULE OF TOPICS AND READINGS

Sessions I & II. A Critique of the Field of Soviet Studies

Feb. 5 & 12

Discussion Topics to Include:

1. History and development of the field
2. The "totalitarianism" paradigm and its historiography
3. Prevailing interpretations of Soviet historical development
4. The possibilities of new (revisionist?) scholarship

Readings:

1. Cohen, "Bolshevism and Stalinism," in *Tucker (ed.), Stalinism,
   pp. 3-29; and Cohen, "Politics and the Past," pp. 137-140
   (xerox copies to be distributed.)

2. One of the following: *Friedrich, Curtis, and Barber, Totalitarianism: Three Views; Spiro and Barber, "Counter-Ideological
   Uses of 'Totalitarianism'," Politics and Society, November 1970;
   or *Hough, The Soviet Union and Social Science Theory, pp. 1-15.

3. *Heer, Politics and History, begin and note especially chap. 8.

Additional Readings:

1. Examine the use of Soviet sources in *Lewin, Russian Peasants,
   chap. 16; *Conquest, Great Terror, chaps. 2 and either 8 or 9;
   and *Medvedev, Let History Judge, chaps. VI and VIII.

2. Browse through *Nechkina (ed.), Ocherki istorii istoricheskoi
   Nauki, Vol. IV, chaps. 1-4, 6; and *Vsesoiuznoe soveshchanie o
   merakh.

*Here and elsewhere, the category "Additional Readings" means
optional, suggested readings for those who wish to pursue a given
subject a little further. Titles in Russian are for those who
will be specializing in Russian/Soviet studies and who want to
sample primary materials or Soviet scholarship on a given subject.

Session III. The Bolsheviks and the Social Revolution of 1917

Feb. 19

Discussion topics to include:

1. Western interpretations of 1917 and the Bolshevik victory
2. The nature of the social revolution
3. The Bolshevik party in 1917 and its rivals. Why did the Bolsheviks win?
4. The legacy of 1917
5. What is to be done on 1917?

Readings:

1. Lenin, What Is To Be Done? and State and Revolution, in *Tucker (ed), Lenin Anthology.

2. One of the following: *Chamberlin, Russian Revolution, Vol. I; Trotsky, The History of the Russian Revolution; *Rabinowitch, The Bolsheviks Come to Power; Liebman, The Russian Revolution; Mel'gunov, Kak bol'sheviki; *Keep, The Russian Revolution, Parts I-III; *R. Medvedev, The October Revolution, Parts I-II. Or combine Radkey, Elections to the Constituent Assembly with the sections on 1917 in *Rosenberg, Liberals in the Russian Revolution; Radkey, Agrarian Foes of Bolshevism; and Getzler, Martov.

Additional Readings:

1. Examine the sections on 1917 in standard Western works on Soviet history. For example, Schapiro, Daniels, Fainsod, Treadgold, Ulam, etc.

2. Familiarize yourself with the sources and arguments in at least one significant Soviet book on 1917. For example, Grunt, Pobeda; Gusev, Krakh partii levykh eserov; Trukan, Oktiabr'; Pershin, Agrarnaia; Volobuev, Proletariat; etc.

3. *Nechkina (ed.), Ocherki, chap. 6, section 1.

4. Browse through the primary materials in collections such as Put' k oktiabriu; Velikaia okt. sots. revoliutsiia; Revoliutsiia 1917 godu; etc.

Session IV. Civil War and the Formation of the Soviet Political
            and Social Order

Feb. 26

Discussion Topics to Include:

1. Western scholarship and interpretations of the civil war
2. The problem of interpreting the interlude between October and
   the outbreak of civil war.
3. Origins and nature of the civil war and of war communism
4. Why did the Bolsheviks win?
5. The civil war as a formative period in Soviet development: the
   immediate and subsequent impact on social and political life
6. What is to be done on the civil war years?

Readings:

1. One of the following: *Chamberlin, Russian Revolution, Vol. II;
   Avrich, Kronstadt; *Gerson, Secret Police; *Schapiro, Origins;
   *Pipes, Formation; Serge, Year One; *Carr, Bolshevik Revolution,
   Vols. I and II (sections on 1918-1921); Footman, Civil War;
   *R. Service, The Bolshevik Party in Revolution, 1917-1923; *T.
   H. Rigby, Lenin's Government: Sovnarkom, 1917-1922; J. Keep
   (ed.), The Debate on Soviet Power; *J. Keep, Russian Revolution,
   Parts IV-V. Or combine the sections on the civil war years in
   *Rosenberg, Liberals; Radkey, Sickle Under the Hammer; and
   Getzler, Martov.

Additional Readings:

1, Examine the sections on the civil war in standard Western histories of the Soviet Union.
2. Familiarize yourself with at least one significant Soviet book
   on the civil war years. For example, Kritsman, Geroicheskii;
   Gorodetskii, Rozhdenie; Gimpel'son, Sovety; Gimpel'son, "Voen-
   nyi kommunizm"; Iroshnikov, Sozdanie; Spirin, Klassy and par-
   tiia; Iz istorii grazhdanskoi voiny; etc.
3. *Pethybridge, Social Prelude, chaps. 2-3.
4. Note the Soviet sources on the civil war in Mazour, Writing of
   History, chaps. IX-X; Naumov, Letopis'; and *Nechkina (ed.),
   Ocherki, chap. 6, section 2.

Session V. NEP Society

March 4

Discussion Topics to Include:

1. Western scholarship and conceptions of NEP society and the 1920s

2. The nature of NEP society: social pluralism and political monopolism?

3. Classes, groups, and attitudes

4. NEP culture

5. Factors of stability and crisis

6. What is to be done on NEP society and the 1920s?

Readings (for sessions V and VI):

1. *Cohen, Bukharin, pp. 270-76.

2. Lenin, "Our Revolution"; "On Cooperation"; "The Question of Nationalities"; "Letter to the Congress"; "How We Should Reorganize the Workers' and Peasants' Inspection"; "Better Fewer, But Better"; "Last Letters", in *Tucker (ed.), Lenin Anthology, pp. 703-713, 719-748.

3. One of the following: *Pethybridge, Social Prelude; Erlich, Soviet Industrialization; Maguire, Red Virgin Soil; *Lewin, Russian Peasants; *Carr, Socialism in One Country, chaps. 1-3, 5-10, 20-24, and his *Foundations, Vol. I and II, chaps. 42-56; Jovarsky, Soviet Marxism; Graham, Soviet Academy; Valentinov, Novaia ekonomicheskaia politika; Reiman, Die Geburtdes Stalinismus.

4. One of the following: *Cohen, Bukharin, chaps 5-9; *Tucker, Stalin as Revolutionary, chaps. 7-14; *Daniels, Conscience, chaps 5-15; *Deutscher, Prophet Unarmed.

5. Carr, "The Legend of Bukharin," TLS, Sept. 20, 1975, or Liebman, "Bukharinism, Revolution and Social Development," *The Socialist Register 1917, pp. 75-94; and Cohen, "Bukharin and the Idea of An Alternative to Stalinism," introduction to Oxford ed. of Bukharin.

Additional Readings:

1. Familiarize yourself with at least one significant Soviet book on the NEP years. For example, Bukharin, Put' k sotsializmu; Preobrazhensky, The New Economics; Voskresenskii, Razgrom; Vaganov, Pravyi uklon; Danilov, Sozdanie; Katorgin, Istoricheskii opyt; Kim (ed.), Novaia ekonomicheskaia politika; *Nechkina (ed.), Ocherki, chaps. 2-6; etc.

Session VI. NEP Politics

March 11

Discussion Topics to Include:

1. The party in the 1920s
2. Lenin's legacy
3. Programmatic ideas and groups within the party: Bukharinism and Trotskyism
4. Why did Stalin win?
5. Political prelude to the events of 1929-33
6. What is to be done on NEP politics?

Readings:

   See above, Session V, items 4 and 5

Session VII.   The Destruction of NEP--Stalin's Revolution From
                     Above (1929-33)
March 18

Discussion Topics to Include:

1. Western interpretations of 1929-33
2. The meaning of "revolution from above"
3. Origins, nature, impact, and outcome of the events of 1929-33
4. Was there a "plan"?
5. Collectivization as a historical problem

Readings:

1. *Lewin, Russian Peasants, chaps 9-17; Lewin, "Society, State,
    and Ideology during the First Five-Year Plan," in Fitzpatrick
    (ed.), Cultural Revolution in Russia, pp. 41-77; *Nove, Eco-
    nomic History, chap. 7-9.

2. Millar and Nove, "Was Stalin Really Necessary? A Debate on
    Collectivization," Problems of Communism, July-August, 1976,
    pp. 49-62.

3. Fitzpatrick (ed.), Cultural Revolution in Russia, pp. 1-7,
    241-53.

Additional Readings:

1. *Fainsod, Smolensk, chaps. 12-16
2. Lewin, "Taking Grain," in C. Abramsky (ed.), Essays in Honour
    of E.H. Carr
3. One of the following Soviet articles (based largely on archive
    materials) on collectivization: Ivnitskii's in Istochnikove-
    denie istorii sovetskogo obshchestva, Vol. I; Ivnitskii's in
    Voprosy istorii, No. 5, 1963; Bogdenko and Zelenin's in Isto-
    riia sovetskogo krest'ianstva (ed. Kim); Danilov's in Istori-
    cheskie zapiski, No. 79 (1966). Or Moshkov, Zernovaia;
    Nemakov, Kom. partiia; or *Danilov (ed.), Ocherki.

Sessions VIII & IX.   Stalinism, 1929-39: Process, System, Interpre-
April 1 & 8   tations

Discussion Topics to Include:

1. Western interpretations of Stalinism and the 1930s: totali-
    tarianism, modernization, historical-cultural traditions, the
    psychological-personality approach, Marxist approaches, etc.

2. Stages in the history of Stalinism: from revolution from above
    to social conservatism

3. The great terror as a historical problem

4. The question of popular support: victims, adherents, benefi-
    ciaries.

5. The cult as religion?

6. Nature of the new social and political system

7. What is to be done on Stalinism and the years 1929-1953?

Readings:

1. *Cohen, Bukharin, chap. 10; and *Conquest, Great Terror, chaps.
    6-13.

2. *Tucker, Soviet Political Mind, chaps. 2-3; and Tucker, "Sta-
    linism as Revolution From Above" and Lewin, "The Social Back-
    ground of Stalinism," both in *Tucker (ed.), Stalinism, pp.
    77-136.

3. Familiarize yourself with the interpretation of Stalinism (or
    the 1930s) in at least one of the following: *Medvedev, Let
    History Judge; *Timasheff, The Great Retreat; *Trotsky, The
    Revolution Betrayed; *Solzhenitsyn, The Gulag Archipelago,
    Vol. I and his Letter to the Soviet Leaders; David Joravsky,
    The Lysenko Affair; T. Von Laue, Why Lenin? Why Stalin?;
    Vera Dunham, In Stalin's Time; Max Shachtman, The Bureaucratic
    Revolution; or *Brzezinski, Permanent Purge.

Additional Readings:

1. Khrushchev, Crimes of the Stalin Era (i.e., secret speech to
    the 20th party Congress)

2. *Fainsod, Smolensk, chap. 11.

3. Beck and Godin, Russian Purge and the Extraction of Confession

4. Nove, "Was Stalin Really Necessary?," in Encounter, April 1962
    (and in his book of the same title).

5. Familiarize yourself with the views in at least one Soviet ac-
    count of the 1930s. For example, Istoriia KPSS, Vol. 4;
    Ivnitskii, Klassovaia bor'ba; Trapeznikov, Istoricheskii;Zhukov,
    Liudi; Ginzburg, Into the Whirlwind; D'iakov, Povest'; Khavin,
    U rulia; Urlanis, Istoriia odnogo pokoleniia; Trifonov, Likvi-
    datsiia; Sharapov (ed.), Rol' rabochego klassa; etc.

Session X.   After Stalin: Reformism and Conservatism in Soviet
April 15   Politics and Society Since 1953

Discussion Topics to Include:

1. Western interpretations of changes in Soviet politics and
    society since 1953
2. Destalinization as reformation from above
3. Leadership politics and relations with society
4. Soviet reformism and conservatism, anti-Stalinism and neo-
    Stalinism
5. Classes, groups, and rival opinions in Soviet society today
6. The reappearance of the oppositionist intelligentsia and other
    recurrent historical patterns
7. What is to be done on contemporary Soviet society?

Readings:

1. *Heer, Politics and History (finish)
2. *Cohen, "The Friends and Foes of Change: Reformism and Conser-
    vatism in the Soviet Union," in Cohen, et al. (eds.), The
    Soviet Union Since Stalin
3. One of the following: *Tatu, Power in the Kremlin; *Linden,
    Khrushchev; Skilling and Griffyths (eds.), Interest Groups;
    *Lewin, Political Undercurrents; Matthews, Class and Society;
    *Roi and Zhores Medvedev, Khrushchev; *Cohen, et al. (eds.),
    The Soviet Union Since Stalin; *R. Medvedev, On Socialist
    Democracy.

Additional Readings:

1. Smith, The Russians; or Kaiser, Russia.
2. One of the following: Reddaway (ed.), Uncensored Russia; Brum-
    berg (ed.), In Quest of Justice; Saunders (ed.), Samizdat;
    Medvedev, On Socialist Democracy; Politicheskii dnevnik
    (2 vols.); Solzhenitsyn, et al., From Under the Rubble;
    Samosoznanie; Dudko, O nashem upovanii; A. Yanov, The Russian
    New Right; M. Meerson-Aksenov and B. Shragin (eds.), The
    Political, Social and Religious Thought of Russian Samizdat.
3. One anti-reformist or neo-Stalinist book. For example, Sovre-
    mennyi pravyi revizionizm; Shevtsov, Vo imia ottsa i syna;
    Kochetov, Chto zhe ty khochesh'?; Trapeznikov, Na krutykh
    povorotakh istorii; etc.

Sessions XI & XII.   Open: Topics and Readings to be Decided by
                     Seminar Participants

Public Affairs 547   Stephen F. Cohen
Soviet Foreign Policy   Spring Term, 1981-82

The seminar examines the history, changing sources, interpretation, and contemporary nature of Soviet foreign policy,
with particular emphasis on East-West relations. Raising
critical-minded questions about these matters is as important
as arriving at "answers." Three sessions are left open in
order to accomodate more specialized interests of students.

Unlike a lecture course, a successful seminar requires
the full participation of students. The requirements are
customary but important. Each member of the seminar is
expected to complete the weekly readings in advance and to
participate in discussions. (Students who are unfamiliar
with the history of Soviet foreign policy should quickly
read as much as possible of either Adam Ulam, Expansion and
Coexistence or George Kennan, Russia and the West Under
Lenin and Stalin.) Each member also will write a seminar
paper (20 to 30 pages) on a topic to be decided in consultation with me.

The following required or optional readings are available,
in paperback editions, at the U-Store:

    A. Ulam, Expansion and Coexistence (2nd edition)
    G. Kennan, Russia and the West Under Lenin and Stalin
    R. Tucker, The Soviet Political Mind
    N. Sivachev and N. Yakovlev, Russia and the United States
    E. Hoffmann and F. Fleron . (eds.), The Conduct of Soviet
       Foreign Policy (2nd edition)
    M. Schwartz, The Foreign Policy of the USSR
    R. Tucker (ed.), The Lenin Anthology
    M. Schwartz, Soviet Perceptions of the United States
    A. Solzhenitsyn, East and West
    A. Solzhenitsyn, The Mortal Danger
    A. Yanov, Detente After Brezhnev
    A. Sakharov, Alarm and Hope
    F. Neal (ed.), Detente or Debacle

Those titles, and other assigned readings, are on reserve
for the seminar in the Woodrow Wilson School library.

WEEKLY SCHEDULE OF TOPICS AND READINGS

I. THE NATURE AND ADMINISTRATION OF THE SEMINAR

        Because students will not have done any assigned
   readings, this first meeting will be given over to a
   discussion of the organization, aims, and requirements
   of the seminar. But as preparation for subsequent
   meetings and discussions, students should read as far
   as possible in Ulam or Kennan, for historical knowledge,
   and all of the readings assigned for the next session.

II. GENERAL EXPLANATIONS OF SOVIET FOREIGN POLICY: HISTORICAL
    AND INTERPRETATIVE OVERVIEW

   Required Reading:

   1. Sivachev and Yakovlev, Russia and the United States,
          chap. 1
   2. Schwartz, Foreign Policy of the USSR, chaps. 3-7
   3. Hoffmann and Fleron, Conduct of Soviet Foreign Policy,
          chaps. 2-3, 7
   4. Tucker, Soviet Political Mind, chap. 9

   Optional Reading:

   1. Ulam, Expansion and Coexistence, chap. 1
   2. Solzhenitsyn, The Mortal Danger
   3. Hoffmann and Fleron, Conduct of Soviet Foreign Policy,
          Parts I-II
   4. S. Bialer (ed.), The Domestic Context of Soviet
          Foreign Policy

   Some Discussion Questions:

   1. What have been the leading interpretations of Soviet
          foreign policy, and its motivations, over the years?
   2. Which of these interpretations are persuasive? Are
          they valid over time or only for certain periods?
   3. Are Western interpretations "value-free," i.e.,
          "objective"? Should they be?
   4. Is a general interpretation possible? Is a comparative
          framework cr theory necessary?

III. THE CHANGING DOMESTIC CONTEXT: THE SOVIET POLITICAL
SYSTEM, 1917-1982

Required Reading:

1. Tucker, Soviet Political Mind, chap. 1
2. R. Tucker, The Marxian Revolutionary Idea, chap. 6
3. S. Cohen, "The Friends and Foes of Change," in Cohen,
   et. al. (eds.), The Soviet Union Since Stalin,
   pp. 11-29

Optional Reading:

1. S. Bialer, Stalin's Successors, Part I
2. R. Tucker (ed.), Stalinism
3. Tucker, Soviet Political Mind
4. J. Hough and M. Fainsod, How the Soviet Union Is
   Governed

Some Discussion Questions:

1. What is the relationship between domestic and foreign
   politics in other political systems? Do we need
   a special conception for the Soviet system?
2. How has the nature of the Soviet political system
   changed over the years? Has the foreign policy
   process?
3. Have these changes been so fundamental as to produce
   different Soviet foreign policies?
4. Which has primacy in the Soviet system -- domestic
   or foreign politics?

IV. REVOLUTION AND FOREIGN POLICY: THE LENINIST TRADITION

Required Reading:

1. Ulam, Expansion and Coexistence, chaps. i-iv; or
   Kennan, Russia and the West, chaps. 1-18
2. Sivachev and Yakovlev, Russia and the United States,
   chaps. 2-3
3. Lenin, "Two Tactics" (pp. 120-47), "Imperialism"
   (pp. 204-74), "Left-Wing Communism" (pp. 550-618),
   and short selections (pp. 619-36) in Tucker (ed.),
   The Lenin Anthology

Optional Reading:

1. Tucker (ed.), The Lenin Anthology
2. F. Borkenau, World Communism
3. E. H. Carr, The Bolshevik Revolution, Vol. 3
4. L. Fischer, The Soviets in World Affairs (2 vols.)
5. T. Uldricks, Diplomacy and Ideology

Some Discussion Questions:

1. What was the Leninist tradition in foreign policy?
   Which factors and/or events shaped that tradition?
2. Do Lenin's writings, notably Imperialism, give a
   comprehensive theory of international relations,
   a "blueprint" for foreign policy?
3. What was the relationship between revolutionary ideas
   (or ideology) and the interests of the Soviet state
   in foreign policy under Lenin?
4. How do Lenin's ideas relate to later concerns in
   Soviet foreign policy -- e.g., national liberation,
   peaceful coexistence, the Brezhnev doctrine, etc.?

V. THE EMERGENCE OF A STALINIST FOREIGN POLICY (1929-1941)?

Required Reading:

1. Sivachev and Yakovlev, Russia and the United States,
   chaps. 3-4
2. Ulam, Expansion and Coexistence, chaps. iv-vi; or
   Kennan, Russia and the West, chaps. 19-22
3. R. Tucker, "The Emergence of Stalin's Foreign Policy"
   and comments by Kennan, Gillette, Dallin, Uldricks,
   and Tucker, in Slavic Review, December 1977, pp.
   563-607 (copies on reserve)
4. Tucker, Soviet Political Mind, chap. 3

Optional Reading:

1. L. Fischer, Russia's Road to War
2. I. Lederer (ed.), Russian Foreign Policy, chap. 7
3. B. Nicolaevsky, Power and the Soviet Elite
4. S. Cohen, Bukharin and the Bolshevik Revolution,
   chap. 10

Some Discussion Questions:

1. Was Stalinist foreign policy in the 1930s outside the Leninist tradition? Or, what was the relationship between Stalinist and Leninist foreign policy?
2. When, how, why did the characteristic features of Stalinist policy emerge?
3. How are important episodes in Soviet foreign policy in the 1930s to be explained -- e.g., Comintern policy, collective security, the Nazi-Soviet Pact?

VI. GREAT POWER AND COLD WAR: THE STALINIST HERITAGE, 1941-1953

Required Reading:

1. Sivachev and Yakovlev, Russia and the United States, chaps. 5-6
2. Ulam, Expansion and Coexistence, chaps. vii-ix (into x)
3. Tucker, Soviet Political Mind, chaps. 4, 10
4. Hoffmann and Fleron, Conduct of Soviet Foreign Policy, chaps. 12-16

Optional Reading:

1. V. Mastny, Russia's Road to the Cold War
2. W. Taubman, Stalin's American Policy
3. C. Gati (ed.), Caging the Bear
4. G. Kennan, Memoirs (2 vols.)
5. M. Shulman, Stalin's Foreign Policy Reconsidered
6. W. LaFeber, America, Russia, and the Cold War
7. D. Yergin, Shattered Peace

Some Discussion Questions:

1. How did WW II and the rise to great-power status affect Soviet foreign policy?
2. What were the causes and nature of the Cold War? Were there alternatives?
3. What was Stalin's legacy in foreign policy?

VII. **GLOBAL POLITICS: SUPERPOWER POLICY UNDER KHRUSHCHEV AND BREZHNEV, 1953-1982**

Required Reading:

1. Sivachev and Yakovlev, Russia and the United States, chap. 7 and Epilogue
2. Ulam, Expansion and Coexistence, chaps. x-xiii
3. Hoffmann and Fleron, Conduct of Soviet Foreign Policy, chaps. 31-33
4. R. Medvedev and Z. Medvedev, "Letter to the West: A Nuclear Samizdat on America's Arms Race," The Nation, January 16, 1982, pp. 38-50 (copies on reserve)

Optional Reading:

1. Schwartz, Foreign Policy of the USSR, chaps. 1-2
2. Hoffmann and Fleron, Conduct of Soviet Foreign Policy, Part IV
3. J. Nogee and R. Donaldson, Soviet Foreign Policy Since World War II
4. A. Rubinstein, Soviet Foreign Policy Since World War II
5. L. Caldwell and W. Diebold, Soviet-American Relations in the 1980s
6. R. Edmonds, Soviet Foreign Policy, 1962-1973
7. R. Slusser, The Berlin Crisis
8. A. Ulam, The Rivals

Some Discussion Questions:

1. Has Soviet foreign policy since 1953 been characterized mainly by continuity or discontinuity with the Stalinist tradition?
2. Has Soviet foreign policy changed fundamentally since the fall of Khrushchev?
3. What have been the main factors and motives of Soviet foreign policy since 1953, since 1964? How are they to be explained?
4. What are the meaning and history of contemporary concepts in Soviet foreign policy -- e.g., peaceful coexistence, detente, parity, ideological struggle, the Brezhnev doctrine?

VIII-X.   THREE OPEN SESSIONS: TOPICS TO BE DECIDED

These sessions can be devoted to closer examination
of topics already scheduled and/or to subjects of special
interest to seminar participants. For example, sessions
might focus on Soviet policy toward a specific area --
the Third World, East Europe, West Europe, China, etc.;
or on specific issues or problems -- strategic policy,
military intervention, SALT, trade, Eurocommunism, etc.
Whichever the choices, these sessions should be decided
and led largely by students, and they should reflect
clusters of student interest. They should be organized,
along with appropriate readings, well in advance of the
meetings.

XI.   CONFLICTING SOVIET PERSPECTIVES ON WORLD AFFAIRS TODAY:
      OFFICIAL AND DISSIDENT

Required Reading:

1. Cohen, "The Friends and Foes of Change" (assigned
      also for Session III)
2. One of the following:
    --M. Schwartz, Soviet Perceptions of the United
       States; and Yanov, Detente After Brezhnev
    --F. Barghoorn, Detente and the Democratic Movement
       in the USSR
    --R. Medvedev, "Problems of Democratization and
       Detente" and "Problems of General Interest"
       (copies on reserve); A. Sakharov, Alarm and
       Hope; and A. Solzhenitsyn, East and West

Optional Reading:

1. W. Zimmerman, Soviet Perspectives on International
      Relations
2. A. Yanov, The Russian New Right
3. A. Sakharov, Sakharov Speaks and My Country and the
      World
4. R. Medvedev, On Socialist Democracy
5. G. Breslauer, Five Images of the Soviet Future
6. USICA, "Soviet Elites: World View and Perceptions
      of the U.S." (September 29, 1981)
7. S. Cohen (ed.), An End to Silence

222

Some Discussion Questions:

1. Are there fundamental disagreements over foreign policy inside the Soviet Establishment?
2. If not, why not? If there are, what are their nature and importance?
3. What has been the nature and importance of dissident debates over foreign policy?

XII. WHAT SHOULD BE AMERICA'S SOVIET POLICY?

Required Reading:

1. F. Neal (ed.), Detente or Debacle
2. A. Solzhenitsyn, The Mortal Danger
3. Hoffmann and Fleron, Conduct of Soviet Foreign Policy, chaps. 18-20, 34, 38

Optional Reading:

1. R. Conquest, et. al., Defending America
2. T. Larson, Soviet-American Rivalry
3. R. Barnet, Real Security and The Giants
4. A. Wolfe, The Rise and Fall of the "Soviet Threat"
5. K. Jowitt, Images of Detente and the Soviet Political Order

Some Discussion Questions

1. Does the United States have a Soviet policy? Has it had one over the years?
2. What should that policy be today? Is it possible?
3. Can American policy influence Soviet domestic and/or foreign policies? Should it try?

Professor Santore
                        Syllabus   Barnard College
                        History 18
                  Italy in the 20th century

I. Introductory Session

September 4:

1. Discussion of syllabus and course requirements.
2. Lecture on Italian geography.

II. Background: Italy in the 19th century, 1815-1900.

September 11:

1. Lecture on Italian unification, 1815-1871.
2. Readings:

Denis Mack Smith, _Italy: A Modern History_, pp, 1-61.
Salvatore Saladino, _Italy From Unification to 1919_, pp. 1-94.

III. The Giolittian Era, 1900-1914.

September 18:

Saladino, _Italy from Unification to 1919_, pp. 94-133.
Shepard B. Clough and Salvatore Saladino (eds.), _A History of Modern Italy: Documents, Readings, and Commentary_, pp. 239-299.
Christopher Seton-Watson, _Italy from Liberalism to Fascism_, pp. 246-54.
Gaetano Salvemini, "An Historian Revisits Italian Democracy in the Making", in A. William Salamone (ed.), _Italy: From the Risorgimento to Fascism_, pp. 437-55.
Benedetto Croce, "Liberalism and Idealism in the Giolittian Era", in Salomone, pp. 306-38.

September 25:

Christopher Seton-Watson, _Italy from Liberalism to Fascism_, pp. 285-324.
Denis Mack Smith, "Regionalism", in Edward R. Tannenbaum and Emiliana P. Noether (eds.), _Modern Italy: A Topical History Since 1861_, pp. 125-146.
Nuncio Pernicone, "The Italian Labor Movement", in Tannenbaum and Noether, pp. 197-213.

William C. Askew, "Italy and the Great Powers Before
the First World War", ibid., pp. 313-336.
Denis Mack Smith, Italy, pp. 272-305.
Clough and Saladino, Documents, pp. 303-26.

First Essay due

IV. The First World War and the Peace Settlement, 1915-1919.

October 2:

Christopher Seton-Watson, Italy from Liberalism
to Fascism, pp. 436-560.
Clough and Saldino, Documents, pp. 326-352.

Second Essay due

V. The Decline of the Parliamentary Regime and the Rise of Fascism,
1919-1922.

October 9:

Christopher Seton-Watson, Italy from Liberalism
to Fascism, pp. 560-612.
Clough and Saladino, Documents, pp. 352-393.
A. Rossi (Angelo Tasca), The Rise of Fascism, 1918-
1922, pp. 1-81.
John M. Cammett, Antonio Gramsci and the Origins
of Italian Communism, pp. 133-155.
John N. Molony, The Emergence of Political Catho-
licism in Italy: Partito Popolare, 1919-
1926, pp. 45-135.

VI. The Fascist Era, 1922-1945.

October 16: The Seizure of Power.

Adrian Lyttelton, The Seizure of Power: Fascist
Italy, 1919-1929, pp. 1-148.
Roland Sarti, Fascism and Industrial Leadership
in Italy, pp. 1-40.

October 23: The Regime in Operation (I)

Alan Cassels, Fascist Italy, pp. 36-116.
Ivone Kirkpatrick, Mussolini: Study of a Demogogue,
pp. 192-263.
Roland Sarti, "Politics and Ideology in Fascist
Italy", in Tannenbaum and Noether, pp.
52-78.
Aldo Garosci, "Italian Communism between the Two
World Wars", in Mario Einaudi, Jean-Marie
Domenach, and Aldo Garosci, Communism in
Western Europe, pp. 154-177.

October 30: The Regime in Operation (II)

    Edward R. Tannenbaum, The Fascist Experience:
        Italian Politics and Society, 1922-
        1945, pp. 59-87, 117-149.
    Roland Sarti, Fascism and Industrial Leadership
        in Italy, pp. 41-69, 134-38.
    Edward Tannenbaum, "The Goals of Italian Fascism",
        American Historical Review, LXXIV, 1183-
        1204.
    Roland Sarti, "Fascist Modernization in Italy:
        Traditional or Revolutionary", AHR, LXXV,
        1029-45.
    Adrian Lyttelton, "Fascism in Italy: the Second Wave",
        Journal of Contemporary History, I, 75-
        100.

        Third Essay due.

November 7: Historical Interpretations of Fascism.

    Renzo De Felice, Interpretations of Fascism (Cam-
        bridge, Mass.: 1977), pp. 3-106, 174-
        192.
    A. James Gregor, Interpretations of Fascism (1974).
    Gilbert Allardyce, "What Fascism is Not: Thoughts
        on the Deflation of a Concept", AHR, vol.
        84, no. 2 (April 1979), pp. 367-398.

        Forth Essay due.

VII. The Republican Era: 1945 to the Present.

November 14: From the Fall of Mussolini to 1948.

    Guisippe Mammarella, Italy After Fascism: A
        Political History, pp. 1-97.
    Aldo Garosci, "The Communist Party During the War
        and After the Restoration of Democracy",
        in Einaudi, et. al., pp. 178-89.
    Clough and Saladino, Documents, pp. 514-556.

November 21: 1948-1963.

    H. Stuart Hughes, The United States and Italy,
        pp. 133-268.
    Clough and Saladino, Documents, pp. 557-615.

December 4: Italy Today.

    Nunzio Pernicone, "The Italian Labor Movement", in
        Tannenbaum and Noether, pp. 213-225.
    Norman Kogan, "Socialism and Communism in Italian
        Political Life", in ibid., pp. 102-124.

Elisa A. Carrillo, "Christian Democracy", in _ibid._,
    pp. 78–100.
Leonard W. Moss, "The Passing of Traditional Peasant
    Society in the South", in _ibid._, pp. 147–169.
The Center for Strategic and International Studies,
    Geogetown University, _The Political
    Instability of Italy_ (1976).
Rosario Romeo and George Uban, "Troubled Italy", _The
    Washington Review of Strategic and International
    Studies_.

Fifth Essay due.

History 147B   Spain and Portugal since 1700   Winter 1979
Mr. Herr
University of California - Berkeley

The course will cover the history of the Iberian Peninsula since the
18th century, but half the course will deal with the 20th century,
  coming down to the transition since the Portuguese revolution
of April 1974 and the death of Franco in November 1975. The three
regular weekly meetings will be devoted to lectures and informal
discussion. A fourth hour, Fridays 3-4, will be used in part to
present material that will illustrate and add depth to the course
(slides, music, documents) and in part to consider questions that
have arisen out of the lectures and reading.

There will be a mid-term and final examination, consisting of essay
questions designed to test the understanding of historical issues.
They will be based on the lectures and required reading. Each
student will also consult with the instructor or reader to select
a topic for a term paper (about 8 pages, due March 5). These topics
may be in any area of the history of Spain or Portugal in the period
covered by the course, and normally will involve some additional
reading · beyond the required reading. A serious review of a significant book is an acceptable paper, but whatever the topic, the
treatment should contain a critical interpretation of a historical
problem. It is not intended to be based on research, but rather
to be a report on the writing and conclusions of some historian(s).

The local bookstores have been ·asked to stock..the_following books,
which contain most of the required reading. (They are also available in Moffitt Library.)

     Gerald Brenan, The Spanish Labyrinth (1943) (Cambridge U.P.
          pbk)

     Richard Herr, An Historical Essay on Modern Spain (1971) (U.
          of Calif. P. pbk)

     George Orwell, Homage to Catalonia (1937) (Harcourt B.J. pbk)

     Stanley Payne, A History of Spain and Portugal (1973) (U. of
          Wisc. P. pbk), Vol. II

     J.A. Pitt-Rivers, The People of the Sierra (1961) (U. of
          Chicago pbk)

General histories for further reading and reference:

     Raymond Carr, Spain 1808-1939 (1966). A professor at Oxford,
Carr is the leading English historian of modern and contemporary
Spain.
     Salvador de Madariaga, Spain (various editions, 1930-58).
A minister in the government of the Second Spanish Republic,
Madariaga became a leader of the moderate opposition to Franco
among Spaniards in exile. He was on the faculty of Oxford.

A. Ramos Oliveira, Politics, Economics and Men of Modern Spain (1946). Also writing in exile after the Civil War, Ramos Oliveira took the viewpoint of the moderate socialists.

Jaime Vicens Vives, An Economic History of Spain (1st ed., 1955). Vicens Vives was the outstanding historian of Spain in the post-Civil War period. He edited and contributed to a longer general work in Spanish: Historia economica y social de Espana y America (5 vols. 1957-59). Vols. IV and V deal with our period.

Charles E. Nowell, Portugal (1973). A brief survey by an American historian of Portugal, the volume stresses modern Portugal.

A.H. de Oliveira Marques, History of Portugal (1972), Vol. II. The best history of modern Portugal, by a leading Portuguese historian.

Course outline and readings:

I. Background and Enlightenment (Jan. 8-17)

Required reading:

Richard Herr, Historical Essay, 1-64

Stanley Payne, History of Spain and Portugal, 351-71, 403-14

J.M. Blanco White, Letters from Spain (1822), 59-134 (the letter is his autobiography)

Additional recommended works:

Raymond Carr, Spain 1808-1939, 1-78

Jaime Vicens Vives, An Economic History of Spain, 9-20 and Part V

Richard Herr, The Eighteenth-Century Revolution in Spain (1948) Part I

David R. Ringrose, Transportation and Economic Stagnation in Spain 1750-1850 (1970)

Michael E. Burke, The Royal College of San Carlos: Surgery and Spanish Medical Reform in the Late Eighteenth Century (1977)

Antonio Dominguez Ortiz, Sociedad y estado en el siglo XVIII espanol (1976)

II. The Impact of the French Revolution and Napoleon (Jan. 19-24)

Required reading:

Herr, Historical Essay, 65-76

Payne, Spain and Portugal, 415-27

Additional recommended works:

Carr, Spain, 79-119

R. Herr, "Good, Evil, and Spain's Rising against
Napoleon," in R. Herr and H. Parker (eds.) Ideas
in History (1965), 157-81

F.D. Klingender, Goya, in the Democratic Tradition

Edith Helman, Trasmundo de Goya, esp. 43-147

Charles E. Nowell, Portugal, 73-86

III. The Struggle for Constitutional Regimes, 1814-1875 (Jan. 26-
Feb. 5)

Required reading:

Herr, Essay, 77-112

Payne, Spain and Portugal, 428-52, 473-86, 513-50

"George Ticknor's Travels in Spain," in T.F. McGann (ed),
Portrait of Spain, 44-56

George Borrow, The Bible in Spain, selection in ibid.,
91-118

John Hay, "A Victorian Yankee Confronts Castile," ibid.,
137-56

Additional recommended works:

Carr, Spain, 129-46 ("The Revolution of 1820"), 277-90
("The Affluent Society")

Jordi Nadal, "The Failure of the Industrial Revolution
in Spain 1830-1914," in C.M. Cipolla (ed.), The Fontana
Economic History of Europe, Vol. IV:2, 532-620

Vicens Vives, Economic History, Part VI (19th Century),
esp. 517-43, 679-88

Miguel Artola, La Burguesia revolucionaria (1808-1869)
(1973)

A.H. de Oliveira Marques, History of Portugal, II, 1-75

Nowell, Portugal, 87-116

C.A.M. Hennessy, The Federal Republic in Spain, 1868-1874
(1962)

230

MIDTERM EXAMINATION: Wed. Feb. 7

IV. Spanish Constitutional Monarchy and Portuguese Republic
    (Feb. 9-16)

    Required reading:

        Herr, Essay, 113-32

        Payne, Spain and Portugal, 550-77

        Gerald Brenan, The Spanish Labyrinth, Part II, 87-228

        Carr, Spain, 366-79 ("Caciquismo and its Consequences")

        Madariaga, Spain, Chap. 7 ("School")

        R. Herr, "Spain," in David Spring (ed.), European Landed
            Elites in the Nineteenth Century (1977), 98-126

        Alberto Jimenez-Fraud, "The'Residencia de Estudiantes,"
            in Image of Spain, a special issue of The Texas Quar-
            terly (1961), 43-54

    Additional recommended works:

        Carr, Spain, 430-72 ("Society 1870-1930"), 524-63 ("The
            Protesters, 1898-1923")

        Madariaga, Spain, Part VI ("The Reign of Alfonso XIII")

        J.B. Trend, The Origins of Modern Spain (1934) (The
            Generation of 1868 and the Institucion Libre de
            Ensenanza)

        Temma Kaplan, Anarchists of Andalusia, 1868-1903 (1977)

        Robert W. Kern, Liberals, Reformers and Caciques in
            in Restoration Spain, 1875-1909 (1974)

        Gerald H. Meaker, The Revolutionary Left in Spain, 1914-
            1923 (1974)

        Stanley G. Payne, Politics and the Military in Modern Spain
            (1967)

        Xavier Tusell Gomez, "The Functioning of the Cacique
            System in Andalusia, 1890-1931," in S.G. Payne, (ed.),
            Politics and Society in Twentieth-Century Spain (1976)

        Stanley G. Payne, "Catalan and Basque Nationalism,"
            Journal of Contemporary History, VI (1971), 15-51

        Oliveira Marques, History of Portugal, II, 119-75

Douglas L. Wheeler, "The Portuguese Revolution of 1910,"
Journal of Modern History, 44 (1972), 172-94

V. Dictatorship, Second Republic, and Civil War in Spain (Feb. 21-
Mar. 2)

Required reading:

Herr, Essay, 133-210

Brenan, Spanish Labyrinth, 229-314

Payne, Spain and Portugal, 645-62

George Orwell, Homage to Catalonia (1938)

Additional recommended works:

Gabriel Jackson, The Spanish Republic and the Civil War
(1965)

Gabriel Jackson, A Concise History of the Spanish Civil
War (1974)

Carr, Spain, 603-51 ("The Second Republic")

Raymond Carr (ed.), The Republic and the Civil War in
Spain (1971) (articles by leading historians on the
parties of the right and left, the army, foreign intervention, and anarchist agrarian collectives)

Raymond Carr, The Spanish Tragedy: The Civil War in
Perspective (1977)

Madariaga, Spain, Book II ("The Republic")

Edward F. Malefakis, Agrarian Reform and the Peasant
Revolution in Spain (1970)

Stanley G. Payne, Falange, a History of Spanish Fascism
(1961), 1-100

Stanley G. Payne, "The Ominous Spring of 1936," in Payne
(ed.), Politics and Society in Twentieth-Century Spain,
120-44

Edward E. Malefakis, "Internal Political Problems and
Loyalties: The Republican Side in the Spanish Civil
War," ibid., 145-59

Pierre Broue and Emile Temime, La Revolution et la
Guerre d'Espagne (1961) (perhaps the most perspective
interpretation; there is an English translation)

Elliot Paul, The Life and Death of a Spanish Town (a
liberal journalist describes a town in Ibiza before
and in the Civil War, 1937)

Ernest Hemingway, For Whom the Bell Tolls (1937)
(Hemingway draws on his experience as a correspondent
in Spain for his novel of the early months of the war)

VI. The Franco and Salazar Regimes (Mar. 5-9)

Required reading:

Herr, Essay, 211-88

Payne, Spain and Portugal, 663-97

J.A. Pitt-Rivers, The People of the Sierra

Gerald Brenan, "Search for a Dead Poet," in McGann,
Portrait of Spain, 243-67

Additional recommended works:

Herbert L. Matthews, The Yoke and the Arrows (1957)
(by a N.Y. Times correspondent unfriendly to Franco)

Benjamin Welles, Spain, the Gentle Anarchy (1965) (by a
N.Y. Times correspondent, friendly to Franco)

Arthur P. Whitaker, Spain and the Defense of the West
(1961) (by a well-known historian)

Elena de la Souchere, An Explanation of Spain (1962)
(by a Spanish exile, unfriendly to Franco)

Carmelo Lison-Tolosana, Belmonte de los Caballeros: A
Sociological Study of a Spanish Town (1966)

Stanley H. Brandes, Migration, Kinship, and Community:
Tradition and Transition in a Spanish Village (1975)

Gerald Brenan, The Face of Spain (1950) (the story of his
return in 1946)

Gabriel Jackson, Historian's Quest (1969) (his experiences
in writing the history of the republic and Civil War)

Juan J. Linz, "An Authoritarian Regime: Spain," in Payne
(ed.), Politics and Society, 160-207

Josep Fontana and Jordi Nadal, "Spain, 1914-1970," in
C.M. Cipolla (ed.), Fontana Economic History of Europe,
6:2, 460-529

Oliveira Marques, History of Portugal, II, 177-224

Antonio de Figuiredo, Portugal: Fifty Years of Dictatorship (1975)

VII. Portuguese Revolution and Spanish Transition (Mar. 12-16)

Reading: None

History 240E   Mr. Loewenberg
Topics in Modern   Spring, 1973
Austrian History, 1848-1938   Mon. 205 P.M.
UCLA/G

Course Outline

This graduate topics course will be a historiographic
and bibliographic survey of the Habsburg Dual Monarch and the
First Austrian Republic. Students will select one work from
the bibliography of each section and guide the discussions of
where that book fits into the literature, the problems it
presents, its strengths and weaknesses, and what contributions
it makes to the understanding of Austrian history.

Each student will choose one area in consultation with
the instructor to write a paper on the historical literature.
Papers will be due on 11 June. There will be no meetings on
9 April, 7 May and 28 May.

April 2- Professor Paul A. Robinson, Department of History,
Stanford University, will present a departmental colloquium on
"The Historical Development of Modern Sexual Thought: Havelock
Ellis, Richard vonKrafft-Ebing, and Sigmund Freud" in the
History Department Conference Room, Ralph Bunche Hall 6275,
2-4 P.M.

April 16- The Habsburg Monarch as Background:

Heinrich Friedjung, The Struggle for Supremacy in Germany, 1859-
1866 (New York, 1966; original in 1897).

-Robert A. Kann, The Multinational Empire: Nationalism and
National Reform in the Habsburg Monarchy, 1848-1918, 2Vols.
(Columbia University Press, 1950; Octogon Books 1964, 1970).

-Oscar Jaszi, The Dissolution of the Habsburg Monarchy
(University of Chicago Press, 1929, 1961)

William A. Jenks, The Austrian Electoral Reform of 1907
(N.Y., 1950)

William A. Jenks, Vienna and the Young Hitler (N.Y., 1960)

Arthur J. May, The Passing of the Hapsburg Monarchy, 1914-1918,
2 Vols. (Philadelphia, 1966)

Peter Pulzer, The Rise of Political Anti-Semitism in Germany
and Austria (N.Y.: John Wiley, 1964)

Sigmund Mayer, Die Wiener Juden: Commerz, Kultur, Politik
(Vienna, 1917)

Rudolph Neck, Arbeitschaft und Staat im Ersten Weltkrieg,
1914-1918 (Vienna, 1964)

Czeike, Felix, Liberale, Christlichsoziale und Sozialdemo-
    Kratische Kommunalpolitik, 1861-1934 dargestellt am
    Beispeil der Gemeinde Wien (Vienna, 1962)
Julius Deutsch, Geschichte der Osterreichischen Gewerkschaft-
bewegungen: Die sozialistische Gewerkschaften von ihren Anfang
bis zur Gegenwart (Vienna 1908)

A.J.P. Taylor, The Habsburg Monarchy, 1809-1918 (London, 1948,
    1964)

Hans Kohn, The Habsburg Empire, 1804-1918 (Princeton University
    Press, 1961; Anvil paperback).

Arthur J. May, The Habsburg Monarchy, 1867-1914 (New York, 1951)

H.W. Steed, The Habsburg Monarch, 2nd ed. (London, 1914)

Jelavich, Charles & Barbara, The Habsburg Monarchy: Towards
    Multinational Empire or National States? (New York, 1959)

Richard Charmatz, Osterreichs aussere und innere Politik von
    1895 bis 1914 (Leipzig, 1918)

Heinrich Benedikt, Die writschaftliche Entwicklung in der
    Franz-Joseph-Zeit, Wiener Historsche Studien, Vol.IV
    (Vienna and Munich, 1958)

A.G. Whiteside, Austrian National Socialism before 1918
    (Hague: M. Nijhoff, 1962)

Adam Wandruzka, The House of Habsburg (Doubleday, 1964)

Z.A.B. Zeman, The Break-Up of the Habsburg Empire, 1914-1918
    (Oxford, 1961)

Z.A.B. Zeman, Twilight of the Habsburgs (American Heritage Press,
    Library of the Twentieth Century).

April 23- Nationalism, Modal Personality, and Socialization
Process:

Hans Mommsen, Die Sozialdemokrtie und die Nationalitätenfrage
    im habsburgischen Vielvölkerstaat.Vol. 1, Das Ringen um
    die supranationale Integration der cisleithanischen
    Arbeiterbewegung (1867-1907) (Vienna, 1963)

Peter Hanak, ed., Die Nationale Frage in der österreichisch-
    Ungarischen Monarchie, 1900-1918 (Budapest, 1966)

A.G. Kogen, "The Social Democrats and the Conflict of
    Nationalities in the Habsburg Monarchy," Journal of
    Modern History, 21 (1949), 204-217.

236

Karl W. Deutsch and William J. Foltz, eds., <u>Nation Building</u>
(New York, 1963); See especially Hermann Weilmann, "The
Interlocking of Nation and Personality Structure," pp. 33-
55.

Walter P. Metzger, "Generalizations about National Character:
An Analytical Essay, in Louis Gottschalk, ed. <u>Generalization</u>
<u>in the Writing of History</u> (1963)

David E. Stannard, "American Historians and the Idea of National
Character: Some Problems and Prospects," <u>American Quarterly,</u>
22 (May 1971), 202-220.

Karl W. Deutsch, <u>Nationalism and Social Communication: An</u>
<u>Inquiry into the Foundations of Nationality</u> (MIT Press,
1953) (MIT 34). See especially pp. 86-122.

Talcott Parsons, "Social Structure and the Development of
Personality: Freud's Contribution to the Integration of
Psychology and Sociology," in Psychiatry, Vol. 21, No. 4
(November 1958), 321-340. Also in <u>Social Structure and</u>
<u>Personality</u> (Collier-MacMillan, 1964), pp. 78-111.

The following is a bibliography of standard historical works on
nationalism, for your reference:

Louis L. Snyder, <u>The Meaning of Nationalism</u> (1954)

Boyd C. Shafer, <u>Nationalism: Myth and Reality</u> (1955)

Carleton J. H. Hayes, <u>Essays on Nationalism</u> (1926)
   "   "   "   " , <u>The Historical Evolution of Modern</u>
<u>Nationalism</u> (1931)
Carleton J.H. Hayes, <u>Nationalism: A Religion</u> (1960)

Hans Kahn, <u>A History of Nationalism in the East</u> (1929)
   "   " , <u>Revolutions and Dictatorships</u> (1939).
   "   " , <u>The Idea of Nationalism</u> (1956).

F. Hertz, <u>Nationality in History and Politics</u> (1944)

Elie Kedourie, <u>Nationalism</u> (1961)

Royal Institute of International Affairs, <u>Nationalism</u> (1939)

R. Rocker, <u>Nationalism and Culture</u> (1937)

W. Sulzbach, <u>National Consciousness</u> (1943)

Aira Kemilainen, <u>Nationalism: Problems Concerning the</u>
<u>Word, Concept, Classification</u> (1964)

April 30 - The First Austrian Republic

K.R. Stadler, The Birth of the Austrian Republic, 1918-1921
(Leyden: A.W. Sijthoff, 1966)

Mary Macdonald, The Republic of Austria, 1918-1934 (London, 1946)

C.A. Macartney, Social Revolution in Austria (Cambridge, 1926)

Heinrich Benedikt, Geschichte der Republik Osterreich (Vienna, 1954)

Walter Goldinger, Geschichte der Republik österreich (Vienna, 1962)

Brita Skottsberg, Der Osterreichische Parlamentarismus
(Göteborg, 1940)

Jürgen Gehl, Austria, Germany, and Anschluss, 1931-1938
(N.Y.: Oxford, 1963)

G.B. Sheperd, Anschluss (Philadelphia: Lippincott, 1963)

May 14 - Conservatism and Christian Socialism:

Leopold Kunschak, Osterreich, 1918-1924 (Vienna, 1934)

Gordon Shepherd, The Austrian Odyssey (London and New York, 1957)

Reinhold Lorenz, Der Staat wider Willen (Berlin, 1940)

Alfred Diamant, Austrian Catholics and the First Republic:
Democracy, Capitalism, and the Social Order, 1918-1934
(Princeton University Press) 1960)

Friedrich Funder, Aufbruch zur christlichen Sozialreform
(Vienna and Munich, 1953)

Kurt Schuschnigg, My Austria (N.Y.: Knopf, 1938)

May 21 - Austrian Social Democracy

Charles A. Gulick, Austria from Habsburg to Hitler, 2 vols.
(Berkeley and Los Angeles, 1948)

Julius Braunthal, The Tragedy of Austria (London, 1948)

Jacques Hannack, Im Sturm eines Jahrhunderts (Vienna, 1952)

Otto Bauer, The Austrian Revolution (London: Leonard Parsons, 1975)

-5-

Norbert Leser, <u>Zwischen Reformismus und Bolshevismus: Der
     Austromarxismus als Theorie und Praxis</u> (Wien, Frankfurt,
     Zürich: Europa Verlag, 1968)

Norbert Leser, "Sozialismus und österreichische Traditionen
     Todes und Lebendiges aus Osterreichs Vergangenheit),"
     in <u>Begegnung und Auftrag</u> (Wieg: Europa Verlag, 1963),
     pp. 215-238.

Joseph Buttinger, <u>In the Twilight of Socialism</u> (N.Y. Praeger,
     1953)

Joseph Buttinger, <u>Am Beispiel Oesterreichs</u> (published as
     manuscript, n.d.)

June 4 - <u>Biography and Autobiography</u>

Franz Stauracz, <u>Dr. Karl Lueger, 10 Jahre Bürgermeister</u>
     (Vienna, 1907)

Rudolph Kupps, <u>Karl Lueger und seine Zeit</u> (Wien, 1933)

Kurt Skalnik, <u>Dr. Karl Lueger: Der Mann zwischen den Zeiten</u>
     (Wien, 1954)

Heinrich Schnee, <u>Karl Lueger: Leben und Wirken eines grossen
     Sozial und Kommunalpolitikers</u> (Berlin, 1960)

Eduard Pichl, <u>Georg Schönerer</u>, 6 vols. in 3 (Oldenburg and
     Berlin, 1938).

Alex Bein, <u>Theodor Herzl: A Biography</u> (Cleveland and New York:
     World Publishing Meridian, 1962); (original Vienna, 1934)

Peter Loewenberg, "Theodor Herzl: A Psychoanalytic Study in
     Charismatic Political Leadership" in B.B. Wolman, ed.,
     <u>The Psychoanalytic Interpretation of History</u> (New York:
     Basic, 1971), pp. 150-191.

Carl E. Schorske, "Politics in a New Key: An Austrian Triptych",
     <u>Journal of Modern History</u>, Vol. 39 (December 1967), 343-
     386.

Ernest Jones, <u>The Life and Work of Sigmund Freud</u>, 3 vols.
     (New York: Basic Books, 1953-1957)

Karl Kautsky, <u>Erinnerungen und Erörterungen</u>, (s-Gravenhage, 1960)

Stefan Zweig, <u>The World of Yesterday</u> (London, 1943)

See also <u>Grosse Osterreicher, Neue Osterreichische Biographic
     ab 1815</u>

239

-6-

Frank Field, The Last Days of Mankind: Karl Kraus and His
    Vienna (N.Y., 1967)

Joseph Redlich, Emperor Francis Joseph of Austria: A Biography
    (Hamden, Conn., 1965)

Klemens von Klemperer, Ignas Seipel: Christian Statesman in
    a Time of Crisis (Princeton University Press, 1972)

Viktor Reimann, Zu Gross für Osterreich: Seipel und Bauer
    im Kampf um die Erste Republik (Wien, Verlag Fritz Molden,
    1968)

Julius Braunthal, ed. and intro, Otto Bauer: Eine Auswahl aus
    seinen Lebenswerk (Wiener Volksbuchhandlung, 1961)

Otto Leichter, Otto Bauer: Tragödie oder Triumph (Wien, Frankfurt,
    Zürich: Europa Verlag, 1970)

Jacques Hannak, Karl Renner und seine Zeit (Vienna, 1965)

Jacques Hannak, Johannes Schober-Mittelweg in die Katastrophe
    (Vienna, 1966)

Oskar Kleinschmied, Schober (Vienna, 1930)

    June 11 - Austrian Culture: An Emerging Synthesis?

Hans Kohn, Karl Kraus, Arthur Schnitzler, Otto Weininger::
    Aus dem jüdischen Wien der Jahrhundertswende (Tübingen, 1962)

Carl E. Schorske, "Politics and the psyche in fin de siecle
    (Vienna: Schnitzler and Hoffmannsthal, " American
    Historical Review, 66:4 (July 1967), 1283-1320

William J. McGrath, "Student Radicalism in Vienna," Journal of
    Contemporary History 2:3 (July 1967), 183-201.

Albert Fuchs, Geistige Strömungen in österreich, 1867-1918
    (Wien: Globus Verlag, 1949)

William M. Johnston, The Austrian Mind: An Intellectual and
    Social History, 1848-1938 (Berkeley and Los Angeles:
    University of California Press, 1972)

This final meeting will be at: 21114 Las Flores Mesa Drive,
Malibu, Tel: 456-3072.

HISTORY 1504: CONFERENCE COURSE (Fall 1983)

MODERNISM IN VIENNA AND MUNICH, 1890-1914

Peter Jelavich

By focusing on Vienna and Munich at the turn of the century, this course seeks to examine the political and social factors that encouraged the rise of modernist trends in literature and the visual and performing arts. Although weekly readings will be centered around specific individuals, the course will attempt to elucidate more general issues, such as: the explicit and implicit sociopolitical dimensions of the arts; artistic ramifications of the crisis of Central European liberalism; explorations of sexuality in social sciences and the arts; and the rise of expressionism and abstraction.

Each student will be expected to: (1) present an oral report on a week's readings; (2) write a short (5-8 page) paper on an assigned topic, due October 26; & (3) write an extended essay (c. 20 pages) on some aspect of the interaction of politics, society and modernist culture in Central Europe, due January 16.

Outline of the course:

I. Vienna:
    1. Habsburg politics and Viennese culture
    2. Arthur Schnitzler and the crisis of liberalism
    3. Hugo von Hofmannsthal: Escape from aestheticism
    4. Populist politics, socialism, and cultural renewal

II. Munich:
    1. Bavarian politics and Munich culture
    2. Frank Wedekind, cabaret, and "Simplicissimus"
    3. Thomas Mann: The writer and bourgeois society
    4. Stefan George: Leaders and followers

III. Arts:
    1. Viennese Secession: Painting, applied art, architecture
    2. Kandinsky: Expression through abstraction
    3. Expressionism in the performing arts
    4. Freud: Psychoanalysis, political sublimation, and the arts

Required reading / viewing / listening:

21 September - Introductory meeting

28 September - Habsburg politics and Viennese culture

Read: Bruce Pauley, The Habsburg Legacy 1867-1939, pp. 1-8 (reserve).
 Robert Kann, History of the Habsburg Empire 1526-1918, pp. 345-49, 356-62, 424-43 (reserve).
 Carl Schorske, "Introduction," "Ringstrasse," and "Politics in a New Key," in: Fin-de-siecle Vienna (purchase).

5 October - Arthur Schnitzler and the crisis of liberalism: Social dissolution and political retreat

Read: Arthur Schnitzler, Anatol (purchase).
 ----------, La Ronde (purchase).
 ----------, Professor Bernhardi (reserve).
 Carl Schorske, "Politics and the Psyche," in: Fin-de-siecle Vienna, pp. 3-15.
 C. E. Williams, The Broken Eagle, pp. 45-59 (reserve).
 Alfred Apsler, "A Sociological View of Arthur Schnitzler," in: Germanic Review, v. 18 (1943), pp. 90-106 (reserve).

12 October - Hugo von Hofmannsthal: Escape from aestheticism

Read: Hugo von Hofmannsthal, "Death and the Fool," in: Poems and Verse Plays, pp. 92-137 (reserve).
 ----------, "The Letter of Lord Chandos," in Selected Prose, pp. 129-141 (reserve).
 Schorske, "Politics and the Psyche," 15-23.
 Michael Hamburger, "Introduction," in: Hofmannsthal, Selected Plays and Libretti, pp. ix-xli (reserve).

Listen to: Richard Strauss / Hugo von Hofmannsthal, Elektra.

19 October - Populist politics, socialism, and cultural renewal

Read: William McGrath, Dionysian Art and Populist Politics in Austria, entire (purchase).

Listen to: Gustav Mahler, Symphony No. 3

26 October - Bavarian politics and Munich culture

Read: Allan Mitchell, Revolution in Bavaria 1918-1919, pp. 3-21 (reserve).
    M. Fischer, "A Century of Architecture," in: Apollo, v. 94 (1971),
     pp. 346-55 (Fogg reserve).
    Robin Lenman, "Politics and Culture: The State and the Avant-Garde
     in Munich 1886-1914," in: R.J. Evans, ed., Society and
     Politics in Wilhelmine Germany, pp. 90-111 (reserve).
    ----------, "Art, Society and the Law in Wilhelmine Germany," in:
     Oxford German Studies, v. 8 (1973-74), pp. 86-113
     (reserve).
    Thomas Mann, "Gladius Dei," in: Stories of Three Decades (reserve).
    Oskar Panizza, The Council of Love (reserve).

2 November - Frank Wedekind, cabaret, and "Simplicissimus:"
      Munich's culture of social criticism

Read: Frank Wedekind, Spring Awakening (purchase).
    ----------, "The Marquis of Keith," in: Corrigan (ed.),
     Masterpieces of Modern German Theater (reserve).
    Sterling Fishman, "Sex, Suicide, and the Discovery of the German
     Adolescent," in: History of Education Quarterly, v. 10
     (1970), pp. 170-88 (reserve).
    Peter Jelavich, "Art and Mammon in Wilhelmine Germany: The Case
     of Frank Wedekind," in: Central European History, v. 12
     (1979), pp. 203-36 (reserve).
    ----------, "Die Elf Scharfrichter: The Political and Sociocultural
     Dimensions of Cabaret in Wilhelmine Germany," in:
     Gerald Chapple and Hans Schulte, The Turn of the
     Century, pp. 507-25 (reserve).
    Gerhard Benecke, "The Politics of Outrage: Simplicissimus 1896-
     1914," in: 20th Century Studies, n. 13/14 (1975),
     pp. 92-109 (reserve).
    Ann Taylor Allen, "Sex and Satire in Wilhelmine Germany:
     'Simplicissimus' looks at Family Life," in: Journal of
     European Studies, v. 7 (1977), pp. 19-40 (reserve).

9 November - Thomas Mann: The writer and bourgeois society

Read: Thomas Mann, "Blood of the Volsungs," "Tonio Kröger," and "Death
     in Venice," in: Death in Venice and Seven other Stories
     (purchase).
    James Cleugh, Thomas Mann, pp. 11-39 (reserve).

16 November - Stefan George: Leaders and followers

Read: Olga Marx and E. Morwitz, eds., The Works of Stefan George, 2nd ed.
(1974), pp. 40-58, 230-44, 257-70, 315-28, 346
(reserve).
Thomas Mann, "At the Prophet's," in: Stories of Three Decades.
Hans Reiss, "Stefan George," in: The Writer's Task from Nietzsche to
Brecht, pp. 18-46 (reserve).
Claude David, "Stefan George: Aesthetes or Terrorists?" in:
M. Baumont, ed., The Third Reich, pp. 287-315 (reserve).

23 November - The Viennese Secession: Painting, applied art, architecture

Read: Carl Schorske, "Gustav Klimt," in: Fin-de-siecle Vienna.
Peter Vergo, Art in Vienna 1898-1918, entire (purchase).

30 November - Kandinsky: Expression through abstraction

Read: Vassily Kandinsky, Concerning the Spiritual in Art, entire (purchase).
----------, "Reminiscences," in: R. Herbert, ed., Modern Artists
on Art, pp. 19-44 (reserve).
----------, "The Problem of Form," in: Kandinsky and F. Marc, eds.,
The Blue Rider Almanach (Fogg reserve).
Kandinsky in Munich: 1896-1914, catalogue, Guggenheim Museum,
entire (purchase).

7 December - Expressionism in the performing arts: Kandinsky, Kokoschka,
Schönberg

Read: Vassily Kandinsky, "The Yellow Sound," in: Blue Rider Almanach.
----------, "On Stage Composition," in: Blue Rider Almanach.
R. Sheppard, "Kandinsky's Abstract Drama Der gelbe Klang," in:
Forum for Modern Language Studies, v. 11 (1975),
pp. 165-76 (reserve).
Oskar Kokoschka, "Sphinx and Strawman," in: V. Miesel, ed.,
Voices of German Expressionism, pp. 119-25 (reserve).
----------, "Murderer the Women's Hope," in: W. Sokel, An Anthology
of German Expressionist Drama, pp. 17-21 (reserve).
Arnold Schönberg, "Relationship to the Text," in: Blue Rider
Almanach.
Carl Schorske, "Explosion in the Garden," in: Fin-de-siecle Vienna.

Listen to: Arnold Schönberg, Book of the Hanging Gardens, op. 15.
----------, Erwartung, op. 17.
----------, Die glückliche Hand, op. 18.

14 December - Sigmund Freud: Psychoanalysis, political sublimation, and the arts

Read: Sigmund Freud, Five Lectures on Psychoanalysis, entire (purchase).
  ----------, Leonardo da Vinci, entire (purchase).
 "Spring Awakening," in: H. Nunberg and E. Federn, eds., Minutes
  of the Vienna Psychoanalytic Society, vol. 1, pp. 111-18
  (reserve).
 Carl Schorske, "Politics and Patricide," in: Fin-de-siecle Vienna.
 William McGrath, "Freud as Hannibal," in: Central European History,
  vol. 7 (1974), pp. 47-57 (reserve).
 Peter Loewenberg, "A Hidden Zionist Theme in Freud's 'My Son, the
  Myops...' Dream," in: Journal of the History of Ideas,
  vol. 31 (1970), pp. 129-32 (reserve).

Istvan Deak   Columbia University   Spring 1982
1229 International Affairs   Md.,Wd., 4:10-5:25
Tel.: 280-4627 or 4008
Office hours: Tu. 1-5

        W 4442y History of Hungary, 1848-1956

Topics and Readings

Jan. 25-27.   Introduction. Sources. The Hungarian background.
                The first Reform Generation.

Feb. 1-10   Reform, revolution, civil war, and the war between
                Austria, Russia and Hungary, 1848-1849.

   Readings:

                C.A. Macartney, Hungary. A Short History. N.Y.:
                Aldine Press, pp. 1-170.

                *Istvan Deak, The Lawful Revolution. Louis Kossuth
                and the Hungarians, 1848-1849. N.Y.: Columbia
                University Press, 1979.

                Paul Ignotus, Hungary. N.Y.: Praeger Publishers,
                pp. 1-75.

Feb. 15-22.   Habsburg constitutional experiments and Hungarian
                passive resistance. The 1867 compromise with the
                dynasty and Austria.

   Readings:
                Same as above.

Feb. 24-   Dualistic Hungary's agricultural and industrial
March 3   revolution. Liberalism, urbanism, secularism
                and assimilation. Budapest during the Dual Monarchy.
                The rise and success of Hungarian Jewry. The
                second Reform Generation (G. Lukacs, O. Jaszi, etc.)
                Constitutional crisis and foreign political turmoil.
                1868-1914.

   Readings:
                Macartney, op. cit., pp. 171-207.

                Ignotus, op. cit., pp. 76-127.

                I.T. Berend and G. Ranki, Hungary. A Century of
                Economic Development. N.Y.: Barnes and Noble,
                pp. 1-90.
                                    OR
                *I.T. Berend and G. Ranki, Economic Development in
                East-Central Europe in the 19th and 20th Centuries.
                N.Y.: Columbia University Press, pp. 1-156.

                              246

*Andrew C. Janos, "The Decline of Oligarchy: Bureaucratic and Mass Politics in the Age of Dualism, 1867-1914," in A.C. Janos and W.B. Slottman, Revolution in Perspective. Berkeley: University of California Press, pp. 1-60.

March 8-24   The First World War, the democratic and the bolshevik revolutions. (1914-1919) István Tisza, Mihály Károlyi and Béla Kun.

Readings:

Ignotus, op. cit., pp. 128-149.

*Ivan Völgyes, ed., Hungary in Revolution. 1918-1919. Nine Essays. Lincoln: University of Nebraska Press, 1971.

Istvan Deak, "Shades of 1848: War, Revolution and Nationality Conflict in Austria Hungary 1914-1920." [This article will be lent to the students. There are enough copies for everyone.]

March 29 -   The Paris Peace Treaties and the end of Greater
April 14   Hungary. White counter-revolution and the regime of Admiral Horthy. Clericals, conservatives, populists, and fascists. Hungary joins the Axis powers. The Second World War. Collaboration, resistance, and the "final solution" of the Jewish problem. The rise of the Arrow Cross and the defeat of Germany.

Readings:

Macartney, op. cit., pp. 209-235.

Ignotus, op. cit., pp. 149-192.

Berend and Ranki, Hungary, pp. 99-182. OR

Berend and Ranki, Economic Development in East Central Europe, pp. 171-342.

*Istvan Deak, "Hungary," in Hans Rogger and Eugen Weber eds., The European Right. A Historical Profile. Berkeley: University of California Press, 1965/1966.

April 19 -   Liberation, democratic coalition and the salami
May 5   tactic. Stalinism in Hungary and the second industrial revolution. The great purge trials. The death of Stalin, the thaw and the drive for reformist communism. Imre Nagy, the revolution of 1956 and the Soviet military intervention. Epilogue: Janos Kadar and "freer" communism.

Readings:

Ignotus, op. cit., pp. 193-310.

Berend and Ranki, Hungary, pp. 184-256. OR

Berend and Ránki, <u>Economic Development in East-Central Europe</u>, pp. 342-365.

Miklós Molnár, <u>Budapest 1956. A History of the Hungarian Revolution</u>. London: George Allen and Unwin, 1971.
OR

*Béla K. Király and Paul Jónás eds., <u>The Hungarian Revolution of 1956 in Retrospect</u>. Boulder, Col.: East European Quarterly, 1978. Distributed by Columbia University Press.

Paul E. Zinner, ed., <u>National Communism and Popular Revolt in Eastern Europe</u>. Program in East Central Europe, Columbia University, 1956.
[This documentary collection will be lent to the students. There are enough copies for everyone.]

<u>Note</u>: Titles marked with an asterisk should be available at the college bookstore. However, all assigned works will be available on reserve in the College Library Reading Room.

. . . .

The course consists of lectures and discussions, and it is open to both graduate and undergraduate students. Familiarity with a European language is not required. The midterm will be optional for graduate students, although all students must take the final examination. The midterm and the final can be either written or oral, according to your individual preference. Graduate students have the option of taking the course for "R" credit.

Rutgers University

HISTORY OF POLAND

This course is a survey of the history of Poland from the formation
of the Polish state through the present. While major emphasis will be
placed on political history, the course will also treat social, economic,
religious, and cultural developments in Poland. Discussion of Polish
literary works will be the focus of several meetings. Students have the
choice between writing a; two midterms and one final, or b; one midterm,
one paper, and one final. Those who choose to write the paper must submit, by
April 4, the title of their choice.

Required Readings:

Jerzy Andrzejewski, Ashes and Diamonds
Neal Ascherson, The Polish August. The Self-limiting Revolution
Krystyna M. Olszer, ed., For your Freedom and Ours. Polish Progressive
    Spirit from the 14th Century to the Present
Boleslaw Prus, The Doll
Piotr S. Wandycz, The Lands of Partitioned Poland, 1795-1918

Books on Reserve:

Vaclav L. Benes & Norman J. G. Pounds, Poland
The Cambridge History of Poland, 2 Volumes, 1971 Edition
Janusz Korczak, Ghetto Diary
Maria Kuncewicz, ed., The Modern Polish Mind. An Anthology
R.F. Leslie, ed., The History of Poland since 1863
Joseph Rotschild, East Central Europe between the Wars
Celina Wieniewska, ed., Polish Writing Today

January 24   Introduction

26   The Polish Land
A brief survey of the geography and ethnography of Poland
before the establishment of a Polish state
            Benes, pp. 21-25

31   The Formation and Consolidation of the Polish state
The Piasts, Mieszko, Conversion to Christianity. King Boleslaw Chrobry.
Polish society before the 13th Century.
            Benes, pp. 25-30
            Cambridge 1, pp. 16-33, 148-154

February 2   Disintegration
The weakening of the Polish state due to internal dynastic
conflicts. The intrusion of the Teutonic knights and the
Mongol invasion.
            Benes, pp. 30-33
            Cambridge 1, pp. 33-59, 85-107, 155-157

7   Restoration
The re-established unity of the Polish state. Kings
Wladyslaw Lokietek and Kazimierz the Great. Polish society,
education, and culture in the 14th Century.
            Benes, pp. 33-40
            Cambridge 1, pp. 108-124, 157-159, 167-187.

February 9	The Polish-Lithuanian Alliance

February 9   The Polish-Lithuanian Alliance
Personal union with Hungary under King Louis. Queen Jadwiga's
marriage to Lithuania's Grand Duke Jagiello, subsequently
crowned as King Wladyslaw II. The battle of Grunwald
(Tannenberg)
        Benes, pp. 40-41
        Cambridge 1, pp. 188-214

14   Poland under the Jagiellos
The Renaissance in Poland. Kings Kazimierz IV and Zygmunt 1.
The growing power of the szlachta (nobility). King Zygmunt
August II and the Union of Lublin.
        Benes, pp. 41-53
        Cambridge 1, pp. 161-166, 215-286, 300-321, 348-368
        Olszer, pp. 17-33

16   The Reformation in Poland
Social and cultural developments in 16th Century Poland.
The Church. The spread of protestantism. Religious tolerance.
A further increase in the szlachta's power. Kings Henry Valois
and Stefon Batory.
        Benes, pp. 53-55
        Cambridge 1, pp. 322-347, 367-415.·

21   The Szlachta's Predominance
Economic conditions and social structure in 17th Century
Poland. Serfs, townsmen, and the sharpening division between
the magnates and the gentry. The Chmielnicki rebellion
and the Swedish invasion. King Jan Sobieski.
        Benes, pp. 55-59
        Cambridge 1, pp. 427-440, 451-569

February 23   Continuing Decline and the Partions
The Saxon Kings. Domestic instability and foreign interventions.
King Stanislaw Poniatowski, Civil War and peasant rebellion.
The first partition. The reform movement. The 1791
Constitution. The second partition. The Kosciusko uprising.
The third partition.
        Benes, pp. 59-70
        Cambridge II, pp. 1-48, 72-176
        Olszer, pp. 37-63

28   Midterm Examination

March 2   Napoleon and the Poles. The Duchy of Warsaw
Napoleon's cynical exploitation of the Poles. The establishment
of Duchy of Warsaw, a Polish client state of France.
        Benes, pp. 70-72
        Wandycz, pp. 24-64

7   Prussian Poland, Galicia, Cracow, and the Kingdom of
Poland (Congress Poland).
Social, economic, cultural, and political developments
in the partitioned parts from the Congress of Vienna through
1830.
        Benes, pp. 72-74
        Wandycz, pp. 65-102

March 9   The Uprisings and the "Great Emigration."
The 1830/31 uprising and its aftermath in the Russian-
dominated Kingdom of Poland. The "Great Emigration"
to England and France. Polish romanticism and messianism.
Adam Mickiewicz, Juliusz Slowacki, and Zygmunt Krasinski.
    Benes, pp. 74-76
    Olszer, pp. 64-105
    Wandycz, pp. 105-150, 180-189.

14   Oppression, Reforms, and the 1863/64 Uprising
Congress Poland at the turn of the 1850's and 60's.
Andrzej Zamoyski and Aleksander Wielopolski. The 1863/64
uprising and subsequent Russian retaliation.
    Olszer, pp. 73-75
    Wandycz, pp. 150-179

16   The Triumph of Realism
Social, economic, cultural, and political developments
during the 1860's, 70's, and 80's in the partitioned
parts. Polish pozitivism.
    Olszer, pp. 106-123
    Wandycz, pp. 193-238, 260-272

28   Discussion of the Novel "The Doll" by Boleslaw Prus.

30   The Renewal of Political Activism
Polish politics in the partitioned parts around the turn
of the century. The National Democrats: Roman Dmowski.
The Socialists: Jozef Pilsudski. Poles at the threshold
of World War I.
    Olszer, pp. 124-173
    Wandycz, pp. 275-303, 308-330

April 4   Polish Participation in World War I
The Polish Legions of Pilsudski. The occupation of Russian
Poland by the Central Powers and their conflicting designs
on Poland's future. The pseudo-independence of a Polish
kingdom created by the Central Powers. Polish activities
on the Entente side. Dmowski and Ignacy Paderewski.
Pilsudski's imprisonment by the Germans. President Wilson's
thirteenth point. Entente victory and the rebirth of an
independent Poland in 1918.
    Olszer, pp. 177-185
    Wandycz, pp. 331-370

6   Midterm Examination

11   The Interwar Period I
Poland at the Paris Peace Conference. Territorial conflicts.
The Soviet-Polish war. The problems of state building.
Polish society in the 1920's. Ethnic and social tensions.
The bankruptcy of the political system. Pilsudski's
coup d'état in 1926.
    Benes, pp. 189-204
    Olszer, pp. 193-213
    Rotschild, pp. 27-55

April 13   The Interwar Period II
Pilsudski's claim to power: moral regeneration (sanacja)
and government by technocratic expertise. His party, the
BBWR. Growing authoritarianism: the colonels' regime.
Pilsudski's death. Marshal Edward Rydz-Smigly. The foreign
policy of Colonel Jozef Beck.
        Benes, pp. 204-241
        Olszer, pp. 218-254
        Rotschild, pp. 55-72

18   Poland in World War II
The Hitler-Stalin Pact. The German invasion of Poland.
Poland's defeat. The occupation policies of the German
General Government. The Polish Underground State. The
Home Army and other resistance groups. The policies of
the Polish Government-in-Exile in London. General Wladyslaw
Sikorski. The systematic extermination of the Jews.
The Warsaw ghetto uprising of 1943. The Warsaw uprising
of 1944. Poland occupied by Soviet troops. The Polish
question at the Yalta Conference. The Provisional Government
of National Unity.
        Benes, pp. 242-258
        Leslie, pp. 209-279
        Olszer, pp. 261-305

April 20   Discussion of the following novel, diary, and short
stories:
Jerzy Andrzejewski, Ashes and Diamonds
Janusz Korczak, Ghetto Diary
Kornel Filipowicz, "A Speck of Dirt" in Kuncewicz
Adolf Rudnicki, "The Crystal Stream" "   "
Jan Szczepanski, "The Tramp"   "   "
Jerzy Zawieyski, "Conrad in the Ghetto""   "
Henryk Grynberg, "The Grave" in Wieniewska
Tadeusz Holuj, "Full Circle" "   "
Stanislaw Stanuch, "King of the Mountains" in Wieniewska

25   Postwar Poland
Territorial charges and economic reconstruction. The
gradual elimination of non-communist opponents and the
concomitant consolidation of communist rule. "The Polish
Road to Socialism." Wladyslaw Gomulka. His purge and
replacement with Boleslaw Bierut. Stalinism in Poland.
        Ascherson, pp. 41-66
        Benes, pp. 261-290
        Leslie, pp. 280-343

27   The Polish October
The Twentieth Congress of the Communist Party of the SU.
"The Thaw" in Poland. Workers' uprising in Poznan.
The reemergence of Gomulka. The events of October, 1956,
and their aftermath.
        Ascherson, pp. 66-79
        Benes, pp. 291-311
        Leslie, pp. 344-366

May 2 **From Liberalization to Stagnation**
Gomulka's rigid dogmatism. Severe economic crisis and
constant frictions with the Catholic Church, Cardinal
Stefan Syszynski. Conflict with the intellectuals. The
unrest of 1968. Campaign of anti-semitism under the guise
of "antizionism." Further deterioration of the economy.
Workers' riots in December 1970. Gomulka's resignation
and replacement with Edward Gierek.
> Ascherson, pp. 80-105
> Benes, pp. 311-338
> Leslie, pp. 367-406

4 **Poland under Gierek**
Gierek's new policies. Rapid economic development until
1975. Institutional reforms. New economic problems after
1975. Workers' riots in 1976. Workers' Defense Committee
(KOR) formed among dissenting members of the intelligentsia.
The corruption of the Party elite.
> Ascherson, pp. 106-125
> Leslie, pp. 407-443
> Olszer, pp. 348-362

9 **Solidarity**
The election of a Polish Pope, Pope John Paul II (Cardinal
Karol Wojtyla) His visit to Poland. Gierek on the defensive.
The formation of Solidarity, August 1980. Lech Walesa.
The Gdansk Agreement. Gierek's resignation. Stanislaw Kania.
Solidarity versus the Party and the Government. Martial
Law, December 1981. The regime of General Wojciech Jaruzelski.
The continuing activities of the Solidarity underground.
> Ascherson, pp. 125-281
> Olszer, pp. 363-367

GPV:lg
4/25/83
10

HISTORY 142
Spring 1982

University of California
Berkeley

Mr. deVries
3222 Dwinelle Hall
Office hours: Tu 2-4
                Th 3-5

HISTORY OF THE NETHERLANDS

The following books have been ordered and should be available for purchase at Ed
Hunolt's Berkeley Book Store and the ASUC Book Store.

Charles Wilson, The Dutch Republic
Pieter Geyl, The Revolt of the Netherlands

These and all other readings are on reserve (2 hour) in Moffitt Library. Reading
assignments preceded by an "R" are included in a reader that can be purchased at
Kinko's.

Evaluation in this course will be based on a mid-term exam, a writing assignment of
8-10 pages, and a final examination.

Geography, Institutions

R   C. T. Smith, A Historical Geography of Western Europe before 1800, pp. 506-524.
R   Jan deVries, "On the Modernity of the Dutch Republic," Journal of Economic History 33
      (1973), 191-202.
R   Gerald Newton, The Netherlands: A Historical and Cultural Survey, Chapter 2 "The
      Dutch Language," pp. 12-28.

General

Charles Wilson, The Dutch Republic, entire. Read this picture book as early in the
      quarter as possible for an introduction to the broad patterns of Dutch history.

The Revolt

Pieter Geyl, The Revolt of the Netherlands, pp. 69-180.
R   J. W. Smit, "The Netherlands Revolt," in Robert Forster and Jack P. Greene, eds.,
      Preconditions of Revolution in Early Modern Europe, pp. 19-54.
R   Geoffrey Parker, Spain and the Netherlands, read: "Spain and her enemies and the
      Revolt of the Netherlands, 1559-1648;" "Why did the Dutch Revolt last so long;"
      "War and Economic Change: The Economic costs of the Dutch Revolt."
R   Herbert Rowan, ed., The Low Countries in Early Modern Times, document nrs: 5-11, 14-21.

The Golden Age

Pieter Geyl, Revolt, pp. 203-259
R   Pieter Geyl, The Netherlands in the Seventeenth Century, Vol I, pp. 38-94; 154-157; Vol
      II, pp. 13-37; 85-106; 121-152.
R   Charles Boxer, The Dutch Seaborne Empire, chapters 2, 3, 4, pp. 31-112.
R   Johan Huizinga, Dutch Civilization in the Seventeenth Century (read only the essay
      of this title).
R   Rowan, Low Countries, document nrs. 22-29, 37-41
    J.L. Price, Culture and Society in the Dutch Republic during the Seventeenth Century,
      chapters 5-7.
R   Immanuel Wallerstein, The Modern World-System, Vol I, pp. 196-221; Vol II, pp. 37-71.

The Decline and Fall of the Republic and the Construction of the Second Dutch State

R   Boxer, Seaborne Empire, ch. 10, pp. 258-294.
R   Charles Wilson, "Taxation and the Decline of Empires, an unfashionable theme,"
       B.M.H.G. 77 (1963), 10-23.
R   E. H. Kossmann, The Low Countries, 1780-1940. pp. 34-47; 82-164; 179-195; 259-309.
R   J.C. Boogmans, "The Netherlands in the European Scene, 1813-1913," in J.S. Bromley
       and E.H. Kossmann, eds., Britain and the Netherlands in Europe and Asia, pp. 138-155.

The Colonial Empire

R   S. L. van der Wal "The Netherlands as an Imperial Power in South-East Asia in the
       Nineteenth Century and After," in Bromley and Kossman, eds., Britain and the
       Netherlands, pp. 191-205.
R   H. Baudet, "The Netherlands after loss of Empire," Journal of Contemporary History
       4 (1969) pp.
R   H. L. Wesseling, "Post-Imperial Holland," Journal of Contemporary History 15 (1980),
       pp. 125-142.

Modern Dutch Society

R   Newton, The Netherlands, "War and Reconstruction," pp. 133-156, "Society and
       Administration," pp. 210-238.
R   J.J.C. Voorhoeve, Peace, Profits and Principles, A Study of Dutch Foreign Policy,
       pp. 3-54.

255

About the Editor

John Santore received his Ph.D. in modern European history from Columbia University in 1976 and has taught at Rutgers University (1976-1977) and Barnard College (1977-1981). In 1981, he served as the Associate Director of the Columbia University Center for Italian Studies and was a lecturer at the New York University School of Continuing Education in 1982-1983. A specialist in twentieth-century Europe, his reviews and articles have appeared in the <u>Canadian Journal of History</u> and <u>History: Review of New Books</u>.

Markus Wiener Publishing announces the publication of innovative, educational materials in history from leading American scholars.

Selected course outlines and reading lists in history as reference books for faculty members, librarians and graduate students.

EUROPEAN HISTORY

Vol. 1 **Ancient History**
edited by Sarah B. Pomeroy
Hunter College of C.U.N.Y.
and Stanley Burstein
California State University of Los Angeles

Vol. 2 **Medieval History**
edited by Penelope Johnson
New York University

Vol. 3 **Early Modern European History**
edited by Jeffrey Merrick
Barnard College, Columbia University

Vol. 4 **Modern European History:**
1789 to the Present
Vol. I: Chronological and National Courses

Vol. 5 **Modern European History:**
1789 to the Present
Vol. II: Topical and Thematic Courses
edited by John Santore
New York University

AMERICAN HISTORY

Vol. 6 **American History I**
Survey and Chronological Courses

Vol. 7 **American History II**
Selected Topics in Cultural, Social and
Economic History

Vol. 8 **American History III**
Selected Topics in Twentieth Century History
edited by Warren Susman and John Chambers
Rutgers University

Vol. 9 **Women's History**
edited by Annette Baxter
Barnard College, Columbia University

For information, write to
Markus Wiener Publishing, Inc.
551 Fifth Avenue, Suite 3210
New York, N.Y. 10176